Poorly Understood

Poorly Understood

WHAT AMERICA GETS WRONG ABOUT POVERTY

Mark Robert Rank, Lawrence M. Eppard,
and Heather E. Bullock

OXFORD
UNIVERSITY PRESS

OXFORD
UNIVERSITY PRESS

Oxford University Press is a department of the University of Oxford. It furthers
the University's objective of excellence in research, scholarship, and education
by publishing worldwide. Oxford is a registered trade mark of Oxford University
Press in the UK and certain other countries.

Published in the United States of America by Oxford University Press
198 Madison Avenue, New York, NY 10016, United States of America.

Library of Congress Cataloging-in-Publication Data
Names: Rank, Mark Robert, author. | Eppard, Lawrence M., author. |
Bullock, Heather E., author.
Title: Poorly understood : what America gets wrong about poverty /
by Mark Robert Rank, Lawrence M. Eppard, Heather E. Bullock.
Description: New York, NY : Oxford University Press, [2021] |
Includes bibliographical references and index.
Identifiers: LCCN 2020039392 (print) | LCCN 2020039393 (ebook) |
ISBN 9780190881382 (hardback) | ISBN 9780190881405 (epub) | ISBN 9780190881412
Subjects: LCSH: Poor—United States. | Poverty—United States. | Public welfare—United
States. | United States—Social conditions | United States—Economic conditions.
Classification: LCC HV91.R364 2021 (print) | LCC HV91 (ebook) |
DDC 362.50973—dc23
LC record available at https://lccn.loc.gov/2020039392
LC ebook record available at https://lccn.loc.gov/2020039393

DOI: 10.1093/oso/9780190881382.001.0001

1 3 5 7 9 8 6 4 2

Printed by LSC Communications, United States of America

One study shows that more than half of Americans will experience poverty at some point during their adult lives. Think about that. This is not an isolated situation. More than half of Americans at some point in their lives will experience poverty.

Former U.S. President Barack Obama, Remarks by the President on Economic Mobility, December 4, 2013.

{ CONTENTS }

SECTION V How Extensive Is Inequality?

SECTION VI Pulling It Together

Introduction

Few topics have as many myths, stereotypes, and misperceptions surrounding them as that of poverty in America. The poor have been badly misunderstood since the beginnings of the country, with the rhetoric intensifying in recent times. Our current era of fake news, alternative facts, and media partisanship has led to a breeding ground for all types of myths gaining traction and legitimacy. The time would appear right to set the record straight.

To our knowledge, *Poorly Understood* is the first book to systematically address and confront many of the most widespread myths pertaining to poverty. Throughout our careers, each of us has encountered these myths on a routine basis. They can be found virtually everywhere—from the political rhetoric emanating out of the highest office in the land to the neighborhood gossip down the street. It would seem as if everyone has a heated opinion about the poor, with the heat rising even higher when the topic of welfare is thrown into the mix.

Yet, as we shall see throughout these chapters, the realities of poverty are much different than the myths. In many ways, they are more disturbing. The idealized image of American society is one of abundant opportunities, with hard work being rewarded by economic prosperity. Consequently, those who fail to get ahead have only themselves to blame according to this argument. It is within this context that America thinks of itself as a fair and meritocratic society in which people get what they deserve in life.

But what if this picture is wrong? What if poverty is an experience that touches the majority of Americans? What if hard work does not necessarily lead to economic well-being? What if the reasons for poverty are largely beyond the control of individuals? Indicative of this is the epigraph quote from President Obama on the front page referring to our research results showing that a majority of Americans will at some point experience poverty.

These are much more disturbing realities to consider because they call into question the very core of America's identity. And perhaps this is one reason that the myths continue. To consider the possibility that people do not get what they deserve is indeed disturbing.

It becomes particularly distressing within the context of the American dream. The American dream has been central to how we as a people like to perceive ourselves and our future.[1] That future is thought to be full of promise as long as we work hard and play by the rules. The playing field is assumed to be level, allowing everyone to compete fairly.

Yet, as we will see, such beliefs can and do blind us to the realities of poverty. They may actually prevent us from addressing and alleviating poverty because they hold out the promise of a better life to come, thereby minimizing the need to correct for the problems of today. To paraphrase Karl Marx, the American dream may be the opiate of the American people. This, then, is one possible reason that the myths of poverty continue despite strong evidence to the contrary.

There may be other reasons as well. Could the maintenance of these myths actually be useful for particularly powerful constituencies? Does the continuation of these myths serve a purpose or function for other segments of the American population? If so, who and what might that be? We will explore these questions in greater detail in later chapters.

It should be noted that poverty and inequality are not acts of nature. Rather, they are strongly influenced by social policies and macroeconomic conditions.[2] Some countries have low rates of poverty and less inequality as a result of their social and economic policies and programs. Other countries, such as the United States, have high rates of poverty and inequality largely as a result of their lack of a strong social safety net. In short, there is nothing inevitable about poverty.

And that is what makes the issue so troubling. The United States has the resources to significantly alleviate poverty. Yet, it chooses not to. As we shall see in later chapters, this approach is, to quote a familiar saying, "penny wise and pound foolish." But once again, poverty myths prevent us from seeing clearly.

That is why we feel the importance of setting the record straight. It is vital to carefully assess the research with a clear mind in order to draw well-reasoned conclusions. We also wish to convey this information in an accessible and direct manner. Now more than ever, we should be firmly guided by grounded facts, not political rhetoric or biased perceptions pandering to particular interest groups. We believe that evidence-based arguments can ultimately dismantle the myths, although the process may be long and tenacious. Yet, as we shall argue in our concluding chapter, paradigm change can and does occur. In fact, we believe we may be on the cusp of such a change. Let us begin.

Organization of the Book

Before we started writing this book, we each sat down and compiled a list of the most common myths regarding poverty that we had encountered. Although there were quite a few, our tallies were remarkably similar. We quickly put together an overall list and began the task of marshaling the best available evidence with respect to the many aspects of poverty that we were addressing. The result is the book that appears before you now. For each of us, the content within this book is very much in our proverbial wheelhouse. It is a subject that we know quite well, and as such, we are eager to share with you this knowledge.

Poorly Understood is divided into six sections. In the first five sections, we examine a wide range of poverty myths, while the sixth section seeks to explore why these myths persist despite overwhelming evidence to the contrary, as well as discussing how we might move forward to effectively confront the realities of poverty.

We have designed each of the chapters to be concise and accessible. They can be read in sequence or as stand-alone pieces. At the end of each chapter are insights provided by an expert in the field regarding the particular subject matter. These short sections are intended to be provocative and add further to your understanding of the many aspects of poverty. We have invited scholars who span a wide range of academic disciplines, representing many of the best researchers in the field of poverty studies today. In some cases we conducted interviews with our invited experts (which were then transcribed), while in other cases the experts submitted their thoughts in writing.

Finally, in the Appendix, readers will find a short list of additional resources for exploring the chapter subject matter in greater detail. These include books and articles, websites, and multimedia sources of information.

We begin in Section I by looking at the characteristics of those experiencing poverty. Section II explores why poverty exists. We address the costs of poverty in Section III. Section IV examines the issue of welfare and the social safety net. In Section V, we turn to the wider context of inequality. And finally, Section VI pulls together our arguments in order to provide a pathway for moving forward in the future.

The chapters themselves are designed to be concise and accessible. We have written them to impart the essential information regarding each topic and to do so in an engaging manner. Each chapter is based on our pulling together the best available research on the subject. For readers interested in delving further into the individual topics, the chapter footnotes contain the original source material used to formulate our conclusions. Curious readers are encouraged to explore these source materials (along with the additional resources in the Appendix) in order to gain greater insights into the subject matter.

Defining Our Terms

There are several terms and concepts that we will refer to frequently throughout this book. The most obvious is the concept of poverty itself. Although poverty can be defined in a number of ways, much our analysis is based on the official definition of poverty used by the U.S. Census Bureau.[3] The Census Bureau defines those living in poverty as being in a household that falls below a specific level of annual income. It is thought that those who are lacking this amount of income cannot purchase the necessary goods and services to maintain a minimally adequate life. In 2019, these levels ranged from $13,011 for a one-person household, to $26,172 for a four-person household, to $52,875 for a household of nine or more people. Each year, the various poverty lines are adjusted upward to take into account inflation. This type of poverty definition is what is known as an absolute measure of poverty. In other words, there is an absolute line drawn with respect to income, and if families fall below that line, they are counted as living in poverty for the year.

Another manner of thinking about poverty is through what is known as a relative measure of poverty. This particular way of defining poverty looks at where someone is in the income distribution relative to where others are, and is used frequently when making comparisons across countries. The most common relative poverty measure is one that counts individuals as poor if they fall below one-half of a country's median income.[4] Consequently, if the median income for a country were $60,000, then households earning less than $30,000 would be considered in poverty. This measure has the advantage of allowing us to make comparisons across countries with respect to the percentage of the population falling into poverty.

A second broad concept that we will be exploring in the chapters ahead is that of economic inequality. We discuss both income and wealth inequality. Income inequality refers to how wide or narrow the overall distribution of annual income is.[5] For example, how far apart are those who are earning at the top 10th percentile of the income distribution from those earning at the bottom 10th percentile? We will also examine wealth inequality. This is analogous to income inequality but is looking at the distribution of economic assets rather than income. Net worth refers to all of one's assets minus all of one's debts. Financial wealth is exactly the same but does not include the equity that one has built up in a home.[6]

A third set of terms that we will be using refer to welfare programs and the social safety net. Welfare programs are generally considered those in which an individual has to be below a certain income and asset level and fall into a particular population group in order to be eligible. These are also known as means-tested programs, with individuals only able to participate if their income and assets are low enough to qualify.[7] They include a wide range of programs, such as Temporary Assistance for Needy Families (TANF), Supplemental Nutrition Assistance Program (SNAP, also known as food stamps), Medicaid, Supplemental Security Income (SSI), Housing Assistance, and several others. The social safety net is a somewhat boarder concept than the welfare system. It includes not only welfare programs but also other government entitlement programs, such as Social Security and Medicare, in which you do not need to be below a particular income level in order to quality.

Finally, there are several terms that we use frequently in discussing the array of research findings that we cover. When making international comparisons, we will often refer to OECD countries.[8] These include the 37 countries that are a part of the Organisation for Economic Co-operation and Development. They are characterized as wealthy nations with highly developed economies. They consist of all European and North American countries, along with Australia, New Zealand, Japan, Korea, and Chile.

Our discussion of research results is intentionally jargon-free and straight-forward. We do, however, refer to a few very basic statistics. With respect to measuring the amount of economic inequality in a country, we make use of what is known as the Gini coefficient or index.[9] This is an overall measure of how unequal the income distribution is, and it ranges from 0 (complete equality) to 1 (complete inequality).

The relationship between two factors is what is known as a simple correlation. It also ranges from 0 to 1. As a correlation approaches 1, the association between two variables is stronger, such that by knowing what one factor is, we can largely know what the other factor is.

Finally, in discussing economic mobility across generations, we refer to the intergenerational elasticity statistic. Again, this ranges between 0 and 1 and indicates how strong the relationship is between parents' income and their children's income.[10]

With this brief tour of the book complete, it is time to start our exploration into the specific myths surrounding poverty and the actual realities that define these topics. We begin at a logical starting point: Who exactly experiences poverty?

{ SECTION I }

Who Are the Poor?

As discussed in Chapter 1, there are many myths and misperceptions surrounding who the poor are. The typical image is of someone who has lived in poverty for years at a time, is Black or Hispanic, resides in an inner-city ghetto, receives two or three welfare programs, and is reluctant to work. On all counts, this image is a severe distortion of the reality.

We begin our examination of poverty myths with several of the most dominant ones regarding who the poor are. The underlying theme tying these myths together is that poverty is often perceived to be an issue of "them" rather than an issue of "us"—that those who experience poverty are viewed as strangers to mainstream America, falling outside acceptable behavior, and as such, are to be scorned and stigmatized.

As we discuss in later chapters, this perspective has helped foster a strong animosity toward those in poverty and an overall reluctance to provide much assistance. Yet, as we shall see throughout these next chapters, the reality of who experiences poverty is, in many ways, more disturbing than the mythology. The truth is that impoverishment is much closer than most of us would like to think.

Most Americans Will Experience Poverty

We begin our dismantling of poverty myths with the widely held belief that most Americans will never experience poverty—that only a small minority of Americans will directly experience impoverishment during the course of their lives and, further, that the use of a social safety net or welfare program is something very much out of the ordinary.

One of the consequences of this myth is that it encourages the idea that those in poverty are somehow different from the typical or average American. For example, survey research has found that in the general population, the words "poverty" and "welfare" often conjure up images of people on the fringes of society—unwed mothers with a multitude of children, inner-city unemployed Black men, high school dropouts on drugs, the mentally disturbed homeless, and so on.[1] The media, political rhetoric, and even at times the research of social scientists often depict the poor as alien and out of step with the rest of America.[2] In short, being poor and using welfare are widely perceived as behaviors that fall outside the American mainstream.

Yet, it turns out that a majority of Americans will experience poverty first hand. Research indicates that most of us will encounter poverty at some point during our lives. Even more surprising, a majority of Americans will turn to public assistance at least once during their adulthood. Rather than poverty and welfare use being an issue of them, it is much more accurate to think of it as an issue of us.

Background

The life course research of sociologists Mark Rank and Thomas Hirschl has helped shed light on this issue. More than two decades ago, Rank and Hirschl were interested in asking a very basic question, "How likely is it that an American will experience poverty first hand?" Furthermore, "What are the chances that an American will use a social safety net program at some point during their adulthood?" To answer these questions, they turned to an invaluable longitudinal data set—the Panel Study of Income Dynamics, otherwise known as the PSID.

The PSID is a nationally representative, longitudinal sample of households interviewed from 1968 onward.[3] It has been administered by the Survey Research Center at the University of Michigan, and it constitutes the longest running panel data set both in the United States and the world. The PSID initially interviewed approximately 5,000 U.S. households in 1968, obtaining detailed information on roughly 18,000 individuals within those households. These individuals have since been tracked annually (biennially after 1997), including children and adults who eventually break off from their original households to form new households (e.g., children leaving home or adults following a divorce). Thus, the PSID is designed so that in any given year, the sample is representative of the entire nonimmigrant U.S. population.

As its name implies, the PSID is primarily focused on household information about economics and demographics. For each wave of the study, there is detailed information about the annual income for each household. Consequently, one can easily determine whether households fell into poverty across the various years of the study. The survey also asks a variety of questions pertaining to whether anyone in the household has used a social safety net or welfare program at some point during the year.

Based on these data, Rank and Hirschl constructed a series of what are known as life tables. The life table is a technique for calculating how often particular events occur during a specific period of time and is frequently used by demographers and medical researchers to assess risk (i.e., the risk of having a heart attack during later adulthood). It allows one to estimate the percentage of the American population that will experience poverty at some point during adulthood.

Risk of Poverty

Using this life table approach, the risk of experiencing poverty for the American population can be assessed. Results indicate that between the ages of 20 and 75 years, nearly 60 percent of Americans will experience living for at least 1 year below the official poverty line, while three-fourths of Americans will encounter poverty or near-poverty (150 percent below the official poverty line).[4] These findings indicate that a clear majority of Americans will directly experience poverty at some point during their adulthood.

Rather than a small fringe on the outskirts of society, the majority of Americans will encounter poverty. Table 2.1 shows the cumulative percentages of the population who will be touched by poverty or near-poverty. Between

TABLE 2.1 Cumulative Percentage of Americans Experiencing Poverty Across Adulthood

Age	Level of poverty		
	Below 1.00 poverty line (%)	Below 1.25 poverty line (%)	Below 1.50 poverty line (%)
20	10.6	15.0	19.1
25	21.6	27.8	34.3
30	27.1	34.1	41.3
35	31.4	39.0	46.9
40	35.6	43.6	51.7
45	38.8	46.7	55.0
50	41.8	49.6	57.9
55	45.0	52.8	61.0
60	48.2	56.1	64.2
65	51.4	59.7	67.5
70	55.0	63.6	71.8
75	58.5	68.0	76.0

Source: Panel Study of Income Dynamics, Rank and Hirschl computations.

the ages of 20 and 35 years, 31.4 percent will have experienced poverty; by age 55 years, 45.0 percent; and by age 75 years, 58.5 percent. Similarly, 76.0 percent of the population will have spent at least 1 year below 150 percent of the official poverty line by the time they reach age 75 years.

This pattern holds up regardless of how we might measure poverty. For example, in a complimentary analysis, Rank and Hirschl relied on a relative measure of poverty: They analyzed the likelihood of Americans falling into the bottom 20 percent of the income distribution as well as the bottom 10 percent. They calculated that 62 percent of Americans between the ages of 25 and 60 years would at some point experience living for at least 1 year below the 20th percentile, while 42 percent would fall below the 10th percentile.[5] Again, the likelihood of poverty was quite pronounced across the life course.

Using a broader definition of economic turmoil that includes experiencing poverty, receiving a social safety net program, or encountering a spell of unemployment results in even higher rates. Consequently, between the ages of 25 and 60 years, 79 percent of the American population experienced one or more of these events during at least 1 year, and 49.8 percent experienced 3 or more years of such turmoil.[6]

The reason these percentages are so high is that over long periods of time, detrimental events are much more likely to happen to people, which can then throw them and their families into poverty.[7] These events include losing a job, families splitting up, or medical and health emergencies, all of which have the potential to start a downward spiral into poverty (discussed in Chapter 4). As we look across broad expanses of time, the probability of one or more of these events occurring increases significantly.

Rank and Hirschl's analyses also indicate that poverty is quite prevalent during childhood and older age. Between the time of birth and age 17 years, 34 percent of American children will have spent at least 1 year below the poverty line, while 40 percent will have experienced poverty or near-poverty (125 percent of the poverty line).[8] In addition, 40 percent of older adults will encounter at least 1 year of poverty between the ages of 60 and 90 years, while 48 percent will encounter poverty at the 125 percent level.[9]

Likelihood of Welfare Use

Having established that a majority of the U.S. population will experience poverty, to what extent do Americans rely on the social safety net in order to help them navigate through these periods of economic distress?

The conventional image of welfare use is one of social deviancy. In fact, few behaviors are as stigmatized in American society as that of welfare use (which we examine in Section IV). Survey research has repeatedly documented the public's considerable animosity regarding welfare programs and its participants.[10] At the heart of this opposition is the belief that welfare recipients are largely undeserving of such assistance. As Martin Gilens writes:

> While no one factor can fully account for the public's opposition to welfare, the most important single component is this widespread belief that most welfare recipients would rather sit home and collect benefits than work hard themselves. In large measure Americans hate welfare because they view it as a program that rewards the undeserving poor.[11]

Accentuating this belief is the pervasive image that those who rely on welfare are predominately minorities, are often plagued by alcohol or drug problems, have large numbers of children, and remain on the dole for years at a time. The visual portrait is of someone quite alien to mainstream America.[12] In short, for many Americans, welfare use is perceived as something that happens to someone else, and welfare recipients as diametrically opposed to the American experience.

Yet, how accurate is this assumption? To what extent will Americans find themselves economically strapped and having to rely on government assistance in order to alleviate their needs? Or, put a slightly different way, to what extent does the welfare system touch the lives of American citizens? We have seen that a majority of Americans will face the experience of poverty. Is the same pattern true of welfare use as well?

It turns out that the likelihood of using a social safety net program is also exceedingly high. Table 2.2 shows that 65 percent of all Americans between the

TABLE 2.2 Cumulative Percentage of Americans Experiencing Various Years of Welfare Receipt Across Adulthood

Age	Number of years				
	1 or more	2 or more	3 or more	4 or more	5 or more
20	14.2	—	—	—	—
25	26.6	18.9	13.9	9.8	6.7
30	33.3	26.5	22.3	17.9	14.2
35	38.7	31.9	27.4	23.3	18.1
40	43.7	36.5	32.4	27.8	21.9
45	47.2	40.6	36.5	31.4	25.3
50	50.9	44.2	40.5	35.2	29.2
55	54.6	48.2	44.1	38.8	32.2
60	58.4	52.7	48.4	42.6	35.5
65	65.0	58.7	54.2	48.0	40.3

Source: Panel Study of Income Dynamics, Rank and Hirschl computations.

ages of 20 and 65 years will at some point reside in a household that receives a means-tested welfare program (e.g., Supplemental Nutrition Assistance Program [SNAP], Medicaid). Furthermore, 40 percent of the American population will use a welfare program in 5 or more years (although spaced out at different points across the life course). As with the dynamics of poverty spells (discussed in Chapter 4), the typical pattern of welfare use is that of short spells. Consequently, only 15.9 percent of Americans will reside in a household that receives a welfare program in 5 or more consecutive years.[13]

One program that has a particularly wide reach is SNAP, better known food stamps. Approximately half (49.2 percent) of all U.S. children between the ages 1 and 20 years will at some point reside in a household that receives food stamps.[14] Childhood thus represents a time of great economic vulnerability for many of America's citizens.

Implications

Poverty has often been understood by the U.S. public as something that happens to others. Yet, by looking across the adult life span, we can see that poverty touches a clear majority of the population. For most Americans, it would appear that the question is not if they will encounter poverty, but rather, when, which entails a fundamental shift in the perception and meaning of poverty. Assuming that most individuals would rather avoid this experience, it is in their self-interest to ensure that society acts to reduce poverty and that a safety net is in place to soften the blow. Such a perspective can be referred to as a risk-sharing argument and has been elaborated most notably by the philosopher John Rawls.[15]

The dynamic here is similar to the reason most of us have automobile insurance. No one plans to have a traffic accident. Yet, we are willing to invest in automobile insurance because we realize that at some point we may be involved in a serious traffic accident that could incur sizable costs. Hence, we are willing to pay for automobile insurance now in order to minimize the risks in the future.

Rather than a traffic risk, poverty can be thought of as an economic risk that accompanies our economic system. If we lose a job, become ill, see our family split up, or experience countless other circumstances, we run a risk of dwindling income, resulting in eventual poverty. Just as automobile insurance is a form of protection against an unforeseen accident, the social safety net is a form of insurance against the accidents that occur around the rough edges of the free-market system.

Despite this, many Americans undoubtedly believe that encountering poverty is only a remote possibility, and therefore they fail to perceive the benefits of an antipoverty policy or of an economic safety net in terms of their own self-interest. The research findings discussed in this chapter directly challenge such beliefs. In doing so they provide a vital piece for making a self-interest argument: Most Americans in fact will be touched directly by poverty.

These findings have an additional implication. Much of the general public's resistance to assisting poor people and particularly those on welfare is that they are perceived to be undeserving of such assistance (examined in Section II). That is, their poverty is the result of a lack of motivation, questionable morals, and so on. In short, poor people are fundamentally culpable and, therefore, do not warrant sacrifices on our behalf.

Although the causes of poverty have not been examined in this chapter, the findings presented here suggest that given its widespread nature, poverty appears systematic to our economic structure. In short, we have met the enemy, and they are us.

Such a realization can cause a paradigm shift in thinking. For example, the economic collapse during the Great Depression spurred a fundamental change in the country's perceptions and policy initiatives as citizens realized the full extent and systematic nature of poverty during the 1930s. Given the enormity of the collapse, it became clear to many Americans that most of their neighbors were not directly responsible for the dire economic situation they found themselves in. This awareness helped provide much of the impetus and justification behind the New Deal.

Or, take the case of unemployment as described by sociologist C. Wright Mills:

> *When, in a city of 100,000, only one man is unemployed, that is his personal trouble, and for its relief we properly look to the character of the man, his skills, and his immediate opportunities. But when in a nation of 50 million employees, 15 million men are unemployed, that is an issue, and*

we may not hope to find its solution within the range of opportunities open to any one individual. The very structure of opportunities has collapsed. Both the correct statement of the problem and the range of possible solutions require us to consider the economic and political institutions of the society, and not merely the personal situation and character of a scatter of individuals.[16]

In many ways, poverty today is as widespread and systematic as in these examples. Yet, we have been unable to see this because we are not looking in the right direction. By focusing on the life span risks, the prevalent nature of American poverty is revealed. At some point during our adult lives, the bulk of Americans will face the bitter taste of poverty. Consequently, unless the general public is willing to argue that the majority of us are undeserving, the tactic of using character flaws and individual failings as a justification for doing as little as possible to address poverty loses much of its credibility.

In short, by conceptualizing and measuring impoverishment over the adult life course, one can observe a set of proportions that truly cast a new light on the subject of poverty in the United States. For the majority of American adults, the question is not if they will experience poverty, but when. Such a reality should cause us to re-evaluate seriously the very nature, scope, and meaning of poverty in the United States.

An Expert Appraisal—Caroline Ratcliffe

Caroline Ratcliffe is trained as a labor economist and was a long-time Senior Fellow at the Urban Institute where she conducted extensive research on issues involving poverty and asset building. She recently transitioned to the Consumer Financial Protection Bureau, where she is a Senior Economist in the Office of Research.

This chapter highlights the reality that poverty and means-tested benefit receipt hits closer to home than many of us realize. A majority of U.S. adults—nearly 60 percent— live in poverty for at least 1 year, and along with this financial insecurity, many experience means-tested benefit programs. Some people have their own private safety net to get through tough times (they have built up a savings cushion or can turn to family or friends), but the data presented in this chapter draw attention to the fact that, for many, their private safety net is not adequate. Driving this home, a recent Federal Reserve survey found that 37 percent of Americans cannot cover a $400 unexpected expense with savings or its equivalence.

This chapter also makes the point that we are not only talking about adults. As adults cycle into and out of poverty, they take their children with them. More than one-third of children will experience poverty between birth and age 17 years. And some of these children spend year after year in poverty. In fact, 10 percent of children spend at least half of their childhood living in poverty. As these children grow up, they are more likely to become unmarried parents, drop out of high school, lack a steady job, and be poor as young adults.

The cost of child poverty is not just borne by the poor. When the expenses related to lost productivity, crime, and poor health are added up, it is estimated that child poverty costs the nation between $800 billion and $1.1 trillion per year. This is vastly higher than the estimated $90 to $111 billion per year it would take to implement a program package that would lift half of children out of poverty.

As rightly pointed out in this chapter, preserving the social safety net will help us if and when we fall on hard times and need it. But beyond this, shoring up safety net programs and investing in poor children and families can be a long-term financially sound strategy for the United States.

{ 3 }

The Poor Tend to Live Outside of Impoverished Inner-City Neighborhoods

An image of the poor often portrayed in the media and elsewhere is that of non-Whites living in high-poverty inner-city neighborhoods.[1] It is a picture that reinforces the idea that the poor are somehow different than other Americans— that they reside in their own neighborhoods, far away from the rest of America. As Paul Jargowsky writes:

> When poverty is discussed, the mental image that often comes to mind is the inner-city, and particularly high-poverty ghettos and barrios in the largest cities. Many people implicitly assume, incorrectly, that most of the nation's poor can be found in these often troubled neighborhoods.[2]

It is certainly true that the United States remains highly segregated on the basis of race and, increasingly, class.[3] Inner cities across the country have been plagued by ongoing economic and social problems. As scholars such as William Julius Wilson have researched and written about over the decades, many of these areas are made up of the "truly disadvantaged."[4]

It is therefore surprising to many people to discover that the vast majority of the poor do not live in high-poverty, inner-city neighborhoods. In fact, only approximately 10 to 15 percent of those in poverty do so. In this chapter, we explore several of these unexpected findings.

Percentage of the Poor Living in High-Poverty Neighborhoods

Based on data from the US Census Bureau, researchers are able to determine what percentage of the poor live in high-poverty neighborhoods. The Census Bureau allows one to analyze these data at the level of what is known as a "census tract" region. A census tract can be thought of as roughly corresponding to a neighborhood, and generally averages about 4,000 people (or about 1,500 housing units).[5] In a densely populated urban area, this might include a 10– by 10–square block area, while in a rural location, a census tract would spread out over a much larger geographical region. High-poverty neighborhoods are frequently defined as census tracts in which 40 percent or more of the residents are living below the poverty line.[6]

Using this definition, Jargowsky has analyzed the percentage of the poor who are living in impoverished neighborhoods.[7] Table 3.1 shows these percentages for 1990, 2000, 2010, and 2015. In 1990, 15.1 percent of the poor were residing in high-poverty neighborhoods. That figure dropped to 10.3 percent by 2000, rose to 13.6 percent for 2010, and then fell to 11.9 percent for 2015.

The second column shows the percentage of all the census tracts in the United States that are considered high-poverty areas. In 1990, 5.7 percent of all census tracts were counted as high-poverty areas. In 2000, this percentage was 3.9 percent; by 2010, it had risen to 5.6 percent, and then it fell to 5.0 percent for 2015. Consequently, although there has been some fluctuation in the percentage of the poor living in high-poverty neighborhoods, most individuals in poverty have not and do not live in such neighborhoods.

In addition, Jargowsky finds that high-poverty neighborhoods have become less concentrated during this period of time. He notes:

Ironically, the concentration of poverty has become deconcentrated, in a sense. In 1990 and the years prior to that, most high-poverty census tracts in a metropolitan area could be found in one or two main clusters. These huge high-poverty, neighborhoods—such as Bedford-Stuyvesant, Harlem, the South Side of Chicago, North Philadelphia, and Watts—have become embedded in the public consciousness as iconic representations of urban poverty. But in the more recent data . . . the individual high-poverty tracts are more decentralized and less clustered.[8]

TABLE 3.1 Percentage of Poor People Living in High-Poverty Census Tracts and Percentage of Overall High-Poverty Census Tracts

Year	Poor people living in high poverty census tracts (%)	Overall high-poverty census tracts (%)
1990	15.5	5.7
2000	10.3	3.9
2010	13.6	5.6
2015	11.9	5.0

Note: High-poverty census tracts are defined as census tracts in which 40 percent or more of residents live below the official poverty line.

Source: Paul A. Jargowsky, personal calculations from U.S. Census Bureau and American Community Survey, 2019.

The overall finding of a minority of the poor living in high-poverty neighborhoods is consistent with the results presented in Chapter 4—that only a small percentage of those experiencing poverty do so for a long, extended period of time. Certainly, it is important to remember those deeply entrenched in poverty when discussing poverty, but it is equally important to keep in mind that they constitute a relatively small proportion of the entire poverty population.

Suburban Poverty

The words "suburban" and "poverty" are rarely uttered together. Yet, it turns out that in terms of sheer numbers, there are now more poor people living in suburban areas of the country than are living in central cities.[9]

Elizabeth Kneebone and Alan Berube addressed this phenomena in their book, *Confronting Suburban Poverty in America*.[10] They analyzed where the poor were living in 100 of the largest metropolitan areas. Approximately two-thirds of the country's population currently reside in these 100 urban areas. Suburbs were defined as those municipalities within a metropolitan area beyond the first-named city. For example, the city of St. Louis would be counted as the city in the region, while the surrounding municipalities such as Ferguson would be counted as suburban.

In Figure 3.1, we can see that the number of poor residents in suburban areas now outnumbers poor residents in city areas. While it is true that poverty rates remain higher in central cities than suburbs, because of the population growth in suburbia over the past 50 years, the actual number of poor people

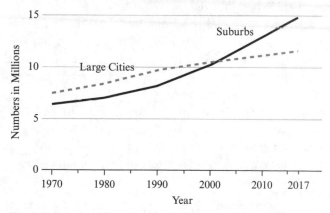

FIGURE 3.1 *Number of poor residents in suburbs and cities, 1970 to 2017.*

Source: Brookings Institution. https://www.brookings.edu/testimonies/the-changing-geography-of-us-poverty/

is now greater in suburban neighborhoods. In discussing these changes, the authors observe:

> *Poverty is a relatively new phenomena in many suburbs . . . As such, it upends deeply fixed notions of where poverty occurs and whom it affects. As poverty becomes increasingly regional in its scope and reach, it challenges conventional approaches that the nation has taken when dealing with poverty in place . . . . Poverty rates do remain higher in cities and rural communities than elsewhere. But for three decades the poor population has grown in suburbs. The especially rapid pace of growth in the 2000's saw suburbs ultimately outstrip other types of communities so that they now account for the largest poor population in the country.*[11]

Much of this poverty can be found in older, inner-ring suburban areas. These were among the first suburbs developed, often at the beginning of the 20th century. By the end of the 20th century, their infrastructure and housing stock were aging and frequently in need of repair. Likewise, some of these communities saw their school districts slowly deteriorate over time. Consequently, these have been many of the areas where the more affluent have left in order to relocate further afield. The result has been a rising number of poor households in these communities.

Rural Poverty

Like suburban poverty, poverty in rural areas is an unlikely image for many people when asked to describe where the poor live.[12] However, it turns out that the most deep-seated poverty in this country is generally found in rural America.[13] Figure 3.2 shows a map of the most persistently poor counties in the United States over the past 40 years. These are counties that have had poverty rates of more than 20 percent from the 1980 Census onward.

We can see that the vast majority of these counties are rural or nonmetropolitan. Of the 353 counties with persistent poverty, 301 are nonmetropolitan. We can also observe from the map that there are certain distinct regions of the country where these counties are found. Each of these areas has a unique historical legacy of poverty.

The area of Appalachia, found predominately in West Virginia and Kentucky, is a region of long-standing White poverty.[14] It is characterized by the dominance and gradual disappearance of the coal mining industry. As a result, service sector types of jobs are often all that remains.[15] In writing about this, Cynthia Duncan notes:

> *There are so few jobs available in these communities, and so many who need work, that people seek fast-food and other part-time retail work in order to*

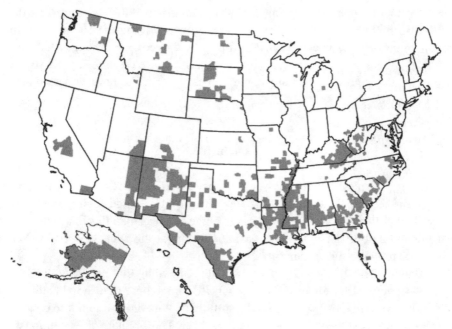

FIGURE 3.2 *Persistently poor counties, 1990 to 2010.*
Source: U.S. Census Bureau, 2019. http://www.ruralhome.org/sct-initiatives/mn-persistent-poverty

*support their families. But the jobs are set up for those who do not need them
to offer a living wage. When household heads do get these jobs, their hours
are always uncertain and unpredictable, always subject to change.*[16]

A second area of deep-seated rural poverty can be found across the Deep South
and the Mississippi Delta region. This is an area with a history of slavery and
cotton plantations. Many of the poor in this region are the descendants of slaves
and sharecroppers. Again, good job opportunities are often few and far between.[17]

The Texas–Mexico border along the Rio Grande constitutes a third area
of deeply entrenched rural poverty. Here one finds a largely Latinx population
with a long history of being exploited.[18] The *colonias* along the border represent largely impoverished communities that are lacking in basic public services.

The Southwest and Northern Plains (including parts of Alaska) are also
marked by high poverty. Much of this poverty is specific to Native Americans,
often on reservations. These counties frequently have some of the highest rates
of poverty in the country.[19] The history here is one of exploitation, broken
treaties, and the decimation of Native people.

Finally, the central corridor of California represents an area of high poverty, especially among migrant laborers. It is a region marked by historically
low wages paid to farm laborers and their families. Most of these workers are
of Hispanic origin.[20]

The fact that poverty is greater in rural than urban America contradicts the bucolic image that we often have of small towns dotting the countryside. In fact, many of these areas have been crippled by the economic changes that have taken place in the past 50 years.[21] Small towns have often seen their main streets bordered up, and small farming communities in particular have witnessed devastating changes.

Conclusion

The image of poverty that many hold in their mind is one of inner-city poverty. While no one should doubt that such poverty is quite real and debilitating, those living in poverty reside in a much wider range of areas than this image implies. In fact, the poor can be found in just about any location across America. Yet, such poverty often seems invisible.

One reason for this is that poverty is not something that people wish to acknowledge or draw attention to. Rather, it is something that individuals and families would like to go away. As a result, many Americans attempt to conceal their economic difficulties as much as possible.[22] This often involves keeping up appearances and trying to maintain a "normal" lifestyle. Such poverty down the block may at first appear invisible. Nevertheless, the reach of poverty is widespread, touching nearly all communities across America.

The myth that poverty is confined to a particular group of Americans, in very specific locations, is corrosive because it encourages the belief that poverty is an issue of "them" rather than "us." As discussed in Chapter 2, poverty strikes a wide swath of the population. In addition, as we have shown in this chapter, it touches Americans in cities, suburbs, and rural communities. Given this, it is much more accurate to think of poverty as affecting us, rather than them.

An Expert Appraisal—Paul A. Jargowsky

Paul A. Jargowsky is Professor of Public Policy at Rutgers University, and is also the director of the Center for Urban Research and Urban Education. Much of his research has focused on the geographic concentration of poverty, as well as patterns of residential segregation by race and class.

When poverty is discussed in the United States, the image that comes to many people's minds is, to use sociologist Elijah Anderson's memorable phrase, the "iconic ghetto." Several myths are bundled together in this mental association. The first myth, as the title of this chapter points out, is that most poor people live in high-poverty ghettos and barrios. The second is that all high-poverty neighborhoods are in the central cities of large metropolitan areas, such as New York, Chicago, and Los Angeles. The third is that all African Americans and Hispanics are poor and reside in such places. This chapter, and many of the others in this volume, do well to tease apart fact and fiction with respect to these topics.

One can hardly blame those who have internalized these ideas. Urban ghettos and barrios—usually depicted as violent and rat-infested—are a staple of movies and TV shows. Depictions of harsh and exploitative neighborhoods are also common in rap music and rags-to-riches memoirs. Politicians looking for votes visit such neighborhoods to push the latest "zone" program promising to revitalize stricken urban cores, only to disappear after the election is over. Judging by the books and articles they write, poverty scholars also seem to focus disproportionately on the urban poor living in high-poverty neighborhoods, often focusing on the question of the effect such neighborhoods may have on children who grow up there.

As this chapter points out, there are now significantly more concentrations of poverty outside central cities. The inner-ring suburb of Ferguson, Missouri, was a mostly White, middle-class suburb as recently as 1990. Now, it is poor and mostly Black, and it recently experienced some of worst racial unrest since the 1960s, ignited by the police killing of Michael Brown. The growth of poverty in suburban locations strains local governments that lack the experience or capacity to provide social services. And poverty in rural areas and Native American reservations seems intractable because of geographic isolation in areas with little economic activity.

Neither the public, the academy, nor the government should focus on the poor residing in high-poverty areas to the exclusion of the larger number of poor residing in less disadvantaged neighborhoods or outside traditional urban cores. Yet, it is worth noting that those poor living in urban high-poverty areas face significant challenges. Not only must they cope with their own lack of resources, but also they reside in neighborhoods that often have low-quality housing stock, vacant buildings, crime and violence, and underperforming schools. Recent research has found significant negative effects on children who grow up in such environments. The existence of these neighborhoods has resulted to a large degree from unwise public policies regarding mortgage lending, exclusionary zoning, and large-scale subsidies for suburban sprawl. While we should improve the social safety net for all poor people, wherever they live, we must also reverse the process that creates economically and racially segregated neighborhoods that make all the problems of poverty worse.

{ 4 }

Poverty Spells Are Short but Frequent

An overriding poverty myth is that the poor are fundamentally different from other Americans. As part of this stereotype, they are often viewed as locked into a pattern of long-term poverty because of their dysfunctional character- istics. The mental image is one of families experiencing poverty year in and year out.

This myth can be seen frequently in media images of the poor. Whether it is about the poverty of single women having numerous children, homeless men living on the streets, or long-term poverty in economically distressed rural America, the story projected is one of chronic poverty. This dovetails closely with a perspective in the social sciences known as the culture of poverty.

The culture of poverty argument asserts that poverty has become a way of life for many of the poor, and that this way of life is passed down from one genera- tion to the next. Perhaps the most popular proponent of this viewpoint today is the author Ruby Paine.[1] Paine has made a career out of advising school districts around the country on how they can best understand and address the needs of poor children in their schools. Her assumption is that such children are locked into long-term poverty and that, as a result, they have developed a completely different way of life and style of learning than their middle-class counterparts.

In sharp contrast, academics over the past 40 years have built up a sizable volume of research measuring the actual length of time that individuals will spend in poverty. They have also estimated how frequently households will experience poverty and the events leading families into and out of poverty. As demonstrated throughout this book, these realities are quite different than the myths.

Most Poverty Spells Are Short

Before the advent of large longitudinal data sets tracking the same people over extended periods of time, it was often assumed that those living in poverty during the current year are roughly the same people who were living in poverty the previous year and who will be the next year. These assumptions were largely based on anecdotal stories. However, beginning in the mid-1970s, social scientists have gathered substantial information from large longitudinal data sets about the actual patterns and length of time that individuals find themselves in poverty.[2] It turns out that a much more accurate picture is that poverty spells tend to be short but frequent. Poverty is more often fluid, rather than the static image portrayed in the myths.

Table 4.1 displays the percentage of new poverty spells in the United States that end within a given number of years. As we can see, within 1 or 2 years, the majority of people escaped from poverty. Within 1 year, 53 percent of new spells ended; 70 percent ended within 2 years, and more than three-fourths within 3 years. Less than 15 percent of spells last more than 5 years.[3] If we consider long-term poverty as lasting 5 or more consecutive years, then the vast majority of American poverty spells do not meet such a standard. As Mary Jo Bane and David Ellwood explained years ago in one of the first analyses of American poverty spells: "Most people who slip into poverty are quite successful in getting out."[4]

Another way of seeing the relatively short-term nature of poverty spells is through a U.S. Census analysis of monthly poverty. Using a large longitudinal data set known as the Survey of Income and Program Participation (SIPP), poverty can be analyzed on a monthly rather than an annual basis. During the 36 months of 2009, 2010, and 2011, 31.6 percent of the U.S. population experienced poverty at some point (defined as being in poverty for 2 or more consecutive months). However, for those experiencing poverty, 72.1 percent did so for 12 months or less, while only 15.2 percent of individuals experienced poverty for more than 24 consecutive months.[5] Again, the vast majority of those experiencing poverty do so over a fairly short period of time.

TABLE 4.1 Spell Length Distribution for New Poverty Spells

Years in poverty	New spells that ended (%)
1	52.5
2	69.7
3	77.9
4	82.9
5	86.1
6	88.3
7	90.1
8	91.3
9	92.3

Source: Ann Huff Stevens, "Climbing Out of Poverty, Falling Back In: Measuring the Persistence of Poverty over Multiple Spells," *Journal of Human Resources* 34, no. 3 (Summer 1999), p. 568.

Research has also shown that poverty entrances and exits are most often caused by changes in employment status and/or financial resources. This could involve getting laid off from a job or having one's hours cut. Other causes of entrances/exits include changes in family structure (e.g., divorce/marriage, childbirth, or a child leaving home to start their own household), changes in disability status, educational attainment, and regional employment conditions (e.g., the number of jobs available and wage levels).[6] These are common events that most of us will experience over the life course. Some Americans live closer to the poverty line than others, however, making these events more consequential in their lives. But they can happen to any of us, and for those close to the line who fall into poverty as a result, most fight hard to escape poverty and succeed relatively quickly.

Poverty spells triggered by moving out of one's parents' house tend to be the shortest, while spells triggered by the birth of a child tend to be the longest. Employment, education, and marriage are helpful in both avoiding poverty and exiting faster if one does become poor. African Americans, women, female single-parent households, and those with low educational attainment are at higher risk of new spells, multiple spells, and longer lasting spells.[7]

While short-term poverty is the norm, long-term poverty is nevertheless a concern. Some analyses show that, at any given moment, a majority of the poor are enduring long-term poverty spells of 10 years or more.[8] How could this be, if most new poverty spells end within 1 or 2 years? Bane and Ellwood explain with a helpful metaphor:

> Consider the situation in a typical hospital. Most of the persons admitted in any year will require only a very short spell of hospitalization. But a few of the newly admitted patients are chronically ill and will have extended stays in the hospital. If we ask what proportion of all admissions are people who are chronically ill, the answer is relatively few. On the other hand, if we ask what fraction of the number of the hospital's beds at any one time are occupied by the chronically ill, the answer is much larger. The reason is simple. Although the chronically ill account for only a small fraction of all admissions, because they stay so long they end up being a sizable part of the hospital population and they consume a sizable proportion of the hospital's resources.[9]

So, while most Americans who find themselves in poverty will be there for only a matter of a few years, persistent poverty is in fact a concern. This minority of the poor does indeed present unique challenges to policymakers compared with the majority of those experiencing short-term poverty.

The risk of experiencing multiple spells is also a concern. Despite the norm of short spells for most people, slightly more than half of those who escape poverty will return for an additional spell within 5 years. The longer one experiences poverty, the harder it is to escape, and the more likely one is to return to poverty. While a majority will exit poverty within the first year, the likelihood of escaping declines rapidly after that. For those who have been in poverty for 5 years, their likelihood of exit is less than 20 percent. And of those who have been in poverty for at least 5 years before exit, more than two-thirds will return within 5 years.[10]

Data on time spent on government assistance is also helpful to this discussion. A little more than one-fourth (27 percent) of Americans use at least one major means-tested program—Medicaid, Supplemental Nutrition Assistance Program (SNAP), Supplemental Security Income (SSI), Temporary Assistance for Needy Families (TANF), and/or General Assistance (GA)—at some point during the year. Participation within a given year is higher for female single-parent households (58 percent vs. 20 percent for married couples), African Americans and Hispanics (49 and 46 percent vs. 18 percent for Whites), children (47 percent vs. 23 percent for working-age adults), those without a high school degree (45 percent vs. 29 percent for high school graduates), and unemployed individuals (42 percent vs. 11 percent for full-time workers). Within a 4-year period, a majority of participants (57 percent) use these programs for 3 years or less. Medicaid and SNAP are the most heavily used programs (15 percent and 13 percent monthly participation, respectively).[11]

The program that Americans most often strongly associate with "welfare"—TANF—is used much less than other programs (1 percent of the population monthly, 1.7 percent over a 4-year period).[12] Spells on TANF are also very short: about half (49 percent) end within 4 months, and more than three-fourths (78 percent) end within a year. Additionally, the vast majority of TANF participants (72 percent) use the program for 2 years or less in a given 10-year period.[13]

Economic Insecurity Is Widespread

In addition to the myth that most poverty spells are long, the belief that encountering economic insecurity is an outlier experience is false. Economic insecurity is in fact something that happens to most of us. As shown in Chapter 2, a majority of Americans will experience poverty (58 percent) and near-poverty (76 percent) for at least 1 year in their lifetimes.[14] Additionally, by age 60 years, a majority will have been unemployed for a spell (67 percent), a sizable minority (45 percent) will have had to rely on welfare, and an overwhelming majority (79 percent) will have experienced some form of economic insecurity (poverty/near poverty, unemployment, and/or welfare use) for at least 1 year.[15]

Furthermore, substantial proportions of the American population will experience multiple years of economic insecurity as well as consecutive years. More than half of the population will experience at least 2 (62 percent) or 3 (50 percent) total years of economic in security, while more than one-third will

experience at least 4 (42 percent) or 5 (35 percent) total years.[16] In terms of
consecutive years, approximately one-half (51 percent) experience 2 or more
consecutive years, about one-third (34 percent) endure 3 or more, and nearly
one-fourth (24 percent) experience 4 or more consecutive years of economic
insecurity.[17] Again, the pattern is that economic insecurity will strike a majority
of the population but will do so for a relatively short period of time.

In fact, regardless of which period of adulthood one examines, whether it is
early in one's career or as when approaching retirement, "during any 10-year
age period across the prime working years, at least half of the population will
experience one or more years of significant economic insecurity."[18]

Punishing Life Events

What these data tell us is that "the reach of economic distress is quite wide, but
its grip is less severe. The typical life course pattern is that individuals tend to
move in and out of economic turmoil, depending on the changing conditions
in their lives."[19] Some groups are likely to be poor more frequently and for a
longer duration than others. For millions of Americans who are living paycheck to paycheck and precariously close to the poverty line, normal life events
like the birth of a child or temporary loss of a job can send them below the
poverty line. But poverty spells tend to be short, and they are caused by the risk
associated with normal events that happen to most of us across the life course.
They are just more catastrophic for some than for others. Indicative of how
close many Americans are to poverty, a recent study by the Federal Reserve
Bank found that 37 percent of Americans do not have enough savings put aside
to protect them from a $400 emergency.[20]

What is abnormal about this situation is not that people experience these
events, but that we have collectively chosen as a society to punish these normal
life events so severely. Because of this, poverty is a much more normal and
systemic feature of the American experience than it is in many other wealthy
countries.

David Brady and colleagues have shown this to be empirically the case across
29 rich democracies. The authors focused on four major risks of poverty—low
education, single motherhood, young adults heading a household, and unemployment. They found that although the prevalence of these risks in the United
States is actually below the average in other countries, the rate of poverty in
the United States is the highest. The reason is that "the penalties for risks in
the United States are the highest of the 29 countries. An individual with all
four risks has an extremely heightened probability of being poor in the United
States."

Take the examples of single parents and young parents. In one cross-national
analysis of single-parent family poverty rates, the country that penalized

single-parent families the least (Denmark) boasted a single-parent family poverty rate of only 8 percent. In the country that penalized these families the most (the United States), the rate was about 4 times higher at 33 percent.[21] In another analysis of poverty rates for young-parent families in rich democracies, the penalty was twice as high or higher for young headship in the United States compared with countries like Australia and Japan.[22] This is largely because of the different contexts in which these family structures occur. In some countries, social policies are designed to protect a wider variety of families than in the United States, regardless of their structure. In the United States, we have collectively decided that we are not going to protect all families to the same degree, and this is reflected in our social policies and resulting poverty rates for these families.

Consider another example—education. It is true that in most countries, as in the United States, a higher level of educational attainment is typically associated with a lower risk of economic insecurity. But the penalties associated with low levels of educational attainment, and the rewards associated with high levels of attainment, vary significantly by country. Full-time workers without a high school degree in Finland, for instance, report the same earnings as those with a high school degree. In the United States, however, these workers experience a 24 percent earnings penalty for not completing high school.[23] In Norway, a college degree yields only a 20 percent earnings increase over a high school degree for full-time workers, versus a much higher 68 percent increase in the United States.[24] The percentage of those with a high school degree earning at or below the poverty threshold is more than 4 times higher in the United States than in Belgium.[25]

Finally, consider the example of unemployment (as shown in Figure 4.1). There are 19 rich democracies that have a higher prevalence of unemployment than the United States, and only nine that have a lower prevalence. What is different about the United States is not the prevalence of unemployment, but the penalty associated with it. We can see in Figure 4.1 that there are only four rich

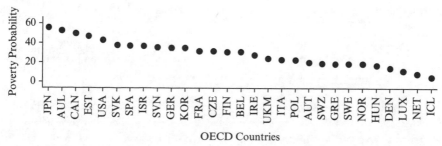

FIGURE 4.1 *Increased poverty probability for the unemployed across 29 rich democracies.*

Source: David Brady, Ryan M. Finnegan, and Sabine Hübgen, "Rethinking the Risks of Poverty: A Framework for Analyzing Prevalences and Penalties," *American Journal of Sociology* 123, no. 3 (November 2017), p. 753.

democracies that penalize unemployment more severely than the United States, and 24 that penalize it less severely. Unemployed workers are much more likely to fall into poverty in countries like the United States, Canada, and Japan, compared with countries such as the Netherlands and Iceland.

Conclusion

To truly alleviate poverty on a large scale, we must fix a system in which normal life experiences such as childbirth can translate into economic insecurity. Most of the poor are not unexplainable anomalies in an otherwise well-functioning society. Instead, they are the normal consequence of structural arrangements guaranteed to produce economic insecurity.

Yet, it may be easier to believe that poverty is something that happens to deficient "others" who are hopelessly locked into a vicious cycle of their own doing. It eases our minds, assuring us that our own personal risk is minimal. It also helps us to avoid the stressful notion that significant systemic failings persist in our country. This, of course, has the potential to undermine our empathy, distort our understanding of how society works, and in the process hamper social progress.

In contrast, poverty is something that most Americans will experience for a short period of time as a consequence of very "normal" occurrences—the loss of a job, the birth of a child, the transition to adulthood, the dissolution of a marriage, and so on. This suggests that the poor are not some deviant group of different "others" that cannot be helped. Instead, they are generally everyday people like you and me who hit a bump in the road and fall on hard times. Once there, the vast majority fight hard to escape poverty and succeed in a short period of time. If we as a society can better manage this systemic problem, we can better manage the risks of new entry into poverty, make them less common, and make the experience of poverty less severe.

An Expert Appraisal—Signe-Mary Mckernan and Kassandra Martinchek

Signe-Mary McKernan is trained as an economist and is currently the co-director of the Opportunity and Ownership initiative at the Urban Institute. Kassandra Martinchek is a research analyst at the Urban Institute.

Any notion of the poor as a permanent underclass in the United States is a myth. Most Americans will experience poverty, and most people who become poor do not spend a long time in poverty. Believing this myth is damaging—it shapes the way we perceive our public benefits programs, our neighbors, and even our own financial security.

Believing that the poor in America are a permanent underclass can warp our beliefs about how our social safety net works and how people fall into poverty, as well as the development of policies that meaningfully address these issues. It implies that safety net programs are largely ineffective because those in poverty remain so for long periods of time. In contrast, SNAP receipt reduces the likelihood of being food insecure by roughly 30 percent, and the safety net (TANF, SNAP, and Medicaid/Children's Health Insurance Program [CHIP]) reduces material hardship by 48 percent.

Nevertheless, we may adopt stories about the behavior of people who experience poverty to explain why they face hardship. We may falsely believe that people in poverty do not work. Or, we may adopt a "welfare queen" view, another myth that most poor people are manipulating the system. However, fraud is rare.

By relying on the myth of a permanent poor underclass, we often develop policies that have unintended consequences. Asset limits (or savings penalties) are designed so that only the most vulnerable can access public benefit programs. However, in practice, they discourage low-income households from having a checking or savings account and building a savings cushion. Relaxed asset limits increase low-income household savings and mainstream financial market participation.

This myth can also warp the way we perceive our own financial security and well-being. If we believe poverty is rare, we may adopt financial behaviors that undermine our financial security and well-being—such as saving for a rainy day.

In summary, despite the common myth that the poor in the United States are a permanent underclass, evidence shows that poverty will affect a significant number of us. Most individuals will escape quickly, but there is a good chance some will get thrown back into poverty later in life. Our public safety net can help reduce the number of material hardships experienced by families, and we must realize that we all have a stake in the success of such programs.

Whites Are the Largest Racial Group
Experiencing Poverty

Close your eyes and think about a "typical" person experiencing poverty. Who do you imagine? A woman or man? An adult or child? A person of color or someone who is White? If you are like many people, whom you envision may not align with the reality of people actually living in poverty. This is particularly the case when it comes to racial demographics. Although White Americans make up the largest number of individuals living below the poverty line in the United States, the tendency to equate poverty with people of color, particularly African Americans, persists. In this chapter, we delve into this myth, separating racialized stereotypes from reality, and attending closely to the role of media in perpetuating this pervasive misconception.

Race and Poverty Demographics

In thinking about who specifically in the U.S. population experiences poverty, there are at least two ways of approaching this question. The first is to focus on which groups have a higher or lower rate of poverty compared with the general population. This allows us to examine to what extent various population characteristics are associated with the risk of poverty.

The second approach looks at the overall poverty population with respect to group composition. This informs us about what the face and makeup of poverty look like. Each of these approaches tells us something slightly different about who the poor are.

Let us consider the example of race. Non-Whites (specifically African Americans, Hispanics, and Native Americans) have much higher rates of poverty than Whites. However, the majority of the poor are White. How can this be? The answer is that Whites account for a much larger segment of the overall population, and therefore, even though their rate of poverty is lower than that of non-Whites, they still make up a majority of the poor.

Table 5.1 shows how the rate of poverty and the composition of the poor population vary by race. It should be noted that "Hispanic" is considered an ethnic rather than a racial category. Consequently, one could self-identify as both White and Hispanic, or as Black and Hispanic.

For Whites (not of Hispanic origin), the poverty rate in 2019 was 7.3 percent. In contrast, the rate for other groups was considerably higher: The poverty rate for Blacks was 18.8 percent; for Hispanics, 15.7 percent; for Native Americans, 23.7 percent; and for Asian and Pacific Islander Americans, 7.3 percent.

These differences reflect the disparities found across many economic measures. They include significant racial and ethnic differences in income, unemployment rates, net worth, educational attainment, and occupational status.[1] The result is a much higher overall rate of poverty for non-Whites compared with Whites.

On the other hand, we can also see that approximately two-thirds of the poor self-identify as White. As noted previously, this is primarily the result of the relatively larger size of the overall White population, so that while the face of poverty is largely White, the risk of poverty is much greater for non-Whites.

The bottom line is that Whites comprise the largest share of the population in both poverty and the overall U.S. population, while communities of color consist of smaller shares of both groups yet are significantly more likely to experience poverty. Relative to their shares of the total population, African Americans, Hispanics, and Native Americans are overrepresented among people experiencing poverty, with poverty rates more than double that of Whites. Nevertheless, Whites make up the largest share of the population in poverty because their overall size in the general population is much larger.

Many of the same demographic patterns and misperceptions that distort understandings of poverty are also evident in stereotypes about safety net programs and their recipients. An exchange between President Donald Trump and the U.S. Congressional Black Caucus vividly illustrates the tendency to

TABLE 5.1 Poverty Rates and Racial Composition of the Poor, 2019

Demographic characteristics	Poverty rate (%)	Percentage of poor population
Total	10.5	100.0
Race and ethnicity		
Whites	9.1	66.2
Not of Hispanic origin	7.3	41.6
Blacks	18.8	23.8
Hispanics	15.7	28.1
Native Americans	23.7	1.7
Asian and Pacific Islander Americans	7.3	4.3

Source: U.S. Census Bureau, 2020.

equate welfare receipt with people of color. When one of the caucus members observed that welfare reform would harm her constituents and noted, "not all of whom are Black," President Trump queried, "Really? Then what are they?"[2] As is the case with poverty, they are probably White. For example, White Americans make up the largest percentage of people participating in the Supplemental Nutrition Assistance Program (SNAP), which provides food assistance to low-income individuals and families. In 2017, 35.8 percent of SNAP recipients were White, 25.4 percent were African American, 16.5 percent Hispanic, and 3.2 percent Asian American.[3] Whites also account for the largest number (23.5 million) and percentage (41 percent) of people who are not senior citizens and receive health care through Medicaid, a program that serves low-income individuals and families.[4] People of color are overrepresented in these programs, but Whites again make up the largest share of recipients.

Temporary Assistance for Needy Families (TANF), which provides cash assistance to low-income families with children and is the program most often associated with "welfare," diverges from this pattern. The largest share of TANF recipients in 2018 were Hispanic (37.8 percent), followed by African Americans (28.9 percent), White Americans (27.2 percent), and Asian Americans (1.9 percent).[5] However, reviewing demographic trends over time reveals that this has not always been the case. Before the passage of the Personal Responsibility and Work Opportunity Reconciliation Act of 1996 (PRWORA), Whites typically made up a larger share of cash aid caseloads than Hispanics and a similar share as African American recipients. Some researchers attribute these shifting demographics to restrictive welfare reform regulations that discourage all but those with the least resources and opportunities from applying for assistance and push recipients who can to exit the program and to do so as quickly as possible. As a consequence, families of color and other recipients with limited social and human capital may be more likely to receive TANF.

Media and the Persistence of Racialized Poverty Myths

Media plays a powerful role in encouraging and reinforcing the association of people of color, especially African Americans, with poverty and safety net programs. The overrepresentation of Blacks and the relative invisibility of Whites in news stories about poverty and welfare is well documented. In a content analysis of 2015–2016 television, print, and online news stories, 59 percent of poor people who were discussed or portrayed were African American, yet they accounted for just 27 percent of people experiencing poverty at the time.[6] Conversely, Whites constituted 66 percent of the low-income population but were depicted in just 17 percent of news media stories.[7] These skewed representations were present in both right- and left-leaning news sources.

Over time, there has been little change in these representations. In Martin Gilens' study of portrayals of race and poverty in three high-circulation news magazines published between 1988 and 1992, African Americans represented 62 percent of the poor people depicted, over twice their actual proportion of 29 percent.[8] A follow-up examination of the same news magazines documented the continued overrepresentation of African American poverty between 1992 and 2010.[9]

Not surprisingly, racial misrepresentations are also common in media portrayals of welfare recipients. In Maura Kelly's analysis of television news coverage of welfare reform, 58 percent of the public assistance recipients profiled were African American, a sizable overrepresentation of the 39 percent of aid recipients during this time period who were African American.[10] Another analysis found that 55 percent of welfare recipients pictured in news magazines were Black, when they actually made up 38 percent of program participants.[11] As Gilens notes, "This distorted portrait of the American poor cannot help but reinforce negative stereotypes of blacks as mired in poverty and contribute to the belief that poverty is primarily a 'black' problem."[12]

Importantly, media does much more than communicate—and in this case distort—the prevalence of poverty among diverse racial groups. It also conveys powerful messages about which low-income groups "deserve" assistance. African Americans are less likely to appear in news stories about poverty that cover sympathetic topics (e.g., employment programs, health care) or to be portrayed as members of "deserving" groups (e.g., people who are working or actively looking for employment, children, senior citizens).[13] Instead, by depicting African Americans as part of an urban underclass and providing limited information about the structural causes of poverty, common media representations are unlikely to generate empathy for people experiencing poverty or support for antipoverty initiatives.[14] The overrepresentation of African Americans as poor, in and of itself, has been found to undermine support for antipoverty initiatives by activating racist and classist stereotypes about laziness and lack of motivation among African Americans and people experiencing poverty (see also Chapter 6).[15]

Consistent with media representations, the public exaggerates the association of people of color with poverty and welfare receipt. Public opinion polls document both the durability and prevalence of this association. For example, when asked whether certain demographic groups tend to be rich or poor, 31 percent of poll respondents in 1994 believed that almost all African Americans were poor or near-poor; a sizable 20 percent of respondents held this same belief in 2014.[16] At both time points, only 1 to 2 percent of respondents believed that almost all Whites lived in or near poverty.[17] Along these same lines, welfare receipt among people of color is overestimated, with one poll finding that only 21 percent of Americans were able to correctly identify that there are more White SNAP recipients than Black recipients.[18] Collectively, these findings further underscore the minimization of White poverty and the tendency to associate being Black with being poor.

Fundamental social psychological processes contribute to the persistence of racialized poverty myths including the tendency to equate poverty with people of color. People tend to remember information that is consistent with their preexisting beliefs and may even misremember information to maintain a sense of consistency (discussed in Chapter 19). For instance, after watching a videotaped story, Franklin Gilliam found that White respondents were less likely to remember seeing a White than a Black welfare recipient.[19] In such cases, people may be unaware of the associations they are making between race, poverty, and welfare.

Mental representations of race and welfare receipt were further probed in an innovative series of visual imaging studies by Jazmin Brown-Iannuzzi and her colleagues.[20] The researchers created a morphed composite of a White woman, a Black woman, a White man, and a Black man, adding various characteristics to create many different versions. Participants were then presented with pairs of faces and asked to select which looked more like a "welfare recipient." Compared with the image of the "average" nonrecipient, the image of the "typical" welfare recipient was perceived as more African American (less White) and as aligning more closely with common stereotypes of both welfare recipients and African Americans (e.g., lazy, incompetent).[21] In turn, participants allocated less support to the hypothetical person depicted in the image of the prototypical welfare recipient (who was viewed as more African American) than to the hypothetical person in the nonrecipient image.

Furthermore, when White Americans' sense of economic advantage over racial minorities is threatened, they express greater opposition to welfare programs, but only if these programs are portrayed as primarily benefiting people of color and not Whites.[22] These findings make clear the important role of racial resentment in stoking opposition to welfare programs. However, with Whites making up the largest number of SNAP and Medicaid beneficiaries, their support for program cuts is likely to cause greater harm to in-group members than anticipated.

Conclusion

Annual poverty statistics and participation rates in safety net programs tell a very different story about race and poverty than what we learn from the media. The consequences of minimizing poverty among Whites and overestimating its prevalence among people of color has far-reaching consequences, from reinforcing deep-rooted racism to undermining support for social welfare programs. Challenging myths that surround race and poverty will require not only debunking racist stereotypes but also providing accurate media coverage of poverty and use of welfare programs.

In their book, *Fighting Poverty in the U.S. and Europe: A World of Difference*, economists Alberto Alesina and Edward Glaeser note:

> *Experimental evidence shows that people tend to be more sympathetic to individuals of the same race, so a less generous welfare state is in part due to the fact that the white majority does not want to redistribute in a way that would favor racial minorities. Racial differences between rich and poor facilitated the propagation of views such as "all poor are lazy" precisely because racist views associate laziness with different skin colors. In Sweden, say, where 95 percent of the population has the same race, ethnicity, and religion, it is much more difficult to identify the poor with some racial characteristics.[23]*

They go on to argue:

> *Racial conflicts can also be used strategically by political entrepreneurs interested not so much in "hating blacks" but in preventing redistribution. By convincing even the not so rich whites that redistribution favors minorities, they have been able to build large coalitions against welfare policies. In other words, some poor whites are willing to vote against redistribution that would favor them because their racial animosity wants to prevent blacks from getting the same redistribution.[24]*

An example of this comes from President Lyndon Johnson. As he explained to an aide in 1960, "I'll tell you what's at the bottom of it. If you can convince the lowest white man that he's better than the best colored man, he won't notice you picking his pocket. Hell, give him somebody to look down on, and he'll empty his pockets for you."[25]

Clearly then, distorted perceptions of the racial makeup of the poverty and welfare populations further attenuates the tendency to be less generous toward the collective needs in a racially heterogeneous society such as the United States. It helps to partially explain why the United States has been such an outlier with respect to its minimal welfare state.

An Expert Appraisal—Alice O'Connor

Alice O'Connor is Professor of History and the Director of the Blum Center on Global Poverty Alleviation and Sustainable Development at the University of California at Santa Barbara. She is the author of *Poverty Knowledge: Social Science, Social Policy, and the Poor in Twentieth-Century U.S. History*.

We have to think about the terminology of poverty. If people think about poverty broadly—as economic struggle, hardship, needing to get by, and not being able to pay the bills—I actually think that there is a much wider recognition among the public that economic hardship is a problem of the economy. Economic hardship is a problem of the vast inequity not just in terms of low wages, but also in the fact that individuals do not have any control over the economy or jobs and wages. I think there is a widespread sense of that.

On the other hand, when people talk about poverty they continue to think about what they consider to be expressions of some kind of economic or cultural pathology. They tend to think about things like the underclass, the visible homeless, or persons of color. And that is where they draw distinctions. That it is not the same as the type of economic hardship that a lot of people are facing who cannot pay the bills—the sort of falling off by the wayside. People still tend to associate the word poverty with the outcasts in society. That is my broad sense.

Researchers continue to do surveys where they ask people to make such distinctions. It would be interesting to see in the future if there has been much of a change in that. I know there has been a shift in the sensibility of economic hardship and how many people experience it. No question about that. In terms of what images poverty brings to mind, my sense is that we still have people drawing a line, and that poverty is pathology, whereas economic hardship is something that a whole lot of people in this country are going through right now.

There is currently more sympathy and more of a structural understanding of economic hardship. But I still think people continue to draw the line between that and poverty, which they consider to be people who are off the rails and are somehow culturally dysfunctional. This serves as a form of cultural affirmation in a lot of ways— especially if you can explain that level of hardship through not, "There but for the grace of God go I," but instead as something "I am never going to experience because I have the character to avoid that situation." Thinking about poverty the way we do reaffirms our own sense that, "I did this on my own, I had the character and work ethic to make it."

Why Is There Poverty?

We now turn to a second major area where poverty myths abound. It revolves around the question, "Why does poverty exist?" This question is fundamental because the answer will largely determine our response to addressing poverty.

The myths surrounding this question have generally centered on the belief that poverty is the result of individual failing. This takes many different forms—the poor are not working hard enough, have made bad decisions in life, have not acquired necessary skills or education, are not smart enough, have questionable morals, are addicted to alcohol or drugs, and so on. The underlying theme is that the causes of poverty can be understood through the lens of individual failure and pathology.

The consequence of this mindset is the belief that the poor must get their own house in order—that only they can pull themselves out of poverty through motivation and hard work. On the other hand, government assistance is often viewed as making the problem worse by fostering dependence.

These myths dovetail with the wider emphasis placed in American society on the importance of individualism. America was founded on the ideal of rugged individualism and self-reliance. The aspirations of conquering a frontier were premised on these values. Thus, it should not be surprising that they also color the types of explanations that people give when asked why poverty exists.

{ 6 }

Hard Work Is Insufficient

"Hard work is the key to success." It is an adage that we have heard from early childhood onward. "As long as you work hard, you can accomplish almost anything!" one is often told. Americans have long been steeped in the ethos of hard work, with the Protestant work ethic profoundly shaping the character of the country.[1]

The phrase, "Pull yourself up by your own bootstraps" is also one embedded in the American lexicon, and is the predominant mindset when it comes to explaining poverty.[2] There is a widespread belief that with hard work and effort, anyone can avoid poverty.[3] Yet, how important is hard work in terms of falling into or getting out of poverty? In this chapter, we explore the widely held myth that the primary cause of poverty is a lack of hard work and effort.

Over the past decades, each of us in our research projects has talked about this topic with hundreds of people from many walks of life. Based on these interviews, as well as other research in the field, we have reached an overall conclusion that hard work is generally a necessary but not a sufficient condition for getting ahead. In other words, hard work and effort are typically important ingredients for reaching one's goals in life, but they do not guarantee success in and of themselves.

We can think about this relationship in the following way. It is difficult to imagine individuals doing well in life without a decent amount of effort and work. Even for those born into wealth, hard work and motivation are generally required for reaching one's goals. And for those starting with much less, hard work and initiative would appear to be essential.

On the other hand, we have interviewed scores of people who have worked very hard throughout their adult lives but have struggled to achieve economic success. Each of us has talked with women and men who have worked extremely hard but nevertheless found themselves in poverty or close to poverty. In these cases, a multitude of factors, such as the lack of opportunities, racial or gender discrimination, the process of cumulative disadvantage, or simple randomness, may have hindered their success and mobility. Consequently, working hard and being motivated by no means guarantee individual success.

Hard Working Examples

Someone who has seen this pattern play out repeatedly is Madeline McBride, who was interviewed in Mark Rank's book, *Chasing the American Dream*.[4] Madeline has worked in various capacities on issues affecting lower income individuals and families, including her current job as a state legislator representing an urban working-class district. In much of this work, she has witnessed firsthand how the goal of economic well-being has too often been beyond the reach of the downtrodden and less advantaged. She has seen countless individuals who have worked extremely hard their whole lives but have struggled to get ahead financially. Madeline talked about such individuals, including her own father. She was asked about how the general notion of the American dream stacked up against the economic realities that she had seen.

> *I think for most people it's sort of a Horatio Alger's thing of going from rags to riches. That anybody through their own hard work can pull themselves up in this country. But I think a whole lot of people have worked really hard and not been able to pull themselves up.*
>
> *My dad worked really, really hard. And the only reason he had $10,000 in the bank when he died is because his brother died and left him some. And then his house sold for a little over $20,000. And this is from a guy who worked his tail off his whole life long. He had paid employment until after age 80 despite his physical disabilities. So, hard work doesn't necessarily get you ahead. I know that.*

When asked how this experience has affected her sense of fairness, Madeline replied:

> *Well, it makes me mad that things are not fair and that we don't value hard work. And, in fact, one of the surest indicators for how hard you'll have to work is your income. The people with lower incomes will have to work harder from a standpoint of backbreaking physical labor.*
>
> *You know, I make a lot more money than Elaine Nelson from my church. But she mops floors down at St. Peters Hospital and changes sheets and makes sure that the operating room is sanitary so that people can go home without a staph infection. Her work is really essential, but she's only making like $9 or $10 an hour to do that kind of work. And I take her to places to get help with her utilities and take her to the food pantry at my church now and then 'cause she doesn't have a car. And she's faced an eviction so many times since I've known her.*

> *And to me, that's just so unfair that a person that does really important work that cares for our community. . . . You know, having a safe, clean hospital is a very important thing. Why don't we reward that adequately? It makes me really mad.*[5]

Similar issues came out in a focus group conducted for the *Chasing the American Dream* book. This particular group was discussing some of the experiences of poverty, when Jane Wu made this observation:

> *I think what I've noticed from my own experience, and from many of the clients that we serve, living in poverty is exhausting! You're constantly functioning in crisis mode. And that wears on you physically, emotionally, spiritually, and it's a never ending battle and fight to try and just stay where you are, let alone improving your circumstances.*

At that point, Maria Gonzalez joined the conversation to talk about the circumstances of a woman she had come to know through her volunteer work:

> *She works as a health aide at one of the nursing homes. Can anyone imagine what that would be like? I mean it's cleaning people up and emptying the bedpans, and not only that, sometimes taking verbal abuse from people from whom you're doing this work. People who are perhaps in dementia and are saying things that they would never say. You know, racial insults and so forth for somebody that's actually doing this.*
>
> *This is exhausting work and draining work and at the same time this person is trying to figure out how to go to community college to climb the ladder, which the next step would be an LPN [licensed practical nurse]. You know before an RN [registered nurse] is a LPN. But if there's been like a lapse of time before going to community college, then there's the necessity of getting the prerequisite just to be prepared to go to community college or to pass the LPN test.*
>
> *So there's this long road of patience, and I'm just so admirable of her tenacity. Because she's taking the classes to prepare herself to take a test to be an LPN. And at the same time imagine the full time work of taking care of a highly demanding four year old? Working at that kind of work throughout the hours exhausts me to think about it. In addition to preparing oneself intellectually to rise to be able to take a test that, you know, can be hard if you've been out of the academic system. And then entering a program that's intensive and that requires study, requires all the energy. So it's just a layering and a piling. She's working a lot of hours but she's not making enough money.*
>
> *And then there's exposure. Think of the viruses and the bacteria that you're exposed to every day, you know health things, with minimal sick time leave for yourself, let alone the sick time leave for your child.*[6]

What Madeline McBride, Jane Wu, and Maria Gonzalez are discussing relates to the fact that there is simply a lack of enough decent-paying jobs to support all Americans. One can work extremely hard at a job and still remain in poverty. In Chapter 7, we will rely on the analogy of musical chairs to illustrate the mismatch between the number of individuals in need of a decent-paying job versus the limited number and availability of such jobs. The result is that for some Americans, no matter how hard they work, they still may not be able to get ahead economically.

This dynamic was written about 50 years ago in a book titled, *Tally's Corner*, by the anthropologist Elliott Liebow. Liebow describes the types of dead-end, backbreaking jobs that working-class Black men in Washington DC were often destined to be employed at. He writes:

> *[T]he man does not have any reasonable expectation that, however bad it is, his job will lead to better things. Menial jobs are not, by and large, the starting point of a track system which leads to even better jobs for those who are able and willing to do them. The busboy or dishwasher in a restaurant is not on a job track which, if negotiated skillfully, leads to chef or manager of the restaurant. The busboy or dishwasher who works hard becomes, simply, a hard-working busboy or dishwasher. Neither hard work nor perseverance can conceivably carry the janitor to a sit-down job in the office building he cleans up.*[7]

Furthermore, we would argue that the role of skill and talent in getting ahead can also be largely understood as a necessary but not a sufficient condition. In order for individuals to do well in life, they often need to develop their individual talents and skills (whatever they may be) and apply those skills to the real world. Consequently, whether individuals have an aptitude for working with their hands, writing music, or creating software, the development and application of such skills and talents is important for achieving personal success. However, developing one's skills and talents does not necessarily guarantee success.

In addition, the ability to develop one's skills and talents may be highly dependent on the types of opportunities that one has available.[8] For example, children growing up in poverty are much less likely to have the range of opportunities that are available to children from well-to-do backgrounds. Consequently, some children will greatly benefit from more opportunities to develop their talents and skills compared with other children.

The Numbers of Low-Wage Jobs

Another way of understanding that hard work will not eliminate poverty is by the fact that approximately 40 percent of jobs currently in the United States are considered low-paying jobs, that is, paying less than $16 an hour.[9] Many of these jobs are lacking in key benefits such as health insurance. In addition, low-paying jobs are often structured as part-time work, allowing employers to forgo benefits to their employees. Approximately six million Americans are currently working at a part-time job but want to be working full-time instead.[10] Because of the nature and structure of the labor market, an individual could be working at two or even three of these jobs and still live in poverty.

The recent economic collapse as a result of the coronavirus pandemic has resulted in millions of Americans facing unemployment and underemployment. In such an environment, it matters little how hard one works, given the scarcity of work in the first place.

Elise Gould has examined the employment patterns for those in poverty between the ages of 18 and 64 years. She found that 35.3 percent of such individuals were not eligible for work because they were either in school, disabled, or retired. For those who were eligible for work, nearly two-thirds were indeed working and employed.[11]

An additional component to consider in thinking about employment is the factor of time. As noted in Chapter 4, individuals move in and out of poverty. Similarly, individuals move in and out of employment. Virtually all of those who are currently experiencing poverty have worked in the past or will work in the future. Life-course patterns of employment have shown this to be the case.[12] Consequently, it is important to keep in mind that although someone may be currently out of work, that represents only a small slice of the person's entire work history.

Another important point to be raised in the context of time and the role of hard work is that incomes are volatile over time. Research has shown that they can rise and fall across adulthood.[13] Individuals who have seen income losses are probably working as hard as when they were seeing income gains. Hard work in and of itself cannot satisfactorily explain the various upward and downward movements that are typical of life-course earnings.

Conclusion

America has emphasized the importance of individualism and self-reliance since its beginnings. It is no wonder, then, that poverty is viewed through the lens of individual effort and hard work. In a land of opportunity, poverty is seen as the logical result of not working hard and failing to take advantage of those opportunities that America provides. This is a deeply entrenched and, at the same time, flawed myth.

A much more accurate and nuanced view is that hard work is a necessary but not a sufficient condition for getting ahead. Yes, it is generally the case that in order to do well in life and reach one's personal goals, effort and hard work are required. However, the key point is that hard work by itself does not ensure that one will reach those goals. Reaching such goals is also dependent on a wide range of factors that we will explore in the next few chapters. They include aspects of life that are often beyond our control, such as socioeconomic background, race, and gender.

A final point regarding the myth of hard work and poverty is that this myth is particularly powerful because it implies a sense of justice and fairness. Those who do well in life through their hard work are seen as deserving, and those who do not do well in life through their lack of hard work are also seen as deserving of their fate.[14] There is something comforting about the idea that people get their just rewards. Unfortunately, neither the world nor poverty is fair. As Michael Harrington wrote in his 1963 book, *The Other America*:

> *The real explanation of why the poor are where they are is that they made the mistake of being born to the wrong parents, in the wrong section of the country, in the wrong industry, or in the wrong racial or ethnic group. Once that mistake has been made, they could have been paragons of will and morality, but most of them would never even have had a chance to get out of the other America.*[15]

An Expert Appraisal—Elise Gould

Elise Gould is a Senior Economist at the Economic Policy Institute in Washington DC. She has written and researched extensively around the topics of wages, poverty, jobs, and economic mobility.

Policymakers too often make the assumption that poor people are impoverished simply because they refuse to work enough to secure a decent living. However, a significant share of poor families are willing and able to work, even to work full-time. But what keeps their annual earnings low are insufficient opportunities to work consistently enough and at a high-enough hourly wage to lift them out of poverty. This means that policies that boost employment opportunities and wages can be an important tool for reducing poverty.

According to the Census Bureau, about 34 million people in the United States live below the poverty line, including 19 million adults 18 to 64 years old. Nearly one-fifth of those nonelderly adults in poverty have a disability, and well over one-third work. A full one-third of the working poor work full-time, year-round. Data from the Congressional Budget Office show that more than two-thirds of income for the bottom one-fifth of the nonelderly household income distribution comes from wages, benefits, or wage-related tax credits. In the most basic way, poor families are a lot like their middle-class peers—they rely overwhelmingly on paychecks and labor market opportunities to make their way.

These labor market opportunities are strongly conditioned by policy choices. A worker at the federal minimum wage of $7.25 per hour is paid only $15,080 for full-time, full-year work, below the poverty line for any family type of at least two people. Not surprisingly, research finds that minimum wage increases are associated with significant reductions in poverty.

One of the clear signs that the bottleneck to low-income adults working more results from their lack of opportunities is provided by looking at their hours of work over the business cycle. When the economy is strong and jobs are plentiful, low-income workers are more likely to find work, find work with higher pay, and be able to secure more hours of work than when the economy is weak. In 2000, when the economy was close to genuine full employment, the unemployment rate averaged 4.0 percent and the poverty rate was 11.3 percent; but in 2010, in the aftermath of the Great Recession, the unemployment rate averaged 9.6 percent and the poverty rate was almost 15.1 percent. What changed in those years was not poor families' attitudes toward work but simply the availability of jobs. Among the bottom one-fifth of nonelderly households, hours worked per household were about 40 percent higher in the tight labor market of 2000 than in recession-plagued 2010.

Given the opportunity for work or additional work hours, low-income Americans work more. A full-employment agenda that increases opportunities in the labor market, alongside stronger labor standards such as a higher minimum wage, reduces poverty.

Raising Education and Skill Levels Will Not Solve Poverty Alone

One of the most enduring poverty myths across the political and ideological spectrum is that if we were able to provide individuals with enough education and skills, poverty could be eliminated. Much of U.S. social policy aimed at the poor has been based on this idea. The emphasis on imparting skills through job training programs and acquiring a GED degree for those without a high school diploma are predicated on such thinking.[1]

The idea is deeply rooted in an economic perspective known as human capital theory.[2] It holds that poverty is largely a result of an individual's lack of human capital. Human capital consists of those skills and resources that each of us brings into the labor market. They include the quantity and quality of education we have attained, job training received, acquired skills and experience, aptitudes and abilities, and so on. The labor market is conceptualized as a competitive system, in which wages are determined by supply and demand as well as the resources or human capital that people possess.[3]

Those who do well in the labor market do so primarily as a result of the valuable human capital they have accumulated. Such people are in greater demand and hence enjoy brighter job prospects. In contrast, those living in poverty are lacking in human capital and therefore cannot compete as effectively in the labor market. As a result, they wind up working in low-paying, dead-end jobs, or not working at all. The acquisition of more marketable human capital would enable them to attain better quality jobs.[4]

According to this perspective, the way to reduce poverty is therefore to concentrate on upgrading individual skills and education. This might include ensuring graduation from high school, teaching people viable trades, enabling them to build job experience, and so on.

And indeed, it is the case that those in poverty (on average) have less education and fewer skills than the overall population.[5] For example, one of the most consistent findings in the social sciences has been the strong positive association between education and income.

TABLE 7.1 Median Income and Poverty Rates by Level of Education for Those 25 Years and Older

Education (yr)	Income ($)	Poverty rate (%)
<12	32,324	23.7
12	35,630	11.5
13–15	40,558	7.8
≥16	65,161	3.9

Source: U.S. Census Bureau, 2020.

Table 7.1 shows the strength of this relationship. As individuals gain in education, they earn more money. Those with less than 12 years of education earn a median of $32,324 a year, while those with 16 or more years of education earn a median of $65,161. Similarly, individuals with lower levels of education are more likely to experience poverty. They range from a high of 23.7 percent for those without a high school diploma, to a low of 3.9 percent for college graduates.[6]

Perhaps, then, we have arrived at our answer for eliminating poverty—by increasing everyone's education and skills. And in fact, it is unquestionably the case that increasing an individual's education and skills is a very good strategy for that particular individual. On average, they will have a much better chance of avoiding poverty.

However, there is fatal flaw to this argument—as an overall macro strategy for reducing poverty, it will be ineffective unless we also increase the overall quantity and quality of opportunities, particularly job opportunities, in society. In other words, by providing an individual with greater education, we have made them more competitive in the job market, but only at the expense of someone else. In this sense, the strategy is played as a zero-sum game.

What greater education and skills allow an individual to do is to move further up in the overall queue of people looking to find a well-paying and rewarding job. However, because of the limited number of such jobs, only a set amount of people will be able to land such jobs. Consequently, one's position in the queue can change as a result of human capital, but the same amount of people will still be stuck at the end of the line if the overall opportunities remain the same.

Lack of Opportunities

The argument made here is that the fundamental problem of poverty lies in the fact that there are simply not enough viable opportunities for all. Although it is certainly true that particular individual shortcomings, such as the lack of education or skills, helps to explain who is more likely to be left out in the competition to locate and secure good opportunities, it cannot explain why there is a shortage of such opportunities in the first place. To answer that question we must turn to the inability of the economic and political structures to provide the supports and opportunities necessary to lift all Americans out of poverty.

The most obvious example of this is the mismatch between the number of decent-paying jobs and the pool of labor in search of such jobs. Over the past 45 years, the U.S. economy has been producing more and more low-paying jobs, part-time jobs, and jobs that are lacking in benefits.[7] It is estimated that approximately 40 percent of all jobs in the United States in 2018 were low-paying jobs, that is, jobs paying less than $16 an hour.[8] And of course, beyond these low-paying jobs, there are millions of Americans who are unemployed at any point in time.

For example, during the past 50 years, U.S. monthly unemployment rates have averaged between 4 and 10 percent.[9] These percentages represent individuals who are out of work but are actively looking for employment. They do not include discouraged workers who have given up looking for work, or individuals who are working part-time but want to be working full-time. Furthermore, it is important to note that the unemployment rate represents how many individuals are unemployed during a given month in time. If, in-stead, we focus on the likelihood of experiencing a spell of unemployment at some point across the entire period of 1 year, the numbers and percentages are much higher. For example, in 2017, the average number of Americans unem-ployed in any given month was approximately 7 million, representing an un-employment rate of 4.4 percent. However, 15.6 million Americans experienced unemployment at some point during 2017, which translated into an annual unemployment rate of 8.6 percent.[10]

Beyond the lack of good paying jobs, the United States has also failed to offer the types of universal coverage for child care, health care, and affordable housing that most other developed countries routinely provide.[11] The result has been an increasing number of families at risk of economic vulnerability and poverty.

Musical Chairs

The way that we have illustrated this situation in prior work is through the analogy of musical chairs.[12] Picture a game of musical chairs in which there are 10 players but only eight chairs available at any point in time. Who is more likely to lose out at this game? Those more likely to lose out will tend to have characteristics that put them at a disadvantage in terms of competing for the available chairs (such as less agility, not as much speed, a bad position when the music stops, and so on). We can point to these reasons for why the two individuals lost out in the game.

However, given that the game is structured in a way such that two players are bound to lose, these individual attributes only explain who in particular loses out, not why there are losers in the first place. Ultimately, those two people have lost out because there were not enough chairs for everyone who was playing the game.

The critical mistake that has been made in the past is that we have equated the question of who loses the game with the question of why the game produces losers in the first place. They are, in fact, distinct and separate questions. So, while characteristics such as deficiencies in skills or education, or being in a single-parent family, help to explain who in the population is at a heightened risk of encountering poverty, the fact that poverty exists in the first place results not from these characteristics, but rather from a failure of the economic and political structures to provide enough decent opportunities and supports in society.

By focusing solely on individual characteristics such as education, we can shuffle people up or down in terms of their being more likely to land a job with good earnings, but we are still going to have somebody lose out if there are not enough decent-paying jobs to go around. In short, we are playing a large-scale version of musical chairs in which there are many more players than there are chairs.

The recognition of this dynamic represents a fundamental shift in thinking. It helps to explain why the social policies of the past have been largely ineffective in reducing the rates of poverty.[13] We have focused our attention and resources on either altering the incentives and disincentives for those playing the game through various welfare reform measures or, in a very limited way, upgrading their skills and ability to compete in the game through various job-training programs, while at the same time we have left the structure of the game untouched.

When the overall rates of poverty do in fact go up or down, they do so primarily as a result of changes on the structural level that increase or decrease the number of available chairs. In particular, the performance of the economy has been historically important.[14] Why? Because when the economy is expanding, more opportunities (or chairs in this analogy) are available for the competing pool of labor and their families. The reverse occurs when the economy slows down and contracts, as we saw in the Great Recession of 2008 or the recent economic collapse as a result of the coronavirus pandemic. To explain the rise and fall of poverty by the rising or falling levels of individual human capital or motivation makes little sense. Rather, an increase or decrease in poverty has everything to do with improving or deteriorating economic conditions.

Likewise, changes in various social supports and the social safety net can make a significant difference in terms of how well families are able to avoid poverty or near-poverty.[15] When such supports were increased through the War on Poverty initiatives in the 1960s, along with the strong economy, poverty rates declined significantly (see Chapter 9). Likewise, when Social Security benefits were expanded during the 1960s and 1970s, the elderly population's poverty rates sharply declined.[16] Conversely, when social supports have been weakened and eroded, as in the case of children's programs over the past 40 years, the rates of poverty have gone up.[17]

The recognition of poverty as a structural failing also makes it quite clear why the United States has such elevated rates of poverty compared with other high-economy OECD countries (see Chapter 13). These rates have nothing to do with Americans being less motivated or less skilled than those in other countries, but with the fact that our economy has been producing millions of low-wage jobs in the face of global competition and that our social policies have done relatively little to support families economically compared with other industrialized countries.[18]

In thinking about the overall availability of opportunities, we should reiterate that they can vary over time and place. In periods of robust economic growth, when plenty of good-quality jobs are being produced, there may be nine chairs for every 10 players competing in the game. On the other hand, during periods of economic downturn such as the Great Recession of 2008 or the recent economic downturn due to the coronavirus pandemic, it may be that there are only six or seven chairs for every 10 individuals looking for a decent opportunity.

Likewise, the size of one's birth cohort can play a role in this mismatch. A larger birth cohort entering the labor market will be at a greater disadvantage than a smaller birth cohort.[19] There can also be a spatial mismatch between opportunities and individuals. For those living in impoverished inner cities or remote rural areas, there is clearly a mismatch between available job opportunities and the pool of labor in need of such opportunities.[20] The game itself is therefore fluid over time and place. But the bottom line is that in order for Americans to get ahead and avoid poverty, there must be enough good opportunities for all who are in need of them.

In his study of long-term unemployment, Thomas Cottle talked with one man who had worked for 25 years at the same company, only to be downsized. After 2½ years of searching, he eventually found a job at a much lower pay scale, but felt fortunate to have such a job, nonetheless. He referred to his job search using the musical chairs analogy:

> *The musical chairs of work still have me in the game. The music plays, we run around, the music stops and I dive for a chair. Took me two and half years to find this last one, I don't want the music to stop again. I'm only fifty-two, but pretty soon they'll take all the chairs away. Then what? That's the part I don't want to think about.*[21]

Or, as one of the interviewees in *Chasing the American Dream* put it, there's a number of Americans who are thinking "the music's going to stop and they're not going to have a chair. And they're just probably living on the brink. One paycheck away, one car accident away, one unfortunate illness away" from joining those in poverty.[22]

Consequently, we argue that this analogy applies to what has been happening in the U.S. economy. There has been a declining number of jobs that we might consider of good quality (livable wages, benefits, stability, good working conditions). Yet, the pool of labor in search of such jobs is much larger than the number of available jobs, creating a significant mismatch.

On the other hand, a few of the remaining chairs have become more comfortable and spacious. That is, some of the jobs being created in the new economy pay very good wages with solid benefits. Many of these jobs are found in the financial and technology sectors, as well as in several of the professional fields. As we discuss in Section V, the gap between the bottom and top of society has been getting wider, with those in the top 20 percent of the income distribution being the beneficiaries of virtually all of the economic gains over the past 50 years.

Providing More Chairs

From this perspective, then, one of the keys to addressing poverty is to increase the labor market opportunities and social supports available to American households. By doing so, we are able to provide more chairs for those playing the game. What are some of the policies we might consider that could increase the number of chairs in the game? We will take this up more extensively in Chapter 20, but let us briefly mention several of these.

First, there is a need to create enough adequately paying jobs that can support individuals and families above the poverty line. This would include initiatives such as raising the minimum wage to a living wage, increasing the earned income tax credit, and stimulating the creation of good-quality jobs.

Second, it is important to increase the accessibility of key social and public goods. These include quality education (at the primary, secondary, and postsecondary levels), health care, affordable housing, and child care.

Third, policies that encourage the building of assets, particularly for those of modest means, is vital. Likewise, building the assets and resources of lower income communities is important.

Finally, providing a strong and effective social safety net is critical in addressing poverty on a national level. This would include a range of programs and supports designed to allow families to get back on their feet when economic turmoil strikes. All of these strategies have the potential to fundamentally alter the game, rather than simply altering the competitiveness of the particular individuals in the game.

Increasing the population's education and skills is, of course, a worthy goal. There are many reasons for why enhancing skills is important. For example, a population with greater skills and ability may be more innovative, which in turn can create more opportunities. However, we must at the same time expand such opportunities in the first place. The magic bullet of education and skills eliminating poverty is an alluring one, but without a substantial increase in the number and quality of opportunities available, it is only a mirage.

An Expert Appraisal—Steven M. Fazzari

Steven M. Fazzari is the Bert A. and Jeanette L. Lynch Distinguished Professor of Economics at Washington University in St. Louis. His research has focused on rising levels of income inequality, the effects of the Great Recession, and the role of Keynesian macroeconomics in understanding economic performance.

The important myth analyzed in this chapter helps explain why U.S. poverty rates remain high compared with other rich countries. Politicians and policymakers continually attribute the source of poverty to the characteristics of individuals rather than structural features of the American economic system. This mistake leads to proposed solutions that emphasize improving education outcomes for the poor, a popular but inadequate response.

The musical chairs analogy presented here describes the problem forcefully. Yes, those with fewer "skills" in playing the game are the most likely to end up without chairs when the music stops. But raising the skill level through better education on how to play the game will not increase the number of winners unless the number of chairs rises.

In addition, the musical chairs analogy helps us understand why the personal failings myth seems validated in Americans' experience even though it is false. If one watches the outcome of games of musical chairs, one sees that it is the slower, less agile players who usually end up without a chair. Analogously, day-to-day experience shows that those with less education have a greater chance of landing in poverty. It appears to be "common sense" that if we would just raise education levels of the poor, or if the poor would just apply themselves better to develop their own skills, the problem would be solved. But the musical chairs story demonstrates why this view, despite everyday appearances, is fundamentally incorrect.

The chapter makes a solid case that the musical chairs analogy is the right way to understand how education and poverty are linked. Yet, there is an important assumption in this analysis that needs some further exploration. Musical chairs is a zero-sum game: Give one player more skill, and that person will just take a chair from another player. As the chapter recognizes, however, it is possible that more and better education overall could be a positive-sum game. By raising their skills and productivity, better education of the workforce might attract better job opportunities with higher pay and working conditions. That is, better education might actually increase the number of chairs in the game.

A look at the evidence, however, suggests this outcome has not prevailed in recent decades. The share of the noninstitutionalized U.S. population 25 years or older with a high school degree rose from 68.6 percent in 1980 to 89.8 percent in 2018. The share with a college degree increased from 17.0 to 35.0 percent in the same period (U.S. Census data). If the fundamental problem of poverty were inadequate education, one would expect this large increase in the population's educational attainment would have clearly reduced the poverty rate. It has not; the poverty rate averaged across business cycles has been roughly constant since 1980.

One might claim that the historical improvement in education could have just affected the higher parts of the income distribution, with education stagnant for lower income families. This argument can be tested with data from the Panel Study of Income Dynamics (PSID, author's calculations). In the full PSID sample, educational attainment rates for the head of household are quite similar to the Census data. If we look only at lower income households, educational attainment rates are, not surprisingly, somewhat lower. But the striking result is that educational attainment has risen strongly even among lower income households. From 1980 to 2017, the share of high school graduates rose 26 percentage points in the bottom half of the income distribution and 31 percentage points in the bottom quarter of the distribution. (Four-year college degree rates rose 10 points and seven points in these two categories, respectively.) Although lower income households have been getting more educated for decades, incomes have stagnated, inequality has exploded, and poverty rates have hardly budged.

This evidence supports the chapter's conclusion that "the fundamental problem of poverty lies in the fact that there are simply not enough viable opportunities for all." Policy must be designed to confront this reality in order to effectively reduce poverty and inequality.

Decision-Making Is Constrained for Those With Fewer Resources

There is a prevalent myth that poverty is largely the result of bad decision-making. This would include not graduating from high school, having children outside of marriage, failing to hold onto a job, committing a crime, using drugs, and so on. An example of this logic is the work of social scientist Isabel Sawhill. In an article entitled, "The Behavioral Aspects of Poverty," Sawhill writes, "Those who graduate from high school, wait until marriage to have children, limit the size of their families, and work full-time will not be poor."[1] She goes on to say, "we should not pretend that money alone is going to change significantly the lives of these families, beyond easing a few hardships. The challenge is to find ways of providing generous support to the poor without disregarding the unpleasant facts about their behavior."[2]

And in fact, it is true that those who fail to graduate from high school, have children outside of marriage, and so on, are indeed much more likely to experience poverty than their counterparts who do not engage in these behaviors. In the previous chapter, we dealt with this argument in terms of lower education and skills specifically. We argued that there are two levels in which one can understand this dynamic: (1) identifying those who lose out at the game and/or (2) why the game produces losers in the first place.

In this chapter, however, we confront the bad decision-making myth by arguing that the range of decisions and choices available to individuals varies considerably. In addition, how one weighs the positives and negatives of a decision also differs widely across the population. In particular, the social and economic class that one finds oneself in is extremely important in shaping the types of decisions that are made.

How Decision-Making Varies by Social Context

Within our individual lives, we face a multitude of decisions. These range from the mundane choices confronting us on a daily basis, to more consequential life decisions. Each of us exerts a degree of agency during the course of our lives. However, the amount and range of decision-making and agency vary considerably depending on the resources available.

Take the case of going to college. An 18-year-old whose parents have abundant resources will likely have many choices when it comes to where they might go to college. In contrast, an adolescent whose parents are low-income earners will have a much more constrained set of choices. In fact, this adolescent may have no choice at all—college may simply not be an option.

Similarly, should the adolescent whose parents are wealthy make a bad decision, the family's resources may very well shield the adolescent from the full repercussions of that decision—for example, being able to receive treatment for a drug addiction. On the other hand, the same unwise decision for a low-income adolescent may prove to be disastrous and long-lasting.

Many other examples could be given demonstrating how the range of decision-making varies widely across the population. In addition, the manner in which those decisions are weighed can also vary. That is, the positives and negatives of a particular decision may differ depending on one's position in the social hierarchy. For example, giving birth as a teenager for an affluent youth is likely viewed as carrying a profound negative cost, while for an impoverished youth with little hope for economic advancement, the negative costs may be perceived as less. In this chapter, we deal with two areas of decision-making that are strongly correlated with the risk of poverty—working and family formation.

Job Decision-Making

A common perception is that the poor have made a conscious decision not to work. In 2016, a survey from the American Enterprise Institute found that almost two-thirds of Americans believe that most poor people do not hold a steady job.[3] The reality? Most of America's poor who can work are in fact employed in paid labor. A recent analysis by Elise Gould (also discussed in Chapter 6) showed that more than one-third of the poor (35 percent) were not eligible to work because they were either retired, in school, or disabled. For the remaining poor, 63 percent were employed in paid labor. Of those who were working, 71 percent were working full-time, while the other 29 percent were working part-time.[4]

Why are some of the poor not working? There are a variety of factors to take into consideration for those who are not retired, in school, or sick or disabled. One of the most important factors is family responsibilities, such as taking care of children or a relative. This is especially true for poor women, who cite home and family responsibilities as the leading cause of their unemployment.[5]

For those in poverty who are working, why are some only working-part time? Often, this is not a deliberate decision—many are seriously constrained by their specific circumstances and the economy. The most likely reason given by the part-time poor for their lack of full-time work is that they cannot find full-time work, followed by caregiving responsibilities and school—these three reasons together account for more than two-thirds of part-time workers' lack of full-time work.[6]

As we discussed in the prior chapter, during the past 40 years the American economy has increasingly produced larger numbers of jobs that do not pay well, do not provide benefits, and only offer part-time hours.[7] There is nearly twice the proportion of full-time American workers in low-wage work relative to average workers in comparison countries.[8] And in an era when many employers are actively trying to keep their employees part-time in order to reduce the wages and benefits owed to them, finding full-time work is a challenge for many. Furthermore, as we discussed in Chapter 6, although some of the poor may not currently be working, virtually all will have worked in the past or will be working in the future.

In summary, the employment decision-making process for those in or near poverty may be much more constrained than for those not in poverty. The types of jobs may be more limited, and the wages for such jobs are likely to be low.

Marriage and Childbearing Decision-Making

But what about marriage and childbearing? Those in poverty are less likely to be married and more likely to have had a child outside of marriage. How might the environment of poverty shape the types of decisions and choices available to lower income individuals?

Research has indicated that one key factor influencing marriage is the perceived economic stability of a potential partner. Prospective partners are often looking to marry individuals with good prospects for long-term economic security. In addition, the expectations surrounding marriage appear to have risen. Marriage today is often considered a capstone experience that occurs once one's life is felt to be settled and the relationship is perceived to be strong.

While the marital expectations of all Americans have been rising, the economic security and risk of incarceration for those at the bottom (in terms of income and education) have been getting worse. This is not a recipe for a boom in marriage rates among the working-class and poor. Kathryn Edin and her colleagues conclude:

> *We live in an America where the gap between the rich and poor continues to grow. This economic reality has infused poor youth with the sense that they have nothing to lose by an early or ill-timed birth. Until poor young women and men have more access to jobs that lead to financial security, and until there is reason to hope for a rewarding life pathway outside bearing and raising children, the poor will continue to have children far sooner than most Americans think they should, and in less than ideal circumstances. Meanwhile, they will probably continue to defer marriage.*[9]

Couples at the bottom of the socioeconomic status (SES) hierarchy have to wait a long time to feel both financially secure enough to marry and prepared to meet their marital expectations once married. In an age of growing inequality, this means they are becoming less likely to marry, less likely to have children inside of marriage, and more likely to divorce once married.

As family scholar Andrew Cherlin observes, college-educated young adults see a realistic future where they are likely to find a suitable partner and pool two solid incomes. Because of this, they are willing to wait to start a family until that stable point in time. Less-educated women "don't see the possibility of finding partners with good incomes. And many are unwilling to give up the opportunity to have a kid by waiting."[10] Of all of the markers of adulthood—graduating college, finding a good job, moving out of your parents' home, buying your own home, getting married, and having children—having a baby may be the only one that women with a low level of education feel they have accessible to them. According to Cherlin, "this is a way a woman or man can be a successful adult when all other paths are blocked."[11]

But what has happened to the pool of male partners available to low-SES women? Between the 1970s and today, the wages of men with a high school education or less have fallen, while those with at least a 4-year college degree have risen. Men with low levels of education are also much less likely to receive employer-provided health insurance and pension coverage today compared with the 1970s.[12] While labor force participation rates for all men have dropped since the 1970s, the decrease has been particularly steep for men with low levels of education.[13] In 1990, 24 percent of men aged 30 to 49 years with a high school degree or less were economically insecure, a number that has risen to 30 percent in recent years.[14]

For men with a high school degree or less, incarceration rates have also skyrocketed since the 1980s. In one staggering example, consider that only about 15 percent of Black male high school dropouts could expect to spend time in prison by their mid-30s at the beginning of the 1980s, but a remarkable 68 percent in recent years. While White men do not face nearly as high a lifetime risk of incarceration compared with Black men, the incarceration rate for

White male high school dropouts in recent years was more than 7 times what it was at the beginning of the 1980s.[15]

Existing research suggests that men with low educational attainment, earnings, and labor force participation—and/or a criminal record—are less likely to get married, and women are less likely to consider them marriageable partners.[16] This reluctance has only grown with our country's rising marital expectations, growing economic inequality, and increasing incarceration rates in recent decades. At the beginning of the 1970s, for instance, 90 percent of White male high school graduates and 86 percent of high school dropouts aged 35 to 44 years were married—in recent years, those numbers dropped to 58 percent and 51 percent, respectively. For Black males aged 35 to 44 years, the proportions married at the beginning of the 1970s were 70 percent for high school graduates and 66 percent for high school dropouts. In recent years, those numbers dropped to 38 percent and 27 percent, respectively.[17]

This means that for low-SES Americans, the normal experience is for children to be born outside of marriage. For women without a high school degree, 62 percent of their children are born outside of marriage. For women who are high school graduates, the number is 59 percent. For women with an associate's degree or some college, 43 percent of births are outside of marriage. For female college graduates, only 10 percent of births are outside of marriage.[18]

Finally, what about the myth that women on welfare make a conscious decision to have more children in order to receive greater welfare payments? A substantial body of research has demonstrated that this is simply not the case. In fact, women on welfare have a slightly lower fertility rate than women in the general population.[19] The difference is that many more of these births occur outside of marriage.

This myth was debunked nearly 50 years by Johnnie Tillmon, a Black mother receiving welfare. Writing for the *Liberation News Service*, she observed,

> *People still believe that old lie that AFDC mothers keep on having kids just to get a bigger welfare check. On the average, another baby means another $35 a month—barely enough for food and clothing. Having babies for profit is a lie that only men could make up, and only men could believe. Men, who never have to bear the babies or have to raise them and maybe send them to war.*[20]

Decisions in Psychological Context

A significant body of research has emerged in the last decade that has analyzed the cognitive toll that living in poverty has on reasoning and decision-making.[21]

In particular, one line of research has focused on the importance of what is known as psychological bandwidth. Frank Schilback and colleagues define this as "the brain's ability to perform the basic functions that underlie higher-order behavior and decision-making."[22] The basic idea is that each of us has an amount of bandwidth that allows us to solve problems, retain information, focus our attention, make wise decisions, and so on. The more bandwidth we can devote to these tasks, the better we are able to succeed in cognitive activities.

Accordingly, poverty acts to reduce overall available bandwidth. It does this through creating greater stress and worries, reduced nutrition, exposure to toxic environments, and so on. For example, the constant worry of how to survive on a day-to-day basis acts to reduce bandwidth:

> *Being poor means having less money to buy things, but it also means having to spend more of one's bandwidth managing that money. The poor must manage sporadic income, juggle expenses, and make difficult trade-offs. Even when the poor are not actually making financial decisions, these preoccupations can be distracting. Thinking and fretting about money can effectively tax bandwidth.*[23]

This body of research has demonstrated that it is important to understand decision-making not only within the socioeconomic context of individuals' lives, but within the psychological context as well. As we discuss in Section IV, poverty extracts a high cost from individuals and families, with part of that cost being impaired cognitive functioning.

Conclusion

Underlying the bad decision-making myth is the belief that each of us has near-total control over determining the shape of our lives—that each of us can single-handedly determine our fate through a series of freely made decisions. The fact is that the types of decisions and options available must be understood within the broader context in which such decision-making takes place. In particular, the socioeconomic context is paramount in this process. Those with greater socioeconomic resources will be able to exert greater agency in determining the course of their lives, while those with fewer resources will struggle to do so.

This is not to discount the idea that, ultimately, individuals must be held responsible for their decisions—only that those decisions are best understood within the broader environmental context in which they are made.

An Expert Appraisal—David Brady

David Brady is a Professor of Sociology and Public Policy at the University of
California Riverside. He is the Director of the Blum Initiative on Global and
Regional Poverty and is the author of *Rich Democracies, Poor People*.

*The behavioral argument really obfuscates the fact that having a low income and
growing up poor prevent some people from getting a good education, from making
the right "choices" when they are teenagers, from not getting pregnant, from having
marriageable men as an option, and so on. If you are going to look at the options for
marriage in low-income communities, for example, there are real constraints on low-
income people. We cannot underestimate how different the opportunities are for people
growing up poor compared with those growing up more advantaged. When you think
about the families they are raised in, the schools they go to, and the neighborhoods they
grow up in, these circumstances create massive disadvantages that make it dramatically
harder to attain the benchmarks that Isabel Sawhill and others talk about.*

*This argument is getting it all wrong. In some ways, what is striking is not that you
can escape poverty if you do everything right, but that if you do some things wrong
in the United States, your odds of poverty are extraordinarily high. That is what is
exceptional.*

*One dominant way that people think about poverty, both in scholarship and in public
discourse, is to focus on demographic characteristics. This explanation assumes that
there is something wrong with poor people's individual characteristics: that they are
more likely to be single parents, they are not working enough, they are too young, or
they are not well-educated. So, the way to attack poverty, from this perspective, would
be to reduce single-parenthood or reduce the number of people with low education. This
explanation concentrates on the individual characteristics of the poor people themselves
and how they are different from nonpoor people.*

*The problem with this explanation is that it does not adequately explain the
big differences in poverty between countries. For example, think about the big four
individual risks of poverty—single parenthood, becoming a head of household at an
early age, low-education, and unemployment. These are indisputably the four big
characteristics that predict your risk of poverty. If the demographic explanation is
correct, then the United States should have very high levels of single-parenthood, young
headship, low educational attainment, and unemployment. That would explain why we
have high poverty: We have a large number of people with those four characteristics.
The reality, however, is that the United States is actually below average in these areas
compared with other rich democracies.*

*What is different in the United States is not the number of people with those
individual characteristics, but the fact that we punish the heck out of people with
such characteristics. If you have these characteristics, we make it so incredibly hard
to make ends meet. We penalize those characteristics severely even though we do not
see a particularly high prevalence relative to other rich countries. We penalize them by
providing no support. So, if you are a young single mother with little education and are
unemployed, you are almost guaranteed to be poor in the United States. It would be*

very hard for you to escape poverty. In most other rich democracies, you would have a much lower probability of being poor.

Poverty scholarship is obsessed with reducing the number of people with these characteristics, when a more effective way to reduce poverty and a different way to think about it is to say that we choose politically which characteristics we are going to penalize. We choose politically which characteristics we do not penalize. In our country, we have chosen to penalize these characteristics by withholding social policies and withholding systems of support to help these people. Ultimately, it is a political decision to punish those with such characteristics and to withhold help from these people, whereas most other rich democracies make a political choice not to penalize such characteristics as severely as we do.

Poverty Is Preventable

A final myth regarding why poverty exists dates back thousands of years. It is the myth that poverty is simply inevitable. The origins of this myth can be traced to Biblical times, with a well-recited verse from the New Testament. Found in the Gospel of Matthew, Chapter 26, Jesus says to his disciples, "The poor you will always have with you, but you will not always have me."[1]

This verse has been used over the past 2,000 years to argue that poverty will always exist. In searching online for this quote, there are literally thousands of websites where the verse can be found and prominently featured. And it is often what people are likely to recall when asked about how the poor are portrayed in the Bible.

A modern twist on this myth comes from Ronald Reagan. In discussing the government's failure to end poverty during the War on Poverty in the 1960s, President Reagan famously declared, "Some years ago the federal government declared war on poverty, and poverty won."[2] His argument was that government programs aimed at reducing poverty actually made the situation worse.[3] This, of course, has been the standard conservative critique of the welfare state in general, most notably argued in the works of Charles Murray and Lawrence Mead,[4] but going back to at least 1835 with a lecture given by Alexis de Tocqueville on pauperism.[5]

A consequence of this myth is that it implies there really is not much we can do to alleviate poverty. That poverty is simply a part of the overall economic landscape. That like it or not, poverty is here to stay.

In sharp contrast, we argue that this is demonstratively false. Poverty can indeed be alleviated, often dramatically so. It is simply incorrect to argue that poverty cannot be substantially reduced.

Ironically, if we place the quote from Jesus into its wider context, the meaning becomes quite different. Quoting from Deuteronomy, Chapter 15, Jesus says:

> *If among you, one of your brothers should become poor, in any of your towns within your land that the Lord your God is giving you, you shall not harden your heart or shut your hand against your poor brothers, but you*

> *shall open your hand to him and lend him sufficient for his need, whatever*
> *it may be. . . . For the poor you will always have with you in the land.*
> *Therefore, I command you, "You shall open wide your hand to your brother,*
> *to the needy and to the poor in your land."*[6]

Rather than arguing for inaction, Jesus is of course imploring his disciples to be actively engaged in addressing the needs of the poor.

In this chapter, we explore three different examples where poverty has been dramatically reduced: (1) the War on Poverty in the 1960s and early 1970s; (2) elderly poverty over the past 60 years; and (3) single-parent families in the Nordic countries.

A Largely Successful War on Poverty

We begin with the widespread myth that President Lyndon Johnson's declared War on Poverty in 1964 was an abysmal failure. That, as Ronald Reagan proclaimed, "We fought a war on poverty, and poverty won."

In giving his State of the Union address in front of Congress, President Johnson announced:

> *This administration, here and now, declares unconditional war on poverty*
> *in America, and I urge this Congress and all Americans to join me in that*
> *effort. It will not be a short or easy struggle, no single weapon or strategy*
> *will suffice, but we shall not rest until that war is won. The richest nation on*
> *earth can afford to win it. We cannot afford to lose it.*[7]

The War on Poverty put in place a wide array of government programs intended to reduce poverty.[8] They included the Food Stamp Act; Medicare and Medicaid; the Special Supplemental Nutrition Program for Women, Infants, and Children; the School Lunch program; Job Corps; the Elementary and Secondary Education Act; Head Start; and Legal Services, along with several others. All of these programs were designed to provide, as the administration often reiterated, "A hand-up, not a hand-out."[9] In addition to federal programs, there was an attempt on the local level to create greater opportunities through an array of community action programs.[10]

Was poverty eliminated during the War on Poverty? No. Was it dramatically reduced? Absolutely. Figure 9.1 shows the overall rates of poverty in the United States for both the total population and for children from 1959 to 1973. During these years, the overall rate of poverty was cut in half, from 22.4 percent in 1959, to 11.1 percent in 1973. Likewise, poverty for children was dramatically reduced, from 27.3 to 14.4 percent.

We can also see in Figure 9.1 that it was certainly true that the rates of poverty were falling before the 1964 announced the War on Poverty. This was

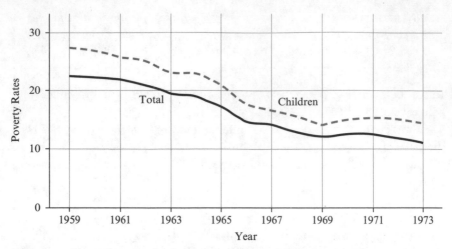

FIGURE 9.1 *Rates of poverty for the total population and children.*
Source: U.S. Census Bureau, 2019.

likely due to the robust economic growth during the period. But our overall point remains the same. The 1960s were a period of time when poverty in the United States was cut in half. This should be seen as a major economic accomplishment. The War on Poverty played an important role in this decline. It demonstrated that the nation's poverty is not immovable and that genuine progress is possible with a concerted effort by the government and a growing economy.

The Case of Elderly Poverty

In 1959, the age group with the greatest risk of poverty was the elderly population. By 2019, the age group with the lowest risk of poverty was the elderly population.[11] What happened? In four words—Social Security and Medicare.

Looking at Figure 9.2, we can see that the 1959 overall rate of poverty for those 65 years and older was 35.2 percent. Consequently, more than one-third of all seniors in the United States found themselves in poverty at the end of the 1950s. The figure displays the dramatic decline in elderly poverty throughout the 1960s and 1970s, with their overall poverty rate falling to approximately 10 percent. By 2019, the rate of poverty for elderly people stood at 8.9 percent.

Elder poverty was reduced by over two-thirds across this span of time. Again, what happened? There was a concerted effort by the federal government to improve the well-being of elderly people. Social Security benefits were increased and expanded, as well as being indexed to the rate of inflation.[12] Consequently, Social Security benefits would keep up with the rising cost of living.

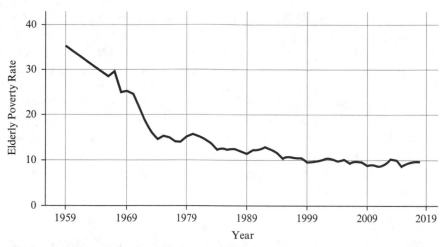

FIGURE 9.2 *Elderly poverty rates from 1959 to 2018.*
Source: U.S. Census Bureau, 2019.

In addition, President Johnson signed into law the creation of the Medicare and Medicaid programs in 1965. Medicare provides universal health care for those 65 years and older, and Medicaid provides health care for lower income Americans.[13] President Nixon also signed off on the creation of the Supplemental Security Income program in 1972. This provided additional financial assistance to seniors who were disabled.[14]

In combination, all of these programs had a dramatic effect on lowering the rate of poverty among elderly people. For example, it is estimated that if there were no Social Security today, the elderly poverty rate would rise from its current 9 percent to approximately 40 percent.[15]

Once again, we can see a dramatic reduction of poverty brought about by a set of targeted social programs. The reduction of poverty among elderly people represents America's greatest success in addressing poverty over the past half century. It demonstrates that poverty can be effectively alleviated provided that the political will exists for such an effort.

Single-Parent Families in the Nordic Countries

A final example illustrating that poverty is not inevitable is the case of single-parent families. The poverty rate for children younger than 18 years in single, female-headed families is currently 36.5 percent in the United States. This compares with 6.4 percent for children in married-couple families.[16] We might look at these statistics and assume that single-parent families have a universal high risk of poverty compared with other families because they do so in the United States.

Yet, if we look beyond the United States, such families are not destined to have a high rate of poverty. We could choose any number of countries, but let us take the case of the Nordic countries, and in particular, Denmark. Here we find that children in single-parent female-headed families have a poverty rate of about 6 percent.[17] In fact, their rates of poverty are lower than those for children in married couples in the United States. The reason for this is that the government of Denmark is proactive in making sure that such families do not fall into poverty. They do this through an array of pro-family, pro-child policies. The result is that regardless of what kind of family children find themselves in, they are unlikely to experience poverty. This pattern is found across the Nordic countries.

We could look at many other OECD countries as further examples showing that poverty does not necessarily have to be high for single-parent families and their children.[18] Poverty can be dramatically reduced through effective social policy. The lesson again is that poverty is not inevitable, but rather is malleable depending on the social, economic, and political conditions within a country.

Conclusion

The inevitability of poverty is a myth that has been around for centuries. It is a narrative that implies it is largely futile to try to reduce poverty. It breeds apathy and an acceptance of the status quo.

In contrast, we have provided three examples in which poverty has been significantly reduced. These examples illustrate the ability of government action to dramatically alleviate poverty. Beyond these three examples, we could have provided many more cases of situations and places where poverty has been dramatically reduced. Perhaps the most monumental in terms of the sheer numbers of people affected has been the recent decline of poverty in China. The estimate is that slightly more than 1 billion people have been raised out of poverty from 1990 to 2015, largely as a result of the growing Chinese economy.[19]

We can also find cases in which poverty has rapidly increased over short amounts of time. For example, the country of Venezuela has experienced an explosion in poverty because of the past policies of its leaders combined with a faltering economy.[20] The point is that poverty is not fixed in time. As we saw with individual movements into and out of poverty in Chapter 4, overall movements can similarly occur within entire countries.

Yet, too often we find public apathy in the United States toward social and political action. The problem is seen as too large and too complex to effectively deal with. Or, there is the deeply held myth that government is not the solution, but rather is the problem. It is certainly true that badly designed government programs are both ineffective and wasteful. But what we are talking about here are well-designed government programs based on research evidence. Such an approach can dramatically reduce poverty.

As we argue elsewhere in this book, the problem is not a lack of solutions. There is considerable evidence demonstrating what strategies are effective in reducing poverty. The problem lies in a lack of political will to implement these strategies. Politicians have used the myth of poverty's inevitability to reinforce their agenda of a smaller federal government footprint.

Yet, when we look at the economic cost of poverty (see Chapter 11), the failure to address the problem is both short-sighted and ill-informed. Investing in the economic well-being of our citizens is one of the smartest deposits that a government can make.

An Expert Appraisal—Lane Kenworthy

Lane Kenworthy is the Yankelovich Endowed Chair Professor in the Department of Sociology at the University of California San Diego. He has conducted extensive research on the topics of inequality and poverty, and his latest book is entitled *Social Democratic Capitalism*.

We often say that government social programs "lift people out of poverty." The way they do so is straightforward—they give money to households with low earnings, and in doing so they raise the income of some of those households enough to be above the poverty line.

How, then, could such programs possibly fail to reduce poverty? The main reason is that a government benefit could discourage people from engaging in as much paid work as they otherwise might. This surely happens with some programs and some people. But the evidence suggests it is not a strong effect. In the United States, a century ago we spent less than 1 percent of our GDP on public social programs. Today we spend nearly 20 percent. Yet, the share of working-age Americans who have a paying job has increased over this period, not decreased. And poverty has gone down. Across the rich democratic nations, those with a bigger welfare state tend to have higher employment rates, and less poverty, than those with a smaller one.

In recent decades, economic developments such as globalization, technological change, shifts in corporate culture, and union decline have weakened employment prospects and slowed wage gains for people on the margins of the labor market. For this reason, increases in income for the least well-off have tended to come mainly from increases in government transfers, not from rising earnings. This is true not just in the United States but also in many other affluent democracies.

"Will there always be poverty?" is an interesting question. But it is also a distraction. A much more important question is, "How can we do better at reducing poverty?" Public social programs that cover more of life's risks and do so more generously are a very effective strategy.

What Is the Cost of Poverty?

In this section, we examine another set of widely held myths. Namely, that the cost of poverty is not a policy concern. This appears in several different forms. One is that the poor in the United States really are not so bad off. After all, poverty is much worse in sub-Saharan Africa, for example. A second myth is that the cost of poverty is borne primarily by those in poverty and perhaps the communities in which they reside. That the toll of poverty to the country as a whole is relatively minor. And third, that poverty can be justified as a result of individual failure—that poverty is a blemish to the individual, not to the country.

In contrast, we will present evidence to show that the poor in the United States are much worse off than their counterparts in other OECD countries. Furthermore, the economic cost of poverty to the country as a whole is enormous. Finally, poverty extracts a toll on the moral fiber of the United States by constituting an injustice of a substantial magnitude.

America's Poor Are Worse Off Than Elsewhere

Every few years a report appears from the Heritage Foundation, a Washington conservative think tank. The author is invariably a policy analyst by the name of Robert Rector. Rector has made a reputation for himself by claiming, among other things, that economic destitution and poverty in the United States are minimal to nonexistent. The Heritage report routinely argues that America's poor are fairly well off, and that they have acquired consumer goods and resources that were unheard of 100 or even 50 years ago. Quoting from the report:

> *The typical poor household, as defined by the federal government, had air conditioning and a car. For entertainment, the household had two color TVs, cable or satellite TV, a DVD player, and a VCR. In the kitchen, it had a refrigerator, an oven and stove, and a microwave. Other household conveniences included a clothes washer, clothes dryer, ceiling fans, a cordless phone, and a coffee maker. The family was able to obtain medical care when needed. Their home was not overcrowded and was in good repair. By its own report, the family was not hungry and had sufficient funds during the past year to meet all essential needs. The overwhelming majority of Americans do not regard a family living in these conditions as poor.*[1]

The report goes on to argue that when compared with those in other countries around the globe, the poor in the United States enjoy a much higher standard of living.[2]

The myth that the poor in the United States are not so bad off can be found in a wide range of places. It basically reflects the idea that those in poverty have nothing to complain about—that given the conditions in less developed countries, things could be much worse.

What we will show in this chapter is that in contrast to this myth, the reality is that the poor in the United States are actually much worse off than those in other high-economy countries. Furthermore, poverty in certain respects may be harsher today than it was in the past.

What Does Living Below the Poverty Line Mean?

As discussed in our introductory chapter, the manner in which poverty is offi-
cially defined in the United States is by falling below a specific level of income.[3]
Households earning less than a minimum-level income are considered to be in
poverty. The actual poverty line that is drawn varies depending on the size of
the household and is updated each year to take into account inflation.

In 2019, the poverty line for a household of three was set just over $20,000
($20,335).[4] Consequently, three-person households that earned less than this
amount would be counted as in poverty. This comes out to an average monthly
income of approximately $1,695. The Census Bureau estimates that poor
families will spend one-third of their income on food and the remaining two-
thirds on other necessities such as housing, clothing, transportation, and so on.

To illustrate what these numbers mean in a day-to-day sense, let us take the
poverty level for a family of three. Using the one-third/two-thirds split, our
hypothetical family would have $6,778 available for food during the year. This
comes out to $130 a week, $18.62 a day, or $6.21 a day for each member of that
family. Assuming that family members eat three meals per day, this works out
to approximately $2.00 per person, per meal, per day.

Taking the remaining two-thirds of the poverty line's threshold—$13,557—
provides our family with $261 per week for all other expenses. Using the MIT
Living Wage Calculator developed by Amy Glasmeier, it is estimated that a
family of two adults and one child in the St. Louis region (which is fairly representative of the country as a whole) would need to earn $39,094 for the year
in order to meet all of their other basic needs beyond food.[5] This comes out
to $752 per week. We can quickly see that a family in poverty falls well short
of what is considered minimally necessary to purchase an adequate basket of
goods and services. Their $261 a week for expenses is only one-third of what
they really need to get by to cover their housing costs, utilities, medical expenses,
and so on. Bringing the poverty line down to this level allows for a more meaningful sense of what these numbers represent in terms of people's lives, and the
extreme difficulty in trying to survive at this level.

However, it is important to keep in mind that this example captures poverty at its most opulent level; that is, families fall to varying degrees below the
poverty line. In 2019, 45 percent of all poor persons were living in households
where their income fell below one-half of their respective poverty thresholds,
otherwise known as extreme poverty.[6] Therefore, rather than an annual income
of $20,335 for a family of three, many are trying to survive on an income of
$10,178 or less for a three-person household. If living at the poverty line is dif-
ficult, imagine trying to live below one-half of the poverty line.

It is also interesting to contrast what Americans feel is the minimum amount
of income needed to get by on versus the poverty line. In 2013, the Gallup

Poll asked a national sample, "What is the smallest amount of money a family of four needs to make each year to get by in your community?" The average amount given was $58,000. In 2013, the poverty threshold for a family of four was $23,550.[7] Consequently, it is obvious that most Americans would perceive surviving below the poverty line as extremely precarious.

Yet another way of translating the meaning of poverty into one's own life can be illustrated with the following statistic. In 2019, the median income for a household of three in the United States was $91,894.[8] On the other hand, as noted, the poverty threshold for such a household in 2019 was $20,335. Therefore, the income for a family of three at the edge of poverty is just 22 percent of the overall median income for such a family.

Some of you reading this book may be near the median in terms of your family income and may occasionally find it difficult to keep up with various household expenses and needs. Now imagine that instead of the income you currently have coming in for this month, next month you will be receiving only 22 percent of your income. The other 78 percent is suddenly gone. That 78 percent is the distance between your current standard of living and the standard of living for those at the edge of poverty. And as noted previously, this represents poverty at its most opulent level. Forty-five percent of poor individuals fall below one-half of the poverty line. For a family of three, this would be $10,168, which represents 11 percent of the national median income.

Finally, in an important respect, today's poverty is harsher than it was 70 years ago. In 1947, the poverty threshold for a family of four would have stood at 69 percent of the median four-person family income. When we began counting the numbers of poor Americans in 1959, it had dropped to just under 50 percent of the median. In 1980, it was 35 percent, and by 2019, the poverty threshold had dropped further to 25 percent.[9] Being categorized as poor has meant living further afield from the economic midpoint than in the past. If we were to apply today the economic distance that families in poverty were from the median income found in 1959, the poverty threshold for a family of four would rise from its current $26,172, to $53,074. As Howard Glennerster notes:

> *Very few American voters can realize that the measure of poverty that dominates political discussion has been getting more and more mean as the years pass. . . . If the present rate of income growth continues and the poverty line remains unchanged, the poverty line will soon be equivalent not to half of median earnings, as it was when Mollie Orshansky invented the number, but to a quarter of median earnings. That would be twice as harsh a measure as other countries in the world adopt.[10]*

We are now at that point. In this sense, poverty has become more severe today than it was 70 years ago.

But What About the United States Compared
With Other Countries?

It is certainly true that if we compare the United States to countries in sub-Saharan Africa, physical poverty in the United States is obviously less extreme.[11] The United States does not have the widespread famine and severe stunting of children that is sometimes found in extremely poor countries. However, most analysts would argue that the more relevant comparison would be the group of other high-economy countries such as those found in the European Union, Canada, Japan, Australia, and so on.[12] In comparing poverty in the United States to these OECD countries, we find that American poverty is both more prevalent and more extreme.[13]

Table 10.1 compares poverty rates across 26 OECD countries.[14] In this table, poverty is being measured as the percentage of the population falling below one-half of a particular country's median household income. This is what is known as a relative measure of poverty and is used extensively in making cross-national comparisons. The first column shows the overall poverty rate for each country; the second column displays the poverty rate for children; and the third column indicates the distance between the average income of those in poverty compared with the country's overall poverty threshold.

What we find is that the U.S. rates of poverty are substantially higher and more extreme than those found in the other 25 nations. The overall U.S. rate using this measure stands at 17.8 percent, compared with the 25-country average of 10.7 percent. The Scandinavian and Benelux countries tend to have the lowest rates of poverty. For example, the overall rate of poverty in Denmark is only 5.5 percent.

Looking at the poverty rates for children, we see similar patterns. The United States again leads all nations in having the highest rates of child poverty at 20.9 percent, while the overall average stands at 11.7 percent. Again, we see the Scandinavian countries having the lowest rates of child poverty, with Denmark seeing only 2.9 percent of its children falling into poverty.

Finally, the third column indicates the poverty gap, which is defined as the percentage by which the average income of the poor falls below the poverty line. This gives us an overall gauge of the depth and severity of poverty in each country. Once again, we find that the United States is at the very high end in terms of this measure. The distance between the poor's average income and the poverty line is nearly 40 percent. Only Italy has a greater poverty gap than the United States.

To summarize, when analyzing poverty as the number of persons who fall below 50 percent of a country's median income, we find that the United States has far and away the highest overall poverty rate in this group of 26 developed nations. Furthermore, the distance of the poor from the overall median income

TABLE 10.1 Extent of Poverty Across 26 OECD Countries

Country	Overall (%)	Children (%)	Poverty gap (%)
Iceland	5.4	5.8	27.2
Denmark	5.5	2.9	31.0
Finland	6.3	3.6	21.0
France	8.3	11.5	23.9
Netherlands	8.3	10.9	31.6
Norway	8.4	8.0	34.3
Switzerland	9.1	9.5	26.2
Sweden	9.3	9.3	22.5
Belgium	9.7	12.3	21.6
Austria	9.8	11.5	35.4
Ireland	9.8	10.8	23.3
Hungary	10.1	11.8	29.2
Poland	10.3	9.3	28.4
Germany	10.4	12.3	26.5
New Zealand	10.9	14.1	26.2
Luxembourg	11.1	13.0	28.9
United Kingdom	11.1	11.8	35.5
Australia	12.1	12.5	28.7
Canada	12.4	14.2	30.4
Portugal	12.5	15.5	29.4
Italy	13.7	17.3	40.8
Greece	14.4	17.6	35.3
Japan	15.7	13.9	33.7
Mexico	16.6	19.8	33.5
Korea	17.4	14.5	35.5
25-Country average	10.7	11.7	29.6
United States	17.8	20.9	39.8

Source: OECD data, 2020. https://data.oecd.org/inequality/poverty-rate.htm#indicator-chart

is extreme in the United States. At the same time, the United States is arguably the wealthiest nation in the world.[15]

This paradox is revealed in additional analyses that have examined both income and wealth inequality across OECD countries.[16] Not surprisingly, the United States has the highest standards of living at the middle and upper ends of the income distribution scale, yet for children at the lower end, their standards of living fall behind most other industrialized nations. The following conclusion can be drawn from these divergent patterns regarding American children:

> *Compared to other high-income counterpart nations, the US constantly experienced higher child poverty rates, regardless of the relative or absolute terms. Social insurance and universal programs in the US tend to be meager*

compared to those in high-income countries, and the overall portion that the
US contributes to reducing its deep child poverty is far lower.[17]

The reasons for such a discrepancy are twofold. First, as discussed in
Chapter 13 and referred to in the above quote, the social safety net in the
United States is much weaker than in virtually every other country listed in
Table 10.1. Second, the United States has been plagued by relatively low wages
at the bottom of the income distribution scale compared with other developed
countries (discussed in Chapter 6). These factors combine to contribute to
both the relative and absolute depths of U.S. poverty in comparison with other
industrialized nations.

The Factor of Time

In reflecting back on the Heritage Foundation report cited at the beginning of
this chapter, there is a another important factor that bears mentioning—that
of time. We have seen in Chapter 4 that most Americans move in and out of
poverty during the course of their lives. The typical spell of poverty is a few
years in duration.[18]

Consequently, it would make sense that individuals and families have acquired some basic goods over time. What the life course patterns of poverty
show is that families may do relatively well for a spell, only to experience occa-
sional setbacks that can throw them into poverty. When these occur, families do
not typically sell off all of their worldly possessions. They attempt to hold out
and make do until better economic times arrive.[19]

An example of this comes from an interview conducted for Mark Rank's
book, *Chasing the American Dream,* with a single mother of two children who
was close to having her home foreclosed by the mortgage company. Her troubles
began when she experienced health problems earlier in the year. As a result, she
was forced to cut back her job hours with a federal agency. In addition, her
mother and son were experiencing their own health difficulties that required
her attention. Finally, her ex-husband stopped paying child support. The combination of these circumstances started her down the road of falling behind on
her house payments, as well as maxing out her credit cards at $14,000. At this
point, the mortgage company began foreclosure proceedings.

I got behind. Everything happened at once. The beginning of the year,
I woke up and couldn't walk. Come to find out, I had bulging discs in my
back. Then turned around, and I guess from all the anxiety of having too
much on me, I thought I was having a heart attack. That turned around. It
wasn't my heart.

They said it must be anxiety because like I said, I have everything to
worry about—my mother and her health and taking care of her making

sure she has her doctor's appointments. Missing hours at work from going to the doctors. Obviously, I had less pay, and then getting laid off on top of it, it was just like boom, boom, boom, one thing right after another. And I fell behind.[20]

Nevertheless, the Heritage Foundation would report this family as having a microwave, a home, and air conditioning. However, the possession of these items would completely obscure the horrific situation that such a household finds itself in.

Social Exclusion and Deprivation

Finally, another way of thinking about the dire condition of American poverty is through the lens of social exclusion and deprivation. The economist and social philosopher Amartya Sen has analyzed poverty in terms of a lack of basic capabilities. Poverty implies an overall absence of individual freedom and agency according to Sen.[21] Using this perspective, one can make a strong argument that the poor in the United States experience much greater levels of exclusion and deprivation than the poverty-stricken in other OECD countries.

For example, life expectancy between the bottom and top of the income distribution is much wider in the United States than in other OECD countries.[22] Similarly, levels of voting and political participation are significantly suppressed for the poverty-stricken.[23] Those in poverty are more likely to experience food insecurity and have unattended health problems, more likely to be incarcerated, more likely to be discriminated against, more likely to be victimized by crime, and more likely to experience predatory lending than their counterparts in other countries.[24]

In addition, the conditions of poverty and use of a safety net program are highly stigmatized in American society.[25] Survey research has repeatedly indicated that the general understanding of poverty is primarily as an individual and moral failing.[26] This stigma and shame are experienced first-hand by those in poverty. It is felt in a variety of settings, from using the Supplemental Nutrition Assistance Program (SNAP) at the grocery store, to being denied health coverage at the doctor's office. This sense of shame permeates the experience of poverty and leads to individuals and families feeling additional levels of social exclusion.[27]

Consequently, not only are the poor worse off economically than those in other OECD countries, but in other aspects of life they may be much worse off. Inner-city residents in an impoverished racially segregated neighborhood may be exposed to much greater levels of stress, anxiety, and social exclusion than their poorer counterparts in many other countries.

We could easily list additional indicators that would show a similar pattern. Suffice it to say that the experience of poverty is far from the good life extolled by the Heritage Foundation. It is marked by the stigma, hardship, and deprivation that epitomizes poverty within a land of plenty.

Conclusion

The myth that the poor are really not so bad off is one that has been persistent and prevalent. After all, goes the argument, this is the greatest country in the world—even those at the bottom are doing alright.

And, in fact, such beliefs are frequently held even by those in poverty. In his book, *Broke and Patriotic: Why Poor Americans Love Their Country*, Francesco Duina explores why poor Americans display such high levels of patriotism and love of one's country. In interviews with residents in Alabama and Montana, individuals repeatedly pointed out that they felt conditions in other countries were much worse than in the United States. As Duina writes, "Being poor in America, then, beats being poor anywhere else in the world."[28]

There was also a strong belief among respondents that although times may be hard, conditions will undoubtedly improve in the future. The faith in the American dream is emblematic of this. As Duina notes, "The promises of a better tomorrow helped diminish the weight of today's problems."[29]

All of these attitudes have worked to maintain the myth that poverty in the United States is nothing to complain about. That economic conditions could be far worse than they are. In sharp contrast, the reality suggests that America's poor are actually much worse off than their counterparts in virtually every other OECD country.

An Expert Appraisal—Amy Glasmeier

Amy Glasmeier is Professor of Economic Geography and Regional Planning at the Massachusetts Institute of Technology. Much of her research has focused on the geography of poverty. In addition, she has created the Living Wage Calculator, which allows Web users to determine basic living expenses in various parts of the country.

The findings in this chapter highlight the daily difficulty individuals and families face as they try to get by being fully employed while unsuccessful in their ability to earn a living wage. Over the past 30 years, American workers have found themselves falling further behind as wages have lagged even as economic output rose. For the past 15 years, the living wage calculator at MIT has tracked the relationship between the cost of living in U.S. counties and cities and the starting minimum wage of Americans working full-time. I regularly receive comments from users who indicate that despite working full-time (40 hours or more a week), they cannot make ends meet and pay their bills. The fact is, over the past 30 years, real wages have been stagnant. Holding down a job that pays the minimum wage leaves people in debt, with individuals and families forced to juggle their bills month to month.

The most significant components of a family's cost of living are housing and child care. For those living in cities, the value of these two components can easily consume more than half of a family's total monthly income. Both have been rising in cost much more rapidly than the average wage rate, particularly in locations where job growth exceeds the national average. Child care and housing costs rise because, in many places, the demand for them exceeds their supply while concomitant changes in wage rates barely break the rate of inflation.

As pointed out earlier in this book, wage rates have been stagnant for much of the past 40-plus years. Americans live precarious lives because of the poor quality of many jobs currently available in the economy. Many citizens are unable to access good jobs that pay above the minimum wage and provide full-time work. Fewer still offer primary benefits such as health care and retirement funds. And for many workers, their positions are part-time, with many of these jobs in franchise operations.

Over the past three decades, jobs in America have shifted from goods-producing to service-producing, with many employed in food services, personal care, and temporary work. To support their families, employees, especially men, are forced to work multiple jobs in landscaping, construction, and other forms of laboring work. These jobs typically do not pay living wages, nor do they offer full-time employment. They pay such low wages that in order to make ends meet, employees must utilize publicly subsidized programs such as SNAP, housing subsidies, and Medicaid.

Historically, one solution to the unevenness of job availability and low relative wage rates has been the ability of Americans to pick up and move in search of economic opportunity. In the past, geographic mobility, while costly, served as a release valve to relieve the consequence of economic decline. Up until the 1980s, the migration machine enabled individuals and families to follow the growth of employment in response to the creation of new industries, the discovery of new natural resources, or the demand for armaments in support of national defense. But, inevitably, economic downturns unfold. And when they do, dislocation occurs, and pools of labor well up. In the past, concentrations of surplus labor were relieved through the valve of migration. Families and individuals could escape to locations of more significant opportunity.

Today, there is no escaping low incomes and the inability to get by in the United States. Among the four U.S. Census regions of the Northeast, Midwest, South, and West, virtually in no counties can individuals cover their necessary costs if paid the minimum wage.

The Economic Cost of Poverty Is Enormous

Clearly, the cost of poverty for those impoverished is high. Substantial research has documented that poverty exacts a heavy toll on those who fall within its grasp. [1] To take but one example, poverty has been shown to exert a powerful influence on an individual's physical and mental health. Those living in poverty tend to have significantly worse health as measured by a variety of indicators compared with the nonpoor. [2]

The effect of poverty on children is particularly destructive. Poverty serves to stunt children's physical and mental development. Poor infants and young children in the United States are far more likely to have lower levels of physical and mental growth (as measured in a variety of ways) than their nonpoor counterparts. [3] As children grow older, and if they continue to reside in poverty, the disadvantages of growing up poor multiply. These disadvantages include attendance at inferior schools, conditions associated with poverty-stricken neighborhoods, unmet health needs, and a host of other hardships. [4]

The result is that poverty exacts a heavy toll on the poor. However, what is perhaps less obvious are the economic costs of poverty to the nation as a whole. To a large extent, we have failed to recognize that poverty places enormous economic, social, and psychological costs on the nonpoor as well as the poor. These costs affect us both individually and as a nation, although we have been slow to recognize them. Too often, the attitude has been, "I don't see how I'm affected, so why worry about it?"

Yet, the issues that many Americans are in fact deeply concerned about, such as crime, access and affordability of health care, race relations, or economic productivity, to name but a few, are directly affected and exasperated by the condition of poverty. As a result, the general public winds up paying a heavy price for allowing poverty to walk in our midst. A report by the Children's Defense Fund on the costs of childhood poverty makes this strikingly clear:

> *The children who suffer poverty's effects are not its only victims. When children do not succeed as adults, all of society pays the price: businesses*

are able to find fewer good workers, consumers pay more for their goods, hospitals and health insurers spend more treating preventable illnesses, teachers spend more time on remediation and special education, private citizens feel less safe on the streets, governors hire more prison guards, mayors must pay to shelter homeless families, judges must hear more criminal, domestic, and other cases, taxpayers pay for problems that could have been prevented, fire and medical workers must respond to emergencies that never should have happened, and funeral directors must bury children who never should have died.[5]

This broad sense of awareness regarding the costs of poverty can be referred to as enlightened self-interest. In other words, by becoming aware of the various costs associated with poverty or, conversely, the various benefits associated with the reduction of poverty, we begin to realize that it is in our own self-interest to combat the condition of poverty.

Alexis de Tocqueville referred to this in his 1840 treatise on America as self-interest properly understood. In fact, the full title of the chapter from his book, *Democracy in America,* is, "How the Americans Combat Individualism by the Doctrine of Self-Interest Properly Understood." His basic premise was that "one sees that by serving his fellows, man serves himself and that doing good is to his private advantage."[6]

This awareness is often accomplished through education because such connections are frequently not self-evident. The case of poverty is a good example. For most Americans, poverty is seen as an individualized condition that exclusively affects those individuals, their families, and perhaps their neighborhoods. Rarely do we conceptualize a stranger's poverty as having a direct or indirect effect on our own well-being. By becoming aware of such impacts through informed knowledge, we begin to understand that reducing poverty is very much in our enlightened self-interest.

The Economic Cost of Childhood Poverty

The question, then, is, "What exactly is the economic cost of poverty?" A recent analysis by Michael McLaughlin and Mark Rank sought to estimate the annual cost of childhood poverty in the United States.[7] To do so, the authors relied on the latest government data and social science research in order to calculate the economic impact that childhood poverty exerted on the country as a whole. In particular, they examined the direct effect that childhood poverty has on lowering future economic productivity, higher health care and criminal justice costs, and increased expenses as a result of child homelessness and maltreatment.

Table 11.1 shows the annual estimated costs of childhood poverty for seven broad areas. Childhood poverty results in an annual loss of $294 billion due to lowered economic productivity through reduced earnings. In addition, increased health costs amount to $192 billion, whereas costs associated with increased crime and incarceration (increased victimization costs of street crime; increased corrections and crime deterrence; increased social costs of incarceration) total $406 billion.

By summing together these costs, the overall estimate is that in 2015, childhood poverty in the United States was costing the nation $1.03 trillion a year. This number represented 5.4 percent of the U.S. annual GDP.

The bottom line is that child poverty represents a significant economic burden to the United States. This is largely because living in poverty stunts the growth and undermines the potential of children. As Martin Ravallion notes, "Children growing up in poorer families tend to suffer greater human development gaps, with lasting consequences for their adult lives."[8] Impoverished children grow up with fewer skills and are less able to contribute to the economy. They are more likely to engage in crime and experience more frequent health care problems. These costs are ultimately borne not only by the children themselves but also by the wider society.

Perhaps a better way of gauging the magnitude of the costs of childhood poverty is to compare it with the total amount of federal spending in 2015. The federal government spent a total of $3.7 trillion in 2015.[9] This included the entire range of programs and agencies supported by the government, including defense spending, Social Security, infrastructure, and so on. The annual cost of childhood poverty—$1.03 trillion—therefore represented 28 percent of the entire budget spent by the federal government in 2015.

Consequently, to argue that we pay a large economic price for having the highest rates of poverty in the industrialized world is actually an understatement. Childhood poverty represents an enormous drain on both the U.S. economy and society as a whole. It results in sizable losses in economic productivity, higher health care and criminal justice costs, and significant costs associated with remedial efforts to address the fallout of childhood poverty.

TABLE 11.1 The Costs of Childhood Poverty

Type of cost	Dollar amount (in billions)
Reduced earnings	294.0
Increased street crime victimization costs	200.6
Increased health costs	192.1
Increased corrections/crime deterrence costs	122.5
Increased child homelessness costs	96.9
Increased social costs due to incarceration	83.2
Increased child maltreatment costs	40.5
Total cost of child poverty	1,029.8

Source: McLaughlin and Rank computations.

One question that naturally arises in a study such as this is, "What would it cost to reduce poverty in the United States?" Moreover, might it be more cost-effective to simply accept the high levels of U.S. childhood poverty rather than pay the price of reducing poverty?

With these questions in mind, two recent analyses have indicated that the cost of reducing childhood poverty is a fraction of what such poverty is costing us. The Children's Defense Fund, in conjunction with the Urban Institute, has estimated that childhood poverty could be reduced by 60 percent at a cost of $77 billion.[10] This would be accomplished through expanding an array of programs that have been shown to be effective in reducing poverty, such as the earned income tax credit, a higher minimum wage, child care subsidies, and so on. Similarly, Luke Shaefer and colleagues have estimated that by transforming the child tax credit into a universal child allowance, childhood poverty could be reduced by 40 to 50 percent, with extreme poverty eradicated, at a cost of approximately $70 billion.[11]

Taking these studies into account, if we assume that childhood poverty could be roughly cut in half through an annual expenditure of $70 billion, that $70 billion would save us approximately half of the $1.03 trillion that we project poverty costs us, or $515 billion. The bottom line is that according to these studies, the ratio of savings to cost is slightly more than 7:1. For every dollar spent in poverty reduction, we would save more than $7 in terms of the economic fallout from poverty.

However, there is a second way of estimating the difference between the price of ending poverty and what it is costing us. It is through a measure known as the poverty gap or the poverty income deficit. This measures what it would cost to lift all poor households with children younger than 18 years to the level of the poverty line. In other words, how much total income is needed to pull every American child out of poverty? According to the U.S. Census Bureau, that figure for 2015 was $86.9 billion.[12] For $86.9 billion, every American household with younger than 18 years in poverty could be raised out of poverty.

We can then compare this figure to our overall estimate of the costs of childhood poverty, which is $1.03 trillion. Combining these two figures results in a ratio of savings to cost of approximately 12:1. Consequently, when using the Census measurement of the costs associated with eliminating poverty, the result is an even higher rate of savings than when using the two earlier mentioned studies.

The bottom line is that reducing poverty is clearly justified from a cost–benefit perspective. Investing in programs that reduce childhood poverty is both smart and effective economic policy.

It should be noted that there were many additional costs that were clearly not accounted for in the McLaughlin and Rank analysis. For example, poverty has been shown to be strongly related to teenage childbearing. In turn, research suggests that the economic costs of teenagers bearing children is high.[13] By reducing childhood poverty, which would lower teenage childbearing, we would bring down these economic and societal costs. Consequently, the estimates should be seen as a lower bound with respect to the costs of childhood poverty.

In addition, there are significant costs associated with poverty during adulthood that were not taken into account at all. The analysis focused only on the costs of childhood poverty. However, as we have seen in Chapter 2, poverty also strikes individuals at various points throughout their lives. In fact, as noted earlier, poverty will affect a majority of Americans at some point during their adulthood. As such, the overall figure of $1.03 trillion a year is undoubtedly a significant underestimate of the true costs of American poverty.

Furthermore, it is important to point out that this analysis has calculated an overall annual cost to the United States. Rather than a one-time cost, the economic cost of childhood poverty is approximately $1 trillion per year. This clearly constitutes a significant ongoing drag on the overall U.S. economy.

Finally, it is pertinent to note that since the early 1980s, the overall rate of poverty for children has ranged between 16 and 23 percent.[14] It has thus remained stubbornly high during this period of time. In fact, children are currently the age group at the highest risk of poverty, and that risk is particularly extreme for younger children. If these trends and patterns continue, the cost of childhood poverty in the future will remain large indeed.

Equality Versus Efficiency?

There is, however, an argument often made with respect to not fully addressing poverty and inequality. It is based on the assumption that there is a necessary trade-off between having a strong economy and having a robust social welfare state. The recent origins of this argument can be traced back to an influential book entitled, *Equality and Efficiency: The Big Tradeoff* by the economist Arthur Okun.

Okun makes the case that the social policy goals of equality and efficiency are generally in opposition to each other. As he states:

> But in this essay I . . . discuss a . . . nagging and pervasive tradeoff, that between equality and efficiency. It is, in my view, our biggest socioeconomic tradeoff, and it plagues us in dozens of dimensions of social policy. We can't have our cake of market efficiency and share it equally.[15]

According to this argument, a country that strives to create a more egalitarian society through a strong welfare state and redistributive policies tends to lower economic efficiency because the incentives for entrepreneurship and economic productivity are reduced—higher taxes and more regulation result in a less efficient and productive economy. On the other hand, a society that seeks to increase its economic efficiency through the lowering of taxes and regulations results in greater levels of inequality and poverty because more laissez-faire capitalism tends to produce bigger winners and losers if left on its own. As Okun states, "We can't have our cake of market efficiency and share it equally."

Based on this, the argument is often made that in order for the United States to have a strong economy, we must have a very limited social welfare state. Yet, is this argument true? It turns out that the past 20 years have put this idea to rest. Some of the most robust economies during this time period have also had very comprehensive social safety nets. The countries of Norway, Germany, Sweden, and the Netherlands quickly come to mind as examples of countries that have been able to achieve both economic efficiency and social equality.[16]

Investing in human resources through a social welfare state turns out to be smart economic policy. As Monica Prasad explains:

> *There are aspects of the welfare state that can benefit economic growth. Health care and education are the most obvious examples: well-educated citizens are more capable of making innovations that lead to productivity gains, and healthy workers lose fewer workdays to illness. More recently, researchers have shown that other kinds of programs, such as food stamps and unemployment insurance, have positive economic effects. The welfare state contributes to productivity and economic growth by avoiding the un-derutilization of the human capital of the poor. A welfare state can also benefit the economy by providing Keynesian stimulus during slumps. The welfare state, Walter Korpi argues, is not a leaky bucket, taking away from productivity, but an irrigation system, ensuring that the economy continues to grow by nurturing the ground from which productivity blooms.*[17]

Furthermore, recent research has indicated that high levels of inequality may actually serve to dampen economic growth.[18] One reason for this is that by underinvesting in a segment of the population, the economy loses some of its potential human capital, as argued previously. On the other hand, social policies that invest in educational, health, and skill development are rewarded with a more dynamic and innovative workforce. This, in turn, helps to create greater economic growth and productivity for the society as a whole.[19] Consequently, one can make a further argument for why the societal cost of poverty is high— it potentially serves as an overall drag on economic productivity.

Conclusion

The bottom line is that the price of childhood poverty is exceedingly high. By allowing poverty to persist at such levels, we wind up spending considerably more in many areas than if poverty were substantially reduced. Impoverishment breeds serious health problems, inadequately educated children, and higher rates of criminal activity. As a result, we pay more for health care, we produce less productive workers, and we divert needed resources into the building and maintaining of correctional facilities. In each of these cases, we are spending our money on the back end of the problem of poverty rather than on the front end, which is almost always a more expensive approach to take.

The old saying, "An ounce of prevention is worth a pound of cure" is certainly apropos. As has been demonstrated, it is not a question of paying or not paying. Rather, it is a question of how we want to pay, which then affects the amount we end up spending. We assume that most of us would prefer to spend our money in a smart and efficient way. That is precisely what we are advocating for in targeting poverty as a priority issue. By making an investment up front to alleviate poverty, the evidence suggests that we will be repaid many times over in the lower costs associated with a host of social problems.

Yet, it is also true that we will not recoup these lower costs overnight. It will take time in order for these savings to become apparent. And therein lies part of the problem. Too often, we base our policy decisions on the short-term rather than the long-term gains. Congressional and presidential terms of 2 or 4 years tend to drive the policy process. Nevertheless, it is the long-term savings that can produce the greatest benefits over time.

Finally, we believe that there is an important psychological benefit to investing our resources in ways that avoid or substantially reduce social problems in the first place, rather than spending our resources on the negative fallout from such problems. Such a benefit is difficult to measure financially, but ask yourself what kind of community you would prefer to live in—one in which we spend our money on building prisons, or one in which we invest in people and their neighborhoods so that they do not eventually wind up in prisons? We believe that most people intrinsically feel better about communities that are characterized by the latter rather than the former. In short, reducing poverty is in our psychological self-interest, as well as in our economic and social self-interest.

An Expert Appraisal—H. Luke Shaefer

H. Luke Shaefer is Professor of Social Work at the University of Michigan, and he is also the director of Poverty Solutions at the University of Michigan. Shaefer is the author (along with Kathryn Edin) of *$2.00 a Day: Living on Almost Nothing in America*.

The costs of child poverty are immense, as the authors eloquently detail in this chapter. A recent consensus study report by the National Academies of Sciences cites Mark Rank's study and another to offer a range for these macroeconomic costs of roughly $800 billion to $1.1 trillion annually. That is a lot of money, in the form of lost economic productivity, health care costs that ultimately trace back to the consequences *of poverty, and crime and other societal challenges. Poverty affects us all, and we have a common interest in addressing it more effectively.*

A challenge with thinking about the cost of childhood poverty (or poverty among any group) is figuring out how to determine who is poor and who is not. My recent research with Richard Rodems uses questions on material hardship to circumvent assumptions about sufficient income. We find that in 2011, 38.4 percent of children lived in households reporting at least one form of material hardship, such as food insecurity, housing, and medical hardship. That is considerably above the rate of children considered poor for that year. Accordingly, our safety net stretches well up the economic ladder— for example, one out of every two infants now uses the Special Supplemental Nutrition Program for Women, Infants, and Children (WIC). Thus, exercises like Rank does to calculate the poverty income deficit are interesting, but incomplete. Lifting everyone above that line would help, no doubt. But our problems will not disappear.

Sometimes, scholars claim that we, as a nation, do not spend much on antipoverty efforts in the United States. My view is more nuanced. In fact, I think we spend a lot on means-tested programs, but that spending is disproportionately located in health care. In my recent essay with Kate Naranjo and David Harris, we find that the federal government spends nearly 3 times as much on health care for low-income Americans as it does on means-tested cash transfers. Why are we, as a nation, willing to spend $450 billion on health care for low-income American, but virtually nothing on cash transfers for the poorest families who are unable to maintain work? I do not, as of yet, have an answer to that question.

Where is the United States most successful in combatting poverty? I would argue that Social Security is our most successful antipoverty program. In my work with Richard Rodems, we find that children are 2.6 times more likely to live in a household reporting material hardship than seniors; they are 3.8 times as likely to live in a household with multiple hardships.

What are the hallmarks of the system we put in place for elderly people? Stability, for one. There is no recertifying for old-age Social Security every 6 months. The system provides fungible cash that seniors can use to meet their needs as they see fit, as well as universalism—virtually everyone is covered.

These insights are why I have become more of a universalist when it comes to tackling poverty than I once was. Someone once said, "Programs for poor people are poor programs." I think that the more you can fold everyone into the same program, the better, the more stable, and the more effective it will be. You circumvent questions about who is and is not poor. You do not create animosity among those who do not get it, and you provide a stability that our current means-tested income transfer programs fail to deliver.

That is what led me to a child allowance, my policy proposal that the authors cite. It is more expensive than other more targeted choices. But I think it is beautiful in its simplicity and could make a transformational impact in reducing the societal costs that the authors detail in this chapter.

{ 12 }

The Moral Ground to View Poverty Is Injustice

Many of the myths that we have been examining throughout this book are connected to the prevailing tendency to perceive poverty as individual failure and inadequacy. If one believes that poverty is the result of a lack of effort and individual failing, then the poor have no one to blame but themselves. In the United States, poverty is typically seen as the fault of the individual—that individuals are largely to blame for their situation and, consequently, that the rest of society bears little responsibility for their plight. The result is a general acceptance of the status quo of high poverty and a lack of initiative to address it. In other words, "It's somebody else's problem and responsibility, not mine."

Examples of using the broad brush of individual blame to paint the poor as undeserving can be found across a wide spectrum. Certainly, it has been the go-to mantra used by many politicians across political parties. From Ronald Reagan, to Bill Clinton, to Donald Trump, the emphasis on individual responsibility has been front and center.[1] Likewise, it is often found in many media portrayals of the poor. And, of course, it can be found sprinkled throughout everyday conversations that touch on issues of poverty and inequality.

As mentioned, one of the pernicious results of this myth is that it provides a comfortable justification for doing nothing to address poverty. If poverty is the result of individual inadequacies, and if the blame for poverty falls squarely on the shoulders of the poor, then we may actually harm the poor by attempting to help them. Such has been the logic of policymakers particularly on the right who have claimed that government is not the solution, government is the problem.

In 1984, the economist John Kenneth Galbraith gave a commencement address to graduating students at American University that was entitled, "The Convenient Reverse Logic of Our Time." The central theme of Galbraith's talk was that rather than moving from diagnosis to remedy in social policy, we have witnessed with greater frequency the rise of employing a reverse logic—that of moving from a preferred remedy to an appropriate diagnosis. As Galbraith explained, "Increasingly in recent times we have come first to identify the remedy that is most agreeable, most convenient, most in accord with major pecuniary or political interest, the one that reflects our available faculty for action; then we move from the remedy so available or desired back to a cause to which that remedy is relevant."[2]

Galbraith went on to illustrate with the example of poverty. Referring to poverty as "our most devastating social failure in this greatly affluent age and land" and "the heaviest burden on our social conscience," he noted that rather than devising social policies that would address the root causes of poverty, we have instead defined the causes of poverty in such a way that are consistent with our preferred policy strategies. These strategies have included cutting back on the role and scope of the federal government, seeking policies that are relatively inexpensive, devolving to the state and local levels, stressing personal responsibility, and so on. Galbraith observed:

> *From this need as to remedy we move back to the new cause of poverty. It is that the poor lack motivation—and they lack motivation because they are already unduly rewarded. That cause, once agreed upon, then calls for reduced expenditure on public services and less aid to the disadvantaged. So, in the recent past we have had, as an antipoverty measure, a broad curtailment of income and services to the poor.*[3]

The myth of understanding poverty through the lens of individual blame is therefore one that is both pervasive and powerful. It is the lynchpin that much of our social policy toward the poor has rested on.

The Concept of Deservedness and Poverty

The concept of deservedness has been applied to the poor across time. This criteria has been used for centuries, particularly since the English Poor Laws of 1601, to divide the poor into the categories of deserving and undeserving.[4] The deserving poor are those deemed worthy of our compassion and assistance because they find themselves in poverty through little fault of their own. As a result, an injustice has occurred. Such persons would include those who have suffered from an unavoidable illness or accident, children, widows, and so on. In general, the deserving poor are considered to represent a fairly small but worthy segment of the overall poverty population.

On the other hand, individuals falling into the undeserving poor category are seen as meriting neither our compassion nor our assistance. They consist of the able-bodied working age poor. As discussed in earlier chapters, such poverty is perceived as being brought on as a result of a lack of initiative, laziness, bad decisions, or some other failing, and therefore impoverishment is a just and fair consequence of prior behavior. The undeserving poor are often portrayed as making up the bulk of those experiencing poverty.

This idea of deservedness is derived from the overall notion of balance found within many theories of justice.[5] Consequently, within a just society, what you deserve in life should reflect your prior efforts, actions, and talents. For example, when someone works hard and plays by the rules, we often hope that he or she will receive their "just rewards." Or, when a crime is committed, justice is seen as being served if the criminal is sentenced to a punishment that fits the nature and severity of the crime.

On the other hand, if an individual commits a serious crime and is neither apprehended nor punished, the feeling is that an injustice has occurred. Thus, in cases in which individuals experience outcomes and consequences that are congruent with their prior actions and behaviors, the world is seen as just. Conversely, in situations in which individuals experience outcomes and consequences that are incongruent with their prior actions and behaviors, the world is viewed as unjust.

Therefore, from this perspective, an individual's current economic situation should be roughly in balance with the individual's prior actions and behaviors. In a just society, those who have worked hard and exerted themselves should do well economically. Likewise, those who have not worked hard and lacked the effort should not do well. Because America is viewed as a land of opportunity (see Chapter 16) with a level playing field (see Chapter 17), anyone who exerts sufficient effort should be able to achieve financial well-being and not be mired in poverty.

The concept of deservedness has also been applied to many other behaviors in American life, including health outcomes, financial success, and academic achievement. In addition, various social problems have been viewed from the lens of social pathology; that is, social problems in the United States are the result of individual shortcomings, and therefore such individuals must be held accountable and are ultimately to blame for their circumstances.

Is Poverty Deserved?

Let us now take the ideas of deservingness and balance and apply them to poverty in the United States. The question becomes, "Are poverty and economic destitution deserved and in balance with prior actions?" We believe that the answer in the vast majority of cases is a resounding no.

A relatively straightforward way to see this is if we simply examine the demographic composition of the poverty population. We can see in Table 12.1 that 30.8 percent of those in poverty in 2019 were children younger than 18 years. We would challenge anyone to make the argument that a 5-year-old child

TABLE 12.1 Composition of the Poverty Population

Demographic characteristic	Percentage
Children (<18 years old)	30.8
Elderly (≥65 years old)	14.3
Disabled (18–64 years old)	9.6
Age 18–64 years with no disability	45.3
Total	100.0

Source: U.S. Census, 2020.

deserves to live in poverty as a result of the child's prior actions. That argument simply cannot be made.

An additional 14.3 percent of the poor are 65 years or older, a category that many people feel is deserving of assistance. A further 9.6 percent of the poor are between the ages of 18 and 64 years and suffer from some type of disability. Again, this is a category that most of us would say deserves some help. Therefore, simply looking at the demographics, we see that more than half (54.7 percent) of people in poverty fall into categories that many would argue are not deserving of impoverishment.

For the remainder of the poor, as we have argued in Section II, research has shown that much of their poverty is the result of failings at the economic and political levels, such as the lack of enough decent-paying jobs to support a family. As mentioned earlier, Elise Gould found that for those between the ages of 18 and 64 years who were eligible for work (i.e., not in school, retired, or disabled), 63 percent were employed.[6] However, because of the nature of low-wage jobs, they were not able to work themselves out of poverty. And for those out of work, research has shown that they have worked in the past and will continue to work in the future.[7]

Ethnographic research has also shown that with respect to work attitudes and motivation, those in poverty exhibit similar behaviors and attitudes to the overall population.[8] Consequently, the basic conclusion is that for the vast majority of the poor, impoverishment cannot be justified in terms of prior negative actions.

Poverty as a Grievous Injustice

In sharp contrast to the perspective of blame, we argue that poverty represents an injustice of a substantial magnitude. Severe deprivation and hardship have been documented in countless studies—not to mention millions of human lives. And as argued in earlier chapters, a large portion of this poverty is the result of failings at the structural rather than the individual level, which places much of the responsibility for poverty beyond that of the individual.

However, what makes poverty particularly grievous is the stark contrast be-tween the wealth, abundance, and resources of America on the one hand and its levels of destitution on the other. Something is seriously wrong when we find that in a country with the most abundant resources in the world, there are children without enough to eat, families who cannot afford health care, and people who are sleeping on the streets for lack of shelter.

This was precisely the contrast that President Johnson was referring to in his inaugural address of 1965, when he spoke about the meaning of America:

> *Conceived in justice, written in liberty, bound in union, it was meant one day to inspire the hopes of all mankind; and it binds us still. If we keep its terms, we shall flourish. First, justice was the promise that all who made the journey would share in the fruits of the land. In a land of great wealth, families must not live in hopeless poverty. In a land rich in harvest, children just must not go hungry. In a land of healing miracles, neighbors must not suffer and die unattended. In a great land of learning and scholars, young people must be taught to read and write.*[9]

It should also be noted that the gap between extreme prosperity and eco-nomic vulnerability has never been wider (as discussed in Chapter 18). The venerable economist, Paul Samuelson, writing in the first edition of his intro-ductory economics textbook in 1948, observed that if we were to make an in-come pyramid out of a child's play blocks, with each layer representing $1,000 of income, the peak would be somewhat higher than the Eiffel Tower, but al-most all of us would be within a yard or so of the ground. By the time of Samuelson's 2001 edition of the textbook, most of us would still be within a yard or two of the ground, but the Eiffel Tower would now have to be replaced with Mount Everest to represent those at the top.[10]

Or, take what has happened with respect to the distance between the average worker's salary and the average CEO's salary. In 1980, the average CEO of a major corporation earned 42 times that of the average worker's pay. Today, it is around 300 times.[11] Adding insult to injury, during the past 40 years, an increasing number of companies have demanded concessions from their workers, including pay cuts and the elimination of health benefits, in order to keep their labor costs down, while those at the top have prospered beyond any sense of decency.

Patterns of wealth accumulation have become even more skewed, as we discuss in Chapter 18. Today in America, we find that the top 1 percent of the U.S. population currently own 46 percent of the entire financial wealth in the country, while the bottom 60 percent of Americans are in possession of less than 1 percent of the country's financial wealth.[12] And, while all of these trends have been happening, our social policies have continued to give more to the well-to-do and less to the economically vulnerable, with the argument that these policies have been helping all Americans.

A new way of thinking recognizes this as a moral outrage. Injustice, rather than blame, becomes the moral compass on which to view poverty amidst abundance. This type of injustice constitutes a strong impetus for change. It signals that a wrong is being committed that cries out for a remedy. A shift in thinking recognizes this and is premised on the idea that social change is essential in addressing the injustices of poverty.

This is in sharp contrast with the old way of thinking, in which the moral focus is on individual blame. This has had the effect of simply reinforcing the status quo of doing little, resulting in continued rates of elevated poverty. The perspective of injustice allows us to actively engage and confront poverty, rather than comfortably settling for the status quo of widespread impoverishment.

Martin Luther King summed this up well with the following passage from his final book, *Where Do We Go From Here: Chaos or Community?* He wrote:

> *A true revolution of value will soon cause us to question the fairness and justice of many of our past and present policies. We are called to play the Good Samaritan on life's roadside; but that will be only an initial act. One day the whole Jericho road must be transformed so that men and women will not be beaten and robbed as they make their journey through life. True compassion is more than flinging a coin to a beggar; it understands that an edifice which produces beggars needs restructuring. A true revolution of values will soon look uneasily on the glaring contrast of poverty and wealth.* [13]

Such a revolution of values must begin with a fundamental shift in how American society understands and ultimately acts toward the issue of poverty.

An Expert Appraisal—Michael Reisch

Michael Reisch is the Daniel Thursz Distinguished Professor of Social Justice in the School of Social Work at the University of Maryland. He has written extensively concerning issues of social justice and the economically disadvantaged.

In the West, the concepts of deservedness and justice are rooted in the idea of virtue, as first expressed by Aristotle. Virtue referred to the presence of certain personal qualities that prioritized the interests of the polis, or community, over those of the individual. Deservedness and justice, therefore, reflected a prior conception of a good society. In ancient Athens, as in 21st-century America, this social construction benefited existing elites and preserved the status quo.

Two millennia later, with the advent of capitalism and its accompanying ideological rationale, based on both religious (largely Calvinist) and secular (e.g., Hobbes, Locke) ideas, that C. B. MacPherson collectively termed the spirit of "possessive individualism," elites developed a new rationale for growing misery in place of former feudal obligations. They created an artificial distinction between the "worthy" and "unworthy" poor that equated deservedness with character and the contribution individuals made both to society and their own condition. For several centuries, this distinction rationalized neglecting the needs of millions of people and ignoring the structural sources of their impoverishment.

In the 20th century, the consequences of global war and economic collapse compelled elites to modify their ideas about deservedness to maintain power and social and political stability. The welfare state was the policy response to this imperative. While Western European countries adopted a more or less universal approach to human needs, the United States maintained the old worthy/unworthy dichotomy, particularly in its income support and health care policies. The contrast between Medicare and Medicaid, and between Social Security and Temporary Assistance for Needy Families (TANF), and even how Social Security benefits are calculated, illustrates the effects of this dualism. The rationale for these distinctions is found in religious beliefs, pseudoscience (social Darwinism), and social science (the culture of poverty). Consequently, the prior equation of individual pathology and deservedness is now applied to entire groups and implicitly regarded as "just."

During the past four decades, the concept of deservedness has been further revised to justify the rollback of assistance for the poor, the dramatic growth of inequality, and the requirements of economic globalization. As John Kenneth Galbraith astutely observed, the work ethic is now applied differently to the wealthy and the rest of society. The former are only required to "work" (i.e., invest) if the return is sufficient to justify the effort. This justified tax cuts, deregulation, and other policies that accrued to elites' benefit. For the 99 percent, however, "work" (i.e., wage labor at whatever salary) became a requirement even to receive social benefits. A critical aspect of this revision is the increased use of racial and gender divisions, and more recently religion and immigration status, to drive a wedge between groups with common interests and sustain the illusion that the provision of aid to one population reflected a zero-sum game in which the "worthy" supported the "unworthy" through their hard-earned taxable dollars.

In the policy sphere, the consequences have been profound. The formerly "worthy," such as children, are denied health care, nutritional assistance, quality education and housing, and fair treatment in the criminal justice system. In the current hyperpartisan environment in which the historical atomistic nature of American society has metastasized to groups, the need to shift the discourse away from individual to collective responsibility and from character flaws to the structural defects that produce growing inequality has never been more compelling.

{ SECTION IV }

Does Welfare Work?

Few behaviors are as stigmatized and vilified in American society as that of using a public assistance or welfare program. In survey after survey, welfare recipients are disapproved of in the general population by a wide margin. The very notion of receiving help from the government cuts against the grain of self-reliance, a core component of the American identity. Therefore, it should come as no surprise that using a safety net program is strongly condemned.

In addition, a wide variety of myths and stereotypes surround welfare recipients and welfare programs. These include the beliefs that the welfare system is overly generous, that welfare fraud is rampant, and that women have more children to get more welfare benefits—and tying many of these myths together, the belief in the stereotype of the welfare queen.

The welfare queen represents the epitome of the myths swirling around this issue. The image is of a woman with a multitude of children living the good life on her generous benefits. She relaxes during the day and parties at night, with the understanding that she is entitled to everything received. She has no intention of ever working and serves as a role model for her many children.

Truth or fiction? We explore several of the most widely held myths surrounding welfare in the pages ahead. To do so, we turn to a sizable body of research that has addressed these topics.

The U.S. Welfare State Is Minimal

It is common to hear complaints about excessive spending on welfare programs and the need to rein in expenses. Yet, how much does the United States actually spend on safety net programs? Is it a large percentage of the overall budget? What does a typical family of three receive in welfare benefits each month? Is it a comfortable amount to live on? When trying to answer these questions, many Americans overestimate how much money the federal government spends on welfare programs and the amount of monthly benefits received by low-income families (just as they overestimate the amount of money spent on foreign aid). In this chapter, we tackle two interrelated myths—the belief that welfare spending is exploding and excessive, and the belief that generous benefits provide recipients with an easy life.

Separating Fact From Fiction in Claims About "Explosive Growth" in Welfare Spending

Attitudes and beliefs about poverty and wealth are highly partisan. For example, a Pew Research Center poll found that Republicans and those leaning Republican were more likely to attribute poverty to a lack of effort than Democrats or those leaning Democrat (48 vs. 18 percent, respectively) and less likely to perceive poverty as resulting from circumstances beyond an individual's control (31 vs. 69 percent).[1] Republicans are also more likely than Democrats to regard the U.S. economy as fair, to believe that welfare creates dependency, and to oppose redistribution of wealth from the rich to the poor.[2] Aligning with these beliefs, Republican policymakers are more likely than their colleagues across the aisle to characterize the U.S. welfare system as bloated and to claim that the lion's share of federal spending is spent on entitlement (mandatory) and discretionary programs for the poor.

Assessing the accuracy of these claims requires considering the range of welfare programs that serve low-income individuals and families. These programs fall into two basic categories—(1) programs that provide health care, such as Medicaid, the Children's Health Insurance Program (CHIP), and tax credits that subsidize marketplace coverage under the Affordable Care Act (ACA); and (2) a wide-range of other programs for low-income individuals and families, such as the Supplemental Nutrition Assistance Program (SNAP), Supplemental Security Income (SSI), housing assistance, the Earned Income Tax Credit (EITC), Temporary Assistance for Needy Families (TANF), and the Low-Income Home Energy Assistance Program (LIHEAP). Because costs associated with health care, both in the public and private spheres, have risen more quickly than other program expenses, it is important to separate low-income programs into these two categories.

Whether looking at longitudinal trends or point-in-time expenditures, there is little evidence to support the myth of runaway welfare spending. While spending on non–health care programs for the poor grew in response to the Great Recession, it subsequently declined in the aftermath.[3] Low-income non–health care spending as a percentage of GDP returned to pre-recession levels in 2018 and is subsequently projected to dip below its 40 year average.[4]

Figure 13.1 shows this historical and projected spending. Federal spending on low-income programs outside of health care was 2 percent of the GDP in 2018, representing 2 cents for every dollar the economy produced.[5] Low-income health care programs—which provide care to an estimated 93 million Americans monthly—were estimated to be 2.4 percent of GDP.[6]

Although additional growth in low-income health care costs is expected, these expenses will be offset by the projected decline in other low-income spending. As a result, a slight decrease in federal spending across all low-income programs is forecasted, from 4.4 percent of GDP in 2018 to 4.3 percent in 2028.

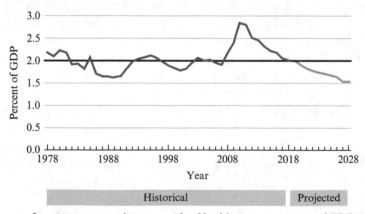

FIGURE 13.1 *Low-income expenditures outside of health care as a percent of GDP.*
Source: Center on Budget and Policy Priorities, 2018.

In addition to GDP, it is also helpful to consider the percentage of the U.S. federal budget dedicated to various programs. In 2019, approximately 8 percent of the federal budget ($361 billion) was spent on low-income programs outside of health care.[7]

Not surprisingly, more is spent on health-related programs, increasing the overall amount. Low-income health care and Medicare spending are often reported together, obscuring that a greater share of the budget goes to Medicare, the program that provides health care to seniors and people with disabilities. In 2019, for instance, spending on health care programs accounted for 25 percent of the federal budget ($1.1 trillion), but close to three-fifths ($651 billion) of these funds were spent on Medicare, with the remaining share on Medicaid, CHIP, and ACA subsidy and marketplace costs.[8] Without a detailed breakdown, spending on low-income health care programs is easily overestimated.

Cross-national comparisons bring limited U.S. investment in welfare programs into sharper focus. Compared with peer OECD countries, the United States has higher rates of relative poverty and inequality, and yet invests less in safety net programs and provides less comprehensive assistance.[9] We can see this pattern clearly in Figure 13.2.

Low U.S. spending on safety net programs comes at an additional cost— child poverty rates are higher in the United States than in countries that spend more on their welfare programs, resulting in higher societal and economic costs (as shown in Chapter 11). Furthermore, U.S. investment levels are headed downward. The United States spends less on poor children today than it did 30 years ago despite ample evidence that childhood participation in welfare programs is associated with improved health and economic productivity during adulthood.[10] In 1990, the federal government spent approximately $8,700

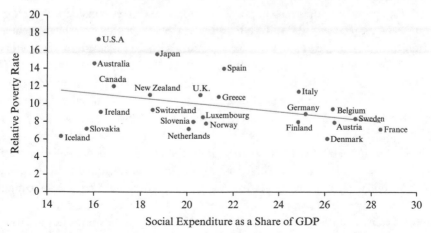

FIGURE 13.2 *Social expenditure and relative poverty rates in selected OECD countries.*
Source: Economic Policy Institute, 2018.

(corrected for inflation) on every child and families in a family without paid employment; by 2015, this figure had dropped to $7,000.[11] Making sense of this decline requires turning our attention to the impact of welfare reform, trends in TANF enrollment and funding, and how restrictive program requirements contribute to the minimal welfare state.

Falling Further Behind: TANF and the Eroding Safety Net

Twenty-five years ago, the Personal Responsibility and Work Opportunity Reconciliation Act of 1996 (PRWORA) changed the structure of the U.S. welfare system for low-income families with children. Making good on President Bill Clinton's campaign promise to "end welfare as we know it," PRWORA replaced Aid to Families With Dependent Children (AFDC), the cash assistance program most commonly associated with welfare, with TANF, which was a new and more restrictive program. As a work-first program, TANF focuses on "ending the dependence of needy parents on government benefits" rather than on ending poverty.[12]

This focus is evident in TANF's implementation of strict time limits on welfare receipt (a federal lifetime limit of 60 months), work requirements that mandate participation in approved employment activities outside of the home, and sanctions that reduce or suspend adult and/or full family benefits for lack of compliance with regulations. Other program changes may go largely unnoticed by recipients but are equally significant. Importantly, PRWORA terminated AFDC's status as an entitlement program, meaning that eligibility for TANF does not guarantee receipt of benefits and that states have the discretion to refuse and/or terminate assistance. As a consequence, eligible families can be turned away if state funds are exhausted and the federal government does not step in to provide additional support. Funding also differs considerably across states. States receive federal TANF funds via block grants and have greater discretion in how they choose to use their funds. State block grants are determined through annual appropriations, with the amount based on states' historical program participation rates rather than on current enrollment and/or need. Despite ongoing increases in the cost of living, TANF funding has remained largely unchanged since 1997, even to account for inflation.

Although U.S. cash aid programs have never been generous, restrictive TANF requirements, reductions in funding, the failure of benefits to keep up with inflation, and marginal state investment in training that could improve employability all contribute to a "perfect storm" of retrenchment. Despite high rates of poverty and ongoing need, TANF's monthly caseload has declined dramatically, from 4.4 million families in 1996 to 1.3 million families in 2017. Particularly noticeable is the fact that TANF reaches significantly fewer poor families than AFDC did and that, under TANF, the number of eligible families served continues to decline (Figure 13.3). Before TANF's enactment in 1996, 68 poor families received assistance for every 100 families living in poverty; by 2017, 23 families received TANF benefits out of every 100 poor families.[13] Further debunking the myth of a bloated welfare system is the estimate that only 3 percent of single female-headed households with two children and earnings below 150 percent of the poverty line access multiple support programs (i.e., EITC, SNAP, and either TANF or housing assistance, or both).[14]

The challenges facing families experiencing poverty are further compounded by the declining value of cash assistance. Cash benefits are extremely low, refuting the well-worn stereotype that generous welfare benefits make it possible for low-income families to live comfortably without working.[15] Although the size of TANF benefits varies from one state to another, the amount of cash aid is consistently much too low to lift a family above the poverty line. According to the Center on Budget and Policy Priorities, "TANF benefits are below two-thirds of the federal poverty in all 50 states and the District of Columbia and at or below 20 percent of the poverty line in 17 states."[16] In 2018, a family of three in the median state received $486 in monthly TANF benefits, and in 14 states, it was less than $300.[17] Without additional sources of income, making ends meet is extremely challenging to impossible.

Although TANF is widely assumed to be a race-neutral program, analyses of racial disparities in access to and receipt of treatment within the welfare system tell a very different story, making clear that the minimal welfare state is even more so for people of color. An analysis by Heather Hahn and colleagues illustrates this point. They found that a larger African American share of a state's total population was associated with less generous TANF benefits (e.g., eligibility criteria, amount of monthly cash aid), more restrictive behavioral

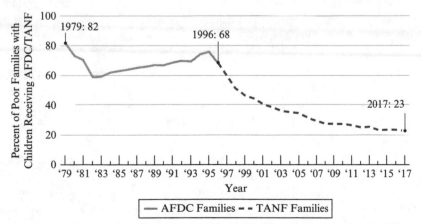

FIGURE 13.3 *Number of families receiving AFDC/TANF benefits for every 100 families with children in poverty.*

Source: Center on Budget and Policy Priorities, 2018.

regulations (e.g., work requirements, school attendance goals, sanctions, family caps), and stricter time limits.[18]

States with larger populations of African Americans also have worse poverty-to-TANF ratios, meaning that fewer families experiencing poverty receive TANF benefits.[19] More specifically, Hahn found that "states with TANF-to-poverty ratios ranking in the bottom half nationally are home to the majority (56 percent) of African American people but only 46 percent of non-Hispanic white people."

Reviewing state disparities in TANF participation brings these inequities into sharper focus. For example, in Vermont, a state with a very small Black population, 78 of every 100 low-income families experiencing poverty received TANF benefits, while in Mississippi, a state with a large Black population, just 10 poor families out of every 100 received TANF benefits.[20] These problematic inequities offer a powerful warning against assuming equal access to or experiences within safety net programs and highlight the urgency of addressing covert and overt racism in the design and implementation of social policy.

The bottom line is that TANF participation rates, estimates of unmet need, and eroding benefits document just how minimal our welfare system is and just how erroneous claims of a bloated welfare state are. Families of color face additional barriers to accessing the limited support that exists. Rather than the safety net being minimal, for some low-income groups it may be nonexistent.

Conclusion

We have spent much of this chapter highlighting how little is spent on U.S. welfare programs, particularly safety net programs outside of health care. It bears noting that expenditures on welfare programs become all the more modest when balanced against the essential nutrition, health, and housing needs of those in poverty. And yet despite their limitations, economic security programs, notably Social Security, food assistance, and tax credits for working families, have reduced the poverty rate by half since 1967.[21] This success is tempered by missed opportunities in reach and impact. For example, if TANF currently served the same share of poor families that it did in 1996, an estimated 3.8 million families would have received assistance in 2017 instead of only 1.3 million, resulting in a lower poverty rate.[22]

Challenging the myth of the bloated welfare state requires tackling multiple intersecting misperceptions, including erroneous portrayals of U.S. welfare expenditures as exorbitant or driving up national spending and debt. It also requires shattering myths that legitimize keeping welfare benefits low. One of the most common arguments against more generous welfare benefits is the fear that larger cash assistance will encourage dependency and reduce interest in seeking paid employment. These concerns are largely unfounded. For instance, in Kjetil van der Wel and Knut Halvorsen's analysis of 18 European countries, commitment to employment increased as social spending grew more generous.[23] Similarly, Abhijit Banerjee's study of cash transfer programs in six developing countries found no evidence that they discouraged work.[24]

An Expert Appraisal—Martin Gilens

Martin Gilens is Professor of Politics at Princeton University. His research has focused on public opinion, particularly with respect to poverty and inequality. He is the author of a number of books, including *Why Americans Hate Welfare: Race, Media and the Politics of Antipoverty Policy.*

I would say that opposition to welfare in the United States stems primarily from the perception that most welfare recipients do not really need it, and that perception is strongly connected to misperceptions about the racial composition of the poor and welfare recipients and the stereotype of African Americans as lazy. We see this manifested in a variety of ways, but the bottom line here is that since the racialization of poverty in the 1960s, Americans' attitudes toward welfare, and White Americans' attitudes in particular, have been thoroughly shaped by their views of Blacks.

The racial diversity of our society makes it more difficult for individual citizens to see the connections between themselves and the rest of society. It is easier to create a sense of us versus them—of people who are paying their taxes versus people who are living off government benefits. These kinds of distinctions can be made more clearly because of the racial diversity and connection between economic stratification and racial group differences.

This is one reason that European welfare states have developed much more generous and robust welfare programs, and also one key reason that some of these programs are under greater threat today with the rise of ethnically, racially, and religiously diverse immigration into those societies than they were a few decades ago.

Having said that, there is still great support for government action as a safety net. Americans do think people should be responsible for themselves, but they also think that when people encounter setbacks, when they have needs that they are unable to meet on their own, that there is an important role for government in providing a safety net.

Welfare Fraud Is Scarce

Do these headlines about welfare sound familiar?

"Woman charged with wrongly receiving more than $10,000 in food stamps, Medicaid benefits"[1]

"Brothers sentenced in $1.4 million grocery store welfare fraud scheme"[2]

"I'm going to make millions! Unrepentant Escalade-driving surfer who lives like a king on food stamps tells how the welfare system has let him strike it rich with his band"[3]

Although such headlines are routine, they are certainly not indicative of the actual prevalence of welfare fraud. For example, the "slacker lifestyle" of Jason Greenslate, the focus of the third headline, received extensive media coverage. Popularly referred to as "lobster boy" and the "food stamp surfer," Greenslate came to prominence when he was profiled in a Fox News series titled, "The Great Food Stamp Binge." Embodying the stereotype of lazy, able-bodied welfare recipients who live comfortably on generous benefits and avoid work, Greenslate boasted about using benefits from the Supplemental Nutrition Assistance Program (SNAP) to pay for sushi and lobster:

> It's not that I don't want a job, I don't want a boss. I don't want someone telling me what to do. I'm gonna live my own life. . . . This is the way I want to live. And I don't really see anything changing. I got the card. It's $200. That's it.[4]

Yet, nearly all SNAP recipients have little in common with the "food stamp surfer." Two-thirds of SNAP recipients are senior citizens, children, and people with disabilities. Among recipients who are able to work, most do.[5] Additionally, SNAP benefits are low, and most recipients do not purchase high-cost items because this would greatly increase their likelihood running out of food before the end of the month, which is nevertheless a common occurrence. In 2018, the average SNAP recipient received $127 monthly in benefits, amounting to $4.17

a day and $1.39 per meal.[6] Not only do these limited funds quickly run out despite careful budgeting, they also belie the stereotype that generous welfare benefits make it possible for recipients to "live large."

Although far from representative of the typical SNAP recipient, Jason Greenslate quickly became the face of the program, with Republican policymakers citing his circumstances as indicative of the need for reform. Emphasis on atypical cases such as this contributes to the overestimation of program abuse and perception of recipients as "takers" who do not contribute to broader society.[7] For instance, during a 2017 speech, President Trump declared, "But welfare reform—I see it and I've talked to people. I know people, they work three jobs and they live next door to somebody who doesn't work at all, is making more money and doing better than the person that's working his or her ass off. And it's not going to happen. Not going to happen."[8]

In one public opinion poll, nearly six in 10 (59 percent) respondents believed that it was very or somewhat common for people to lie and/or misrepresent their eligibility to receive SNAP.[9] Nevertheless, analyses of welfare fraud find that it is relatively rare, making clear that there is a large gap between common beliefs about program abuse and reality.[10]

In this chapter, we contrast prevalence rates of welfare fraud with stereotypes about program abuse, attending to how myths about fraud legitimize restrictive welfare policies, criminalize public assistance, stigmatize recipients, and reduce access to essential safety net programs. Because SNAP is subject to great scrutiny and misperception, we focus on this program.

How Common Is Welfare Fraud?

When people hear the term "welfare fraud," they usually think of individuals who misrepresent themselves or their economic situation so that they can obtain benefits that they are not eligible for or receive more benefits than they are entitled to. Perhaps the most notorious example of this was the so-called "welfare queen" that President Reagan often referred to. In a radio address on October 18, 1976, he described her story:

> *The trail extends through fourteen states. She has used a hundred and twenty-seven names so far, posed as a mother of fourteen children at one time, seven at another, signed up twice with the same case worker in four days, and once while on welfare posed as an open-heart surgeon, complete with office. She has fifty Social Security numbers and fifty addresses in Chicago alone, plus an untold number of telephones. She claims to be the widow—let's make that plural—of two naval officers who were killed in action. Now the Department of Agriculture is looking into the massive*

*number of food stamps she's been collecting. She has three new cars, a full-
length mink coat, and her take is estimated at one million dollars.*[11]

In his book, *The Queen*, Josh Levin describes how this sensational and atypical
case was used to frame the welfare population as undeserving and criminal.

The question, then, is, "How much fraud and abuse actually occur?" Program
abuse can take many different forms. Analyses of SNAP take into account a
range of inaccuracies and misconduct, including (1) trafficking or the illegal
sale of SNAP benefits, which can involve retailers and/or recipients; (2) retailer
application fraud, which involves a wrongful attempt to participate in SNAP
when the store or owner is ineligible; (3) errors and fraud by SNAP applicants
when securing benefits; and (4) errors and fraud by state agencies that result in
inaccurate payments to benefits.[12]

The more holistic approach embodied by these categories shifts the relatively
narrow focus on applicants and recipients to other sources of inaccuracies and
problems within the system, notably service providers and SNAP-authorized
retailers. Moreover, while each category of information is useful, not all of it
is indicative of fraud. Some behaviors, such as trafficking, are always treated
as fraud, while others, such as duplicate enrollment, may reflect fraud or error
depending on intent.[13] Unintentional behaviors, such as a small reporting error
on income or rent, are not considered fraudulent. Yet, when this this information is included in estimates of SNAP overpayments, it can result in exaggerated
perceptions of fraud. We review these different indicators, highlighting the wide
gap between myth and reality. What stands out across different measures is that
fraud in the SNAP program is universally low.

Prevalence Rates of Retailer Trafficking and Application Fraud

One form of retailer trafficking of SNAP benefits occurs when recipients sell
their benefits for cash (typically at a loss) to an owner or employee of a store
that accepts SNAP benefits. Three-year trafficking estimates document that this
is not a common practice. Between 2009 and 2011, it is estimated that 1.34 percent of all redeemed SNAP benefits were trafficked, meaning that they were
sold for cash or exchanged illegally at stores; this figure rose slightly to 1.50 percent between 2012 and 2014.[14] Another way to assess retailer trafficking is to
consider its monetary cost. In 2012 to 2014, an estimated $1.1 billion in benefits
were trafficked annually.[15] While not insignificant, it is also a small share of the
approximately $73 billion spent annually on the program at that time.

The government also tracks the national store violation rate or the percentage
of SNAP retailers who have trafficked benefits at least once during a given time
period. For 2009 to 2011 and 2012 to 2014, these figures were estimated to be
10.5 and 11.8 percent, respectively.[16] This slight increase is attributed to the
rise in small businesses that accept SNAP benefits, particularly convenience

stores, which tend to have higher trafficking rates than larger retailers.[17] Even so, this problem is limited in prevalence and scope. In 2016, less than 1 percent of participating retailers (1,842 of 260,115 stores) rose to the level of being disqualified from accepting SNAP benefits because of trafficking.[18] Fraudulent retail applications are even less common than trafficking, with less than one store sanctioned for every 2,064 participating stores in 2016 for a violation related to integrity standards.[19]

Fraud and Error by Recipients and State Agencies

Despite stereotypes about pervasive welfare abuse, deliberate misrepresentation by recipients is uncommon. For every 10,000 households that received SNAP benefits in 2016, only 14 included a recipient who was investigated and determined to have committed fraud that resulted in an overpayment that had to be repaid.[20] Recipients are far more likely to make reporting errors than engage in fraudulent behaviors, with 181 of every 10,000 SNAP households being overpaid for this reason.[21] Examining dollar outlays further confirms minimal fraud. In 2016, only $11 of every $10,000 paid in SNAP benefits was overpaid because of recipient fraud versus $63 because of recipient error.[22] To put this into perspective, the Internal Revenue Service estimates that about $1 out of every $6 owed in federal taxes is not paid because of tax evasion or fraud.[23]

Congressional testimony by Stacy Dean accurately summarizes findings concerning fraud versus error:

> *The overwhelming majority of SNAP errors that do occur result from mistakes by recipients, eligibility workers, data entry clerks, or computer programmers, not dishonesty or fraud by recipients. In addition, states have reported that almost 60 percent of the dollar value of overpayments and almost 90 percent of the dollar value of underpayments were their fault, rather than recipients. Much of the rest of overpayments resulted from innocent errors by households facing a program with complex rules.*[24]

This separation of error versus fraud rates, and recipients from administrators, is particularly useful in debunking stereotypes because different sources of inaccuracies and problems are disentangled from one another. Unfortunately, other measures such as the highly misunderstood National Payment Error Rate (NPER) tend to garner far more attention. The NPER is an indicator of state "quality control" in making benefit determinations but is frequently misinterpreted as assessing the prevalence of fraud and dollars lost to fraud. Instead, it is a calculation of both overpayments and underpayments of more than $38 (adjusted for inflation annually) due to combined multiple sources (i.e., recipient and agency errors and fraud). Even when overpaid benefits are collected from households, they count toward a state's error rate.[25] In 2017, the

NPER was 6.3 percent, with an overpayment and underpayment rates of 5.2 and 1.1 percent, respectively.[26]

Overall, error rates are low, reflecting the effectiveness of current eligibility and benefit determination practices. Although welfare programs are stereotyped as going largely unchecked, SNAP error rates are closely monitored, and significant federal and state resources are dedicated to assessing program integrity.

The Criminalization of Welfare Receipt and Its Impact

Despite ample evidence to the contrary, the myth of rampant welfare fraud persists. It is heard in ongoing complaints that welfare recipients take advantage of the system and in continued calls for "welfare reform" and greater "program integrity." It is also evident in policies that require welfare recipients to submit to periodic drug tests and finger-imaging to receive benefits. These stigmatizing practices treat low-income individuals and families more like criminals than people in need of assistance, and, not surprisingly, they are more effective at humiliating recipients and deterring prospective applicants than reducing fraud.[27]

Low rates of substance abuse among welfare recipients raise questions about the true purpose of drug testing, leaving little doubt that this practice is more deeply grounded in stereotypes than evidence. SNAP recipients are only slightly more likely than nonrecipients to experience a drug abuse disorder, and as is the case with nonrecipients, alcohol abuse, which is not detected via drug testing, is more common than other forms of substance abuse.[28] In fact, demographic characteristics such as youth are better predictors of substance abuse than SNAP receipt.[29] Drug testing of participants in the Temporary Assistance for Needy Families (TANF) program yields similar findings. In a seven-state analysis, TANF recipients were found to test positively for drug use at lower rates than the general population.[30] Collectively, these studies indicate that the millions of dollars spent on drug testing would be better utilized on job training and other services that move families out of poverty. Nevertheless, some states have sought to make unemployment benefits contingent on drug testing.

Evidence supporting the use of finger-imaging is equally scant. Touted as a strategy for reducing "double-dipping" (i.e., fraudulent submission of multiple welfare applications), finger-imaging became popular in the 1990s.[31] Although its effectiveness in reducing fraud is increasingly questioned, finger-imaging succeeds at humiliating and deterring applicants. As one SNAP applicant explained, "It's basically like when you're going through central booking or something. You're getting booked, and you feel like you're getting fingerprinted, with one finger here and one finger there."[32] Likewise, another recipient observed:

> *I feel that the fingerprinting of welfare clients is another mean-spirited action to "criminalize" poverty and further exclude the lower class from society. When I first heard of the fingerprinting proposal, I was immediately reminded of the identifying and segregating of innocent human beings over fifty years ago, not only in Europe, but, in this country and Canada as well. . . . I am also concerned with the misuse of this information in punitive ways. Whether we segregate and stigmatize by barriers of barbed wire, race or economic standing, we . . . diminish the moral fibre of all of society.[33]*

Drug testing and finger-imaging, along with other restrictive policies (e.g., requiring frequent verification of income), discourage prospective participants from applying for assistance. Stigma and stereotypes associated with welfare, more broadly, are problematic as well. In analyzing survey data from 901 community health center patients, Jennifer Stuber and Karl Kronebusch found that the stigma and stereotypes associated with welfare reduced enrollment in both TANF and Medicaid.[34] Stereotypes associating public assistance programs with dependence and fraud reinforce the perception of welfare recipients as "undeserving takers," a personal identity that few people want to embrace. As a consequence, "stigma is likely to constitute a stronger deterrent to participation than the expected penalty for dishonest claiming, both in discouraging participation and in reducing its duration."[35]

Conclusion

Unfortunately, myths about welfare fraud continue unabated, as does their impact on recipients and social policy. There are currently multiple initiatives underway to curb SNAP enrollment that appear to be fueled by unfounded concerns about fraud, abuse, and waste. President Trump's Executive Order, *Reducing Poverty in America by Promoting Opportunity and Economic Mobility,* sought to expand work requirements for SNAP recipients and establish work requirements for Medicaid recipients.[36] The Trump Administration also proposed lowering SNAP asset limits and ending automatic enrollment in SNAP if an applicant qualifies for another public assistance program such as TANF, a change that would remove an estimated 3 million low-income households from the program.[37]

The push to strictly enforce and lower asset limits appears to be informed by examples such as the highly unusual case of a retired 66-year-old Minnesotan, Rob Undersander, who applied for SNAP benefits to "test" the system. To be eligible for SNAP, households must have a gross household income below 130 percent of the federal poverty line ($34,024 annually for a family of four in 2019) and assets up to $2,250, or $3,500 if at least one household member is 60 years or older or is a person with a disability.[38] These asset limits make it possible for low-earning individuals and families to accrue at least some savings and still access food assistance. To expand access and get benefits to eligible applicants more quickly, Minnesota is one of 34 states that has opted to rely on income to determine eligibility and not conduct asset checks. Undersander met the income criteria for SNAP benefits but had $1 million in property and savings—and his application was approved. Although an unfortunate case, there is no evidence that millionaires or others with significant assets routinely apply for food assistance and receive it; most SNAP households have less than $500 in liquid assets.

Both Rob Undersander and Ronald Reagan's "welfare queen" are classic cases of using isolated examples to paint an entire group as fraudulent. With millions of families now at risk of losing much needed benefits to rout out illusory fraud, the urgency of debunking myths about welfare fraud grows stronger.

Finally, research has demonstrated that a number of poverty-stricken individuals and families who would be eligible for various safety net programs choose not to apply in order to avoid the humiliation, frustration, and stigma associated with welfare.[39] Rather than encouraging fraud, the system would appear to be encouraging nonparticipation instead.

An Expert Appraisal—Noam Chomsky

Noam Chomsky is the Laureate Professor of Linguistics, Agnese Nelms Haury Chair at the University of Arizona. He is generally considered the founder of modern linguistics and is one of the most widely cited scholars and influential public intellectual scholars in the world today.

If you take the people who say they want the government off their back, individualist in that sense, in the same polls, when you ask them if they want to see more spending on education, on health, on aid for mothers with dependent children, they say they support that. So, they also have social democratic inclinations even though they would not call it social democratic.

Take for example welfare. They are opposed to welfare. They are opposed to welfare because it has been demonized, especially by Ronald Reagan with his tales about welfare queens, Black women driving in limousines to steal your money at the welfare office, and all that business. People are opposed to that. But if you ask about the things that welfare performs, you get support for it. It is a complex mixture because of the nature of propaganda, of the dominant culture, and various conflicting elements of that culture. And, of course, it is not uniform by any means.

It is also worth bearing in mind that the United States in many ways remains what it was before World War II—largely a traditional, conservative backwater by international standards. Things have changed somewhat since the Second World War, but only for part of the population.

Another manifestation of this is that a large part of the Trump vote, those people who voted for Obama in 2008 and voted for Trump in 2016, are saying, "We don't want this system anymore. We want it changed. It is harmful to us." Which it is. Real male wages are about what they were in the 1960s. Much of the population, the working class, the lower middle class, this population has been essentially cast aside. Nobody represents them, the policies are harmful to them and have taken away their meaningful jobs, taken away work, dignity, hopes for the future, security, and so on. They are resentful and want to change it. That has been showing up in many ways across both Europe and the United States, and it is dramatic.

Government Programs Can Reduce Poverty

There is a widespread myth that governments can do little to address the problem of poverty (also addressed in Chapter 9). In Joe Feagin's influential 1969 study of American beliefs about poverty and antipoverty programs, he reported that although three-fourths of his respondents supported an all-out federal assault on poverty, only 10 percent were optimistic about the government's effectiveness in actually confronting poverty.[1]

Since that time, cross-national data collection has called this myth into question.[2] As popular as this belief has been, analyses from the Luxembourg Income Study (LIS) and other data sources demonstrate that many wealthy countries are actually quite successful at achieving substantial reductions in poverty through their social programs, even if they do not eliminate it entirely. A number of countries have committed to implementing robust and structurally oriented social welfare policies, and they have been rewarded with lower poverty rates.

These include programs that target poverty specifically, along with ones that manage the economic risks associated with childbearing, illness and disability, unemployment, aging, and other life events. Such policies and programs include (but are not limited to) old-age pensions, income supports, food programs, family and children allowances, subsidized child care, early childhood education, paid parental leave, universal health care, housing assistance, subsidized higher education, unemployment insurance, worker training programs, strong labor unions, public employment, labor market policies, and tax credits.

The United States, of course, has many social policies and programs, implemented at the federal, state, and local levels, which help manage Americans' economic risk. As discussed in Chapter 13, these include Temporary Assistance to Needy Families (TANF), Unemployment Insurance, the Supplemental Nutrition Assistance Program (SNAP), Medicaid, Supplemental Security Income (SSI), Housing Assistance, the Special Supplemental Nutrition Program for Women, Infants, and Children (WIC), the National School Lunch

Program, and the Earned Income Tax Credit (EITC). However, compared with wealthy countries with lower rates of poverty and economic inequality, the United States tends to spend much less on these policies and programs, leaving it "iconically unequal" in the wealthy world.[3]

American social programs also tend to be more individualistically oriented, meaning they implicitly assume that opportunities are plentiful and that poor Americans just need a bit of a "push" in order to land back on their feet, rather than acknowledging that a certain level of disadvantage may in fact be unavoidable unless we change the structure of opportunity in the United States. As a result, American social policies do not achieve the same level of poverty reduction as many other wealthy countries are able to accomplish.

How Well Do Government Programs Work?

Given these patterns, the question becomes, "Exactly how successful have some of these countries been in reducing poverty?" An analysis of poverty reduction among OECD countries by the economist Jared Bernstein demonstrates the impact of welfare states on poverty reduction. As discussed in the introductory chapter, most policy analysts would consider the group of OECD countries to be the proper comparison for the United States. Bernstein's analysis focuses on relative poverty rates among OECD countries before taxes and social welfare programs are calculated (pretax/pretransfer) and after (post-tax/post-transfer).[4] This analysis is shown in Table 15.1. We can see that the average post-tax/post-transfer poverty reduction factor among OECD countries (excluding the United States) is 63 percent. The countries with the largest reduction factors were Sweden (80 percent) and Denmark (78 percent), leaving each tied for the lowest post-tax/post-transfer poverty rate at just 5 percent. While the United States pretax/pretransfer poverty rate of 26 percent was middle-of-the-pack among OECD countries, it displays the highest post-tax/post-transfer poverty rate at 17 percent, and its reduction factor (35 percent) lagged far behind the OECD average of 63 percent.[5] While these data suggest that the United States does a poor job of reducing poverty, this clearly does not have to be the case since many of these countries reduce poverty to a significant degree. If done right, government poverty reduction does indeed work.

A United Nations Children's Fund (UNICEF) analysis found a similar trend for child poverty rates before and after taxes and transfers. The analysis focused on 35 countries, including the United States. The average reduction in child poverty after taxes and transfers was 40 percent across the other 34 countries, while the United States achieved only an 8 percent reduction, leaving it with the second highest post-tax/post-transfer child poverty rate (23 percent), in front of only Romania (26 percent).[6]

TABLE 15.1 Pretax/Pretransfer and Post-Tax/Post-Transfer Relative Poverty Rates Across Selected OECD Countries

Country	Pretransfer poverty rates (%)	Post-transfer poverty rates (%)	Reduction factor (%)
Sweden	26.7	5.3	80.1
Denmark	23.6	5.3	77.5
Austria	23.1	6.6	71.4
Norway	24.0	6.8	71.7
France	30.7	7.1	76.9
Finland	17.6	7.1	59.7
Netherlands	24.7	7.7	68.8
United Kingdom	26.3	8.3	68.4
Switzerland	18.0	8.7	51.7
Belgium	32.7	8.8	73.1
New Zealand	26.6	10.8	59.4
Germany	33.6	11.0	67.3
Italy	33.8	11.4	66.3
Canada	23.1	12.0	48.1
Australia	28.6	12.4	56.6
Greece	32.5	12.6	61.2
Spain	17.6	14.1	19.9
Ireland	30.9	14.8	52.1
Japan	26.9	14.9	44.6
United States	26.3	17.1	35.0
Average (excluding U.S.)	26.4	9.8	62.9

Note: Poverty is defined as less than 50 percent median income.

Source: Jared Bernstein, "International Poverty Comparisons: What Do They Tell Us About Causes?" (2012), http://jaredbernsteinblog.com/international-poverty-comparisons-what-do-they-tell-us-about-causes/.

A similar pattern can be found when examining pretax/pretransfer and post-tax/post-transfer measures of income inequality. Economists Max Roser and Esteban Ortiz-Ospina recently calculated the Gini coefficients of OECD countries pretaxes/pretransfers and compared them to the Gini coefficients of those countries post-taxes/post-transfers. As discussed in Chapter 1, the Gini coefficient is a frequently used measure of income inequality. Values fall between 0 and 1, with a value of 0 representing perfect equality and a value of 1 representing perfect inequality. The higher the value, the more unequal the income distribution in that country. The OECD pretax/pretransfer Gini coefficient average (excluding the United States) was 0.47, putting the United States above average at 0.51 but not in the lead—20 countries were in the same neighborhood (0.48 or higher), and six countries had Gini coefficients greater than the United States. It is after taxes and transfers where the United States really stands out. The U.S. post-tax/post-transfer Gini coefficient was 0.39, tied with Turkey for third highest, in front of only Mexico (0.46) and Chile (0.47). The average for the other OECD countries in the analysis was 0.31. Three countries actually had lower pretax/pretransfer inequality compared with the post-tax/ post-transfer inequality in the United States (Iceland, Switzerland, and South Korea).[7]

Even the risk of poverty for single-parent families (discussed in Chapter 9), which some believe is unavoidably high, is highly dependent on the country in which it occurs. Table 15.2 demonstrates this based on an analysis of 24 countries by Laurie Maldonado and Rense Nieuwenhuis. The average poverty rate for single-parent families pretax/pretransfer across the other 23 non-U.S. countries in this analysis is 42 percent. At 49 percent, the United States is above average, ahead of only five other countries. Yet, when taxes and transfers are taken into consideration, the average single-parent family poverty rate in the other 23 countries falls from 42 percent to 19 percent. On the other hand, the United States only manages to reduce single-parent family poverty by one-third through taxes and transfers, compared with an average reduction of 54 percent across the other 23 countries. The authors interpret their data to indicate that "the U.S. is still an exceptional case due to its lagging policy to address the labor market inequalities—the point being that the United States does not have national policies for paid leave and child allowance and provides little public expenditure on child care and preschool, all consequential to reducing poverty."[8]

A major reason for the post-tax/post-transfer differences in poverty and economic inequality is the level of generosity found in the social programs across these countries. As social welfare scholars Cheol-Sung Lee and In-Hoe Koo explain, "total public expenditures on social policies and overall measures of welfare generosity are highly correlated with relative poverty" among wealthy democracies. "Critics of welfare states have questioned the effectiveness of government poverty programs," they go on to write, but researchers of the welfare state have ultimately provided "more convincing evidence."[9] When countries choose to provide generous social benefits to their citizens, they tend to have less poverty and greater economic equality.

Figure 15.1 demonstrates this trend among affluent democracies. The relationship between welfare generosity and poverty is displayed on the top panel of the figure, while the relationship between welfare generosity and income inequality is displayed on the bottom panel.

The association between welfare generosity and poverty in Figure 15.1 suggests a strong relationship (–0.67), with the negative sign indicating that an increase in welfare generosity is associated with a decrease in poverty rates. There is a similar strong association between welfare generosity and income inequality (–0.58), with an increase in welfare generosity associated with a decrease in Gini coefficients. We can see in both the top and bottom panels of Figure 15.1 that individual countries allocating more resources into their safety nets have lower rates of poverty and inequality.[10]

TABLE 15.2 Single-Parent Family Poverty Pretax/Pretransfer and Post-Tax/Post-Transfer in Selected OECD Countries

Country	Pretax/pretransfer poverty rate (%)	Post-tax/post-transfer poverty rate(%)	Reduction factor (%)
Denmark	37	8	78
United Kingdom	57	13	77
Finland	36	10	72
Norway	39	11	72
Slovak Republic	28	9	68
Netherlands	48	16	67
Ireland	61	22	64
Iceland	51	19	63
Poland	45	17	62
Luxembourg	41	16	61
Australia	54	22	59
France	42	21	50
Czech Republic	39	20	49
Estonia	43	23	47
Greece	38	20	47
Spain	38	20	47
Germany	50	27	46
Canada	47	26	45
Japan	42	23	45
Italy	31	18	42
Slovenia	27	17	37
Israel	41	29	29
Hungary	26	21	19
Average (excluding U.S.)	42	19	54
United States	49	33	33

Note: All data from 2010 except Japan (2008) and Hungary (2012).

Source: Laurie C. Maldonado and Rense Nieuwenhuis, "Single-Parent Family Poverty in 24 OECD Countries: A Focus on Market and Redistribution Strategies" (2015), https://osf.io/preprints/socarxiv/w9htc/.

The data that we have discussed so far suggest that a number of wealthy countries are able to greatly reduce their post-tax/post transfer poverty and economic inequality. In these countries, government programs are working quite well. Although the U.S. government also reduces poverty and economic inequality post-tax/post-transfer, it achieves a much smaller reduction factor compared with governments that are more committed to equality.

Despite this, there are areas where the U.S. government has been particularly effective in reducing the risk of economic insecurity for its citizens. The impact of programs such as Social Security and Medicare on the economic insecurity of seniors are prime examples (also discussed in Chapter 9).

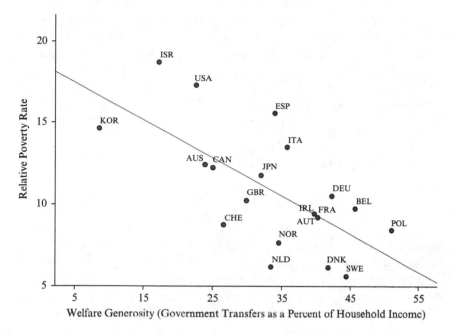

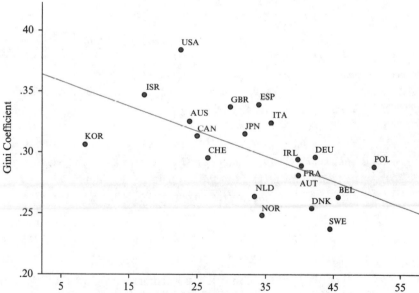

FIGURE 15.1 *Association between welfare generosity and relative poverty/income inequality in 20 affluent democracies.*

Note: Poverty correlation = –0.67 (p < .01), inequality correlation = –0.58 (p < .01).

Source: Calculations by authors in collaboration with David Brady using Luxembourg Income Study data.

As the 1950s drew to a close, more than one-third of American seniors (35 percent) found themselves in poverty. By 2019, that number had fallen to 8.9 percent.[11] Why? The answer is Social Security. In an analysis by economists Gary Engelhardt and Jonathan Gruber, they estimate that increases in Social Security benefits since the 1960s explain all of the elderly poverty reduction during this time period. Based on their analysis, the authors conclude:

> *The most frequently cited "victory" in the war on poverty of the 1960s is the dramatic decline in elderly poverty. This poverty decline is typically attributed to the growth in Social Security over this period. . . . Our analysis suggests that the growth in Social Security can indeed explain all of the decline in poverty among the elderly over this period.*[12]

Without Social Security, the elderly poverty rate in the United States today would climb from its current 8.9 percent to 39 percent.[13] Kathleen Romig notes, "Social Security benefits play a vital role in reducing poverty in every state, and they lift more Americans above the poverty line than any other program."[14] A majority of American seniors (those 65 years and older) depend on Social Security for the bulk of their income. Almost half (48 percent) are economically vulnerable and would be in dire straits without their Social Security income, as David Cooper and Elise Gould explain:

> *Many of America's 41 million seniors are just one bad economic shock away from significant material hardship. Most seniors live on modest retirement incomes, which often are barely adequate—and sometimes inadequate—to cover the costs of basic necessities and support a simple, yet dignified, quality of life. For these seniors, and even for those with greater means, Social Security and Medicare are the bedrock of their financial security. . . . With nearly half of all seniors in the United States falling below the threshold of economic vulnerability, policymakers must be especially careful when considering changes to the social insurance programs—predominantly Social Security and Medicare—that protect this group.*[15]

Medicare is also critically important to the economic security of American seniors. In 1963, before the implementation of Medicare, almost half (48 percent) of seniors were uninsured, a number that dropped to 1 percent by 2016. A recent analysis revealed that seniors today pay 13 percent of their health care costs out-of-pocket, only one-fourth of what they paid in the 1960s.[16]

Finally, a more recent example of government initiatives dramatically reducing poverty can be found in the Coronavirus Aid, Relief, and Economic Security (CARES) Act passed by Congress in March 2020. The CARES Act provided approximately $500 billion in income transfers to those who had lost their jobs as a result of the virus. An analysis by Zachary Parolin and colleagues estimated that without this assistance, poverty would have risen from 12.5 percent to 16.3 percent in 2020. However, as a result of this initiative, poverty was projected to increase only to 12.7 percent.[17] Once again, we see that social policies can indeed have a dramatic effect on reducing poverty.

So What Are We Waiting For?

Governments can reduce poverty and economic inequality significantly if they choose to do so. The existing research makes this clear. As poverty researcher Timothy Smeeding argues, "if one decides to make poverty or inequality an active policy goal, one can make a difference. We have more inequality and poverty than other nations because we choose to have more."[18]

A number of researchers have weighed in on why the United States takes a more minimalist and individualistically oriented approach to social welfare, despite evidence demonstrating its effectiveness. Alberto Alesina and colleagues provide a particularly compelling argument for what sets the United States apart: "Our bottom line is that Americans redistribute less than Europeans because (1) the majority believes that redistribution favors racial minorities, (2) Americans believe that they live in an open and fair society and that if someone is poor it is their own fault, and (3) the political system is geared towards preventing redistribution."[19] American politics are unique when compared with many other wealthy countries, including weaker leftist political parties, lower unionization rates, the outsized influence of money in politics, fewer females in government positions, low voter turnout, and a majoritarian electoral system.

Along with these political variables, racial attitudes play a crucial role as well. Researchers who have investigated this phenomenon have convincingly demonstrated that because many Americans mistakenly believe that poverty is a "Black problem" and believe the false notion that African Americans are not sufficiently committed to the work ethic and traditional morality, they are less willing to support generous and structurally oriented social welfare policies (also discussed in Chapter 5).[20]

Americans are also an exceptionally individualistic people, and this is important as well. Highly individualistic individuals and countries tend to be less supportive of generous and structurally oriented social welfare policies compared with less individualistic individuals and countries.[21]

As Alesina argues, these factors are critical in understanding why the United States has such a minimal welfare state (also see Chapter 13). In addition, as we will see in Chapter 19, these are important factors in understanding why the poverty myths persist despite evidence to the contrary.

Conclusion

The existing research makes it clear that government programs, when done correctly, can be highly successful in reducing poverty and economic inequality. Examples from many OECD countries exist showing dramatic reductions in their rates of poverty as a result of social policy. The United States, on the other hand, has an extremely weak social safety net, resulting in very high levels of poverty and inequality. The myth that government programs do not work in addressing poverty is simply incorrect. The case of Social Security for the elderly population over the past 60 years in the United States is a prime example of a government program effectively reducing the rate of poverty for a vulnerable population group, while countless cross-national examples demonstrate the ability of government policy to reduce overall rates of poverty.

An Expert Appraisal—Jamila Michener

Jamila Michener is an assistant professor in the Department of Government at Cornell University. Her research focuses on poverty, racial inequality, and public policy in the United States.

Poverty and economic deprivation are political choices. They are a reflection of political choices that we have made and that we continue to make over and over again as a society. Are there people who sometimes do not work as hard as they should? Sure. But the idea that cultural deficiencies and individual character attributes explain the contours of poverty and economic deprivation in the United States just does not have solid empirical grounding. This is especially the case if we think about the United States in a comparative context, where many of the things that we believe are the causes of poverty also exist in other countries, but those other countries do not display the levels of poverty and inequality that we have in the United States. The argument that poverty is cultural or about individual people not doing what they need to do just does not hold up.

Instead, the reason for poverty in the United States is about decisions that we make with respect to social policy, specifically how resources are distributed and redistributed, and sometimes decisions that we fail to make. So, when people do not have access to affordable health care, when people do not have access to jobs that pay living wages that allow them to take care of their families, when people do not have access to affordable housing, we end up in a situation where there is dramatic economic inequality and where there are significant levels of economic deprivation. And that is the exact situation that we are in. Health care, housing, employment, and so on are a reflection of policy decisions that we make or do not make.

Those policy decisions that we make or do not make are a reflection of politics, of political coalitions, and of political attitudes and behaviors among the American populous. And so part of this is about who has political power in this country, who has consistently had political power over a long period of time, and who organizes most effectively.

Politics is about the rules of the game. Who are the rules of the game structured to benefit in this country? People who are wealthy, overwhelming men, and overwhelming White Americans. When taken in combination—not just individually, but in combination—a system where the rules of the game are structured to benefit those folks, and where inertia is built into the system through checks and balances and through federalism, and where the design of our politics is such that the people who are the most disadvantaged by inequality and poverty have the least power in our political system—all of those things ultimately are the causes for the outcomes that we are talking about now.

So, what needs to change? A lot. But ultimately, we need a serious reorientation of our political system in a number of different ways before we are going to see big changes in outcomes around economic and material deprivation.

{ SECTION V }

How Extensive Is Inequality?

Having examined a number of myths regarding who the poor are, why they experience poverty, the costs of poverty, and the stereotypes surrounding welfare, we now turn to the wider context of inequality. These topics revolve around the nature of American society and its juxtaposition to poverty.

America has been built on a set of ideals and aspirations. These are epitomized in the concept of the American dream. The American dream asserts that anyone in America can make it with enough hard work and talent. The reason for this is that individuals from all walks of life are seen as being able to climb a ladder of opportunity. They are able to climb that ladder because the playing field is viewed as level. As a result, poverty can be avoided through motivation and skill.

Therefore, according to the mythology, inequality and poverty are neither unjust nor problematic because they represent the importance of individual agency, self-reliance, and meritocracy. Ultimately, American opportunity is believed to provide the mechanism for anyone to succeed. In this section, we delve into the realities of this collection of myths.

{ 16 }

The United States Is No Longer a Land
of Upward Mobility and Opportunity

There has always been a strong conviction that in the United States, upward economic mobility can be achieved through hard work, effort, and talent (see Chapter 6)—that no matter where one starts the race of life, motivation and initiative should provide a vehicle for climbing the ladder of success and eventually attaining economic prosperity.[1]

This has been seen as achievable within America's mythology because the country has viewed itself as a land of boundless opportunity. Horace Greeley's famous advice of, "Go West, young man" and seek your fortune, illustrates the dream of unlimited opportunity. The availability of opportunities has been understood as a key building block on which individuals and families are able to get ahead in life. The image of streets paved with gold, despite its obvious exaggeration, reflects this overall idea, as does the portrayal of climbing a ladder of success.

Indeed, polling data indicate that a clear majority of Americans believe it is possible to rise from rags to riches within one's lifetime. A *CBS News/New York Times* poll has asked Americans over the past 15 years the question, "Do you think it is still possible to start out poor in this country, work hard, and become rich?" The percentage of individuals answering yes has averaged between 70 and 85 percent. In 2012, 71 percent of Americans felt that it was possible to rise from rags to riches through hard work.[2]

Furthermore, Americans are much more likely than those in other countries to believe that work, talent, and skill can guarantee individual success. An international survey of 27 industrialized countries found that 69 percent of Americans (the highest percentage across all countries) agreed with the statement, "people are rewarded for intelligence and skill." Likewise, Americans ranked near the top in terms of believing that "people get rewarded for their effort," and near the bottom in agreeing with, "coming from a wealthy family is essential/very important to getting ahead."[3]

Similarly, as we discussed throughout Section II, Americans are quick to ascribe the reasons for poverty to individual failings. In national survey data collected by James Kluegal and Eliot Smith, the percentage of Americans agreeing that the following factors were either "very important" or "important" in understanding poverty were as follows: lack of thrift—94 percent; lack of effort—92 percent; lack of ability or talent—88 percent; attitudes that keep them from improving their condition—88 percent; loose morals and drunkenness—57 percent.[4] The overall perception is that individuals can indeed succeed and economically prosper as a result of their efforts and skill, and that these individual attributes can help to overcome prior hardships, such as being born into poverty.

One of the most enduring myths of poverty and economic mobility has been the rags-to-riches story. This narrative revolves around individuals beginning their lives in very humble circumstances, but through their hard work, initiative, and skill, eventually accomplishing great success in life. By taking full advantage of the opportunities that come their way, these individuals are able to overcome adversity and climb the ladder of success.

America has long celebrated such individual triumphs, in part to demonstrate that literally anything is possible in this land of opportunity. Horatio Alger wrote dozens of stories about young street urchins in the latter part of the 19th century who were able to achieve great success through their hard work and moral character despite having grown up in impoverished conditions. Although Alger's stories were fictional accounts, there have certainly been real-life rags-to-riches stories over the course of U.S. history. In tracing back each of our own personal family histories, many of us can undoubtedly point to at least one relative who represents a rags-to-riches story.

Nevertheless, the questions that we ask here are, "What is the actual empirical reality of such economic mobility?" "How likely is it that someone can indeed rise from poverty to affluence?" "Is economic mobility more likely in the United States than in other countries?" "What percentage of children will do better economically than their parents, and how has this changed over time?" These are the questions that we touch on in this chapter.

In thinking about economic mobility, we can conceptualize it in at least two different ways. The first is what social scientists refer to as relative mobility. This pertains to how well children are doing as adults in the income distribution relative to where they started with respect to their parents' economic position within the overall income distribution.[5] Consequently, have children as adults moved up or down with respect to their position in the income distribution compared with their parents' position? Absolute mobility is a second way of measuring economic mobility across generations. It refers to whether children are actually earning more in inflation-adjusted dollars than their parents did.[6]

Each measure tells us something somewhat different about the degree of economic mobility.

Relative Mobility

To what extent can parents' earnings predict how well their children will do economically as adults? This has been a question that social scientists have grappled with for decades.[7] If a strong relationship exists between the two, it implies that economic mobility across generations is more difficult, while a weak relationship indicates that economic mobility is more attainable. Researchers employing this approach generally compare an average of 3 to 5 years of earnings for fathers with an overall average of 3 to 5 years of earnings for sons (who are often in their late 30s to early 40s).

One way of examining this relationship is through what economists refer to as an intergenerational elasticity statistic. This statistic ranges between 0 and 1 and shows the overall strength of a relationship. The statistic basically tells us how much of the advantage or disadvantage of the father's economic position is handed down to his son. For example, a value of .5 would indicate that roughly 50 percent of a father's economic advantage or disadvantage is handed down to his son, while a value of .9 would indicate that 90 percent of the father's economic position is inherited by his son.

The Canadian researcher, Miles Corak, has examined dozens of research studies across a number of countries to come up with a comparative analysis of how these values vary internationally. Corak has evaluated the research in each country, adjusted the statistics for comparability to the extent possible, and then taken the "best" estimate from each country for comparison.[8] His results are presented in Table 16.1.

We can see that the United States is near the top of the listing of 15 countries with respect to the strength of its intergenerational elasticity. The United Kingdom, Italy, the United States, and Switzerland represent the countries where fathers' income has the most effect on influencing sons' income. Corak's estimate of the U.S. intergenerational elasticity is .47, indicating that nearly half of the father's economic position is handed down to his son. On the other hand, Canada, Finland, Norway, and Denmark are the countries with the weakest associations between fathers' and sons' incomes, ranging from .19 for Canada, down to .15 for Denmark. Contrary to popular opinion, these results indicate that economic mobility is much more constrained in the United States than in many other economically developed countries. In addition, research by Jonathan David and Bhaskar Mazumder has shown that intergenerational economic mobility has been declining in the United States since 1980 (as measured again by the intergenerational elasticity statistic).[9] Other work by Mazumder

TABLE 16.1 Intergenerational Elasticities Between Fathers' and
Sons' Earnings Across 15 Countries

Country	Earnings elasticity
United Kingdom	.50
Italy	.48
United States	.47
Switzerland	.46
France	.41
Spain	.40
Japan	.34
Germany	.32
New Zealand	.29
Sweden	.27
Australia	.26
Canada	.19
Finland	.18
Norway	.17
Denmark	.15

Source: Adapted from Miles Corak, "Chasing the Same Dream, Climbing
Different Ladders: Economic Mobility in the United States and Canada."
(Economic Mobility Project, the Pew Charitable Trusts, 2010); and Miles Corak,
"Inequality from Generation to Generation: The United States in Comparison"
(Unpublished paper, Graduate School of Public and International Affairs,
University of Ottawa, 2011).

has indicated that the intergenerational elasticity statistic for the United States
may be as high as .60 to .70.[10]

An alternative way of examining the patterns of relative mobility can be
found in Table 16.2. This table is based on an analysis by Markus Jantti and
colleagues.[11] Here, the approach is to divide the income distribution into
fifths, or quintiles. Jantti then examines which quintile sons fall into with
respect to their income, compared with the income quintile that their fathers
fell into. By using this approach, we can observe to what extent sons are able
to rise, fall, or stay roughly the same with respect to their father's overall economic position.

Table 16.2 looks at sons from six different countries who grew up in
households where their fathers fell into the bottom 20 percent of the income
distribution. We can see that in the United States, 42.2 percent of such sons
remained in the bottom 20 percent of the income distribution as adults. This
percentage is much higher than in the other countries examined. For example,
in Denmark, 24.7 percent of sons whose fathers were in the bottom 20 percent
remained in the bottom 20 percent of the income distribution as adults. We
can also see that the likelihood of going from rags to riches varies across the
six countries. Surprisingly, this pattern is least likely in the United States, where
only 7.9 percent of sons growing up in the bottom 20 percent find themselves in
the top 20 percent as adults, compared with 14.4 percent in Denmark.

TABLE 16.2 Intergenerational Economic Mobility Patterns for Sons Growing Up in the Bottom 20% Across Six Countries.

	Sons' earnings in adulthood (%)	
Country	Bottom 20%	Top 20%
Denmark	24.7	14.4
Finland	27.8	11.3
Norway	28.2	11.9
Sweden	25.8	10.9
United Kingdom	30.3	12.2
United States	42.2	7.9

Note: For sons raised in families in which the father's earnings were in the bottom 20% of the income distribution.

Source: Adapted from Markus Jantti, "American Exceptionalism in a New Light: A Comparison of Intergenerational Earnings Mobility in the Nordic Countries, the United Kingdom and the United States" (Discussion Paper 1938, Institute for the Study of Labor: Bonn, Germany, 2006).

Tables 16.1 and 16.2 thus indicate that economic mobility appears to be more constrained in the United States than in many other countries. Whether we examine an overall measure such as an intergenerational elasticity statistic, or the actual upward intergenerational movements in income, the United States has less economic mobility than other industrialized countries. Researchers have commented on the "stickiness" at the bottom and top of the U.S. income distribution.[12] In particular, those growing up in the bottom 20 percent of the U.S. income distribution have a much harder time pulling themselves upward than their counterparts in other countries.

Absolute Mobility

A second approach to measuring economic movement is through what researchers refer to as absolute mobility. Here, the focus is on answering the question, "Are children doing better than their parents in terms of overall household income at the same stage of life?" Consequently, after controlling for inflation, will children earn more and do better financially than their parents did? This measure taps into the American dream ideal that each generation should achieve a higher standard of living than the previous generation.

Here, we turn to work of the economist Raj Chetty and colleagues to shed light on this question. Chetty has been at the forefront of using big data to analyze what has happened to economic mobility in the United States over time. In this analysis, he merged data from the Census Bureau with individual federal income tax returns. The result is a total of more than 10 million parent–child pairs within the analysis. Chetty and colleagues are looking at parents' household income between the ages of 25 and 35 years and comparing that with their child's household income at age 30 years.[13]

In the top panel of Figure 16.1, we can see how well children who were
born in 1940, 1950, 1960, 1970, and 1980 were doing in comparison with their
parent's income. For children born in 1940, nearly all of them earned more
than their parents earned. Obviously, for those whose parents were earning

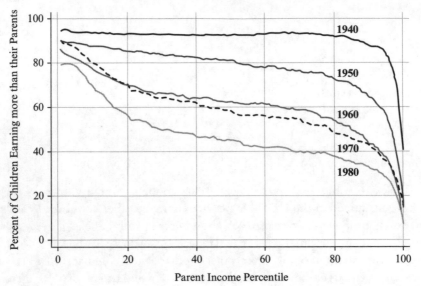

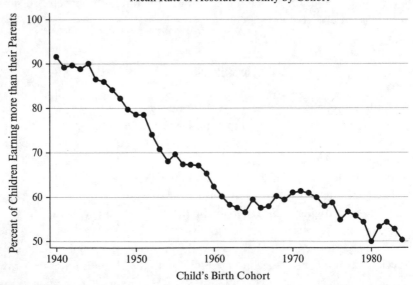

FIGURE 16.1 *Absolute intergenerational mobility for birth cohorts from 1940 to 1980.*

Source: Raj Chetty, David Grusky, Maximilian Hell, Nathaniel Hendren, Robert Manduca, and Jimmy Narang,
"The Fading American Dream: Trends in Absolute Income Mobility since 1940," NBER Working Paper Series,
Working Paper 22910 (Cambridge, MA: National Bureau of Economic Research, December 2016), http://www.
equality-of-opportunity.org/papers/abs_mobility_paper.pdf.

very little (i.e., the 5th percentile), there is little way but up for their children to go. However, regardless of how much their parents were earning, almost all children from the 1940 cohort were earning more as adults. Only for those children whose parents were at the very top end of the income distribution (i.e., the top 95th percentile) do the percentages begin to drop. Altogether, upward of 90 percent of children born in 1940 would go on to earn more than their parents earned.

However, what we can see is that for the 1950, 1960, 1970, and 1980 birth cohorts, there is a steady decline in the likelihood of children earning more than their parents. For each decade, the curve drops lower, such that by 1980, only children whose parents were in the bottom 40 percent of the income distribution were able on average to earn more than their parents.

The bottom panel of Figure 16.1 shows this in a slightly different way. Here, we have the birth cohorts from 1940 to 1984 and the overall average percentage of the entire cohort surpassing their parents' income. We see a dramatic decline over time in the likelihood of children earning more than their parents. As Chetty notes, "Absolute mobility declined starkly across birth cohorts: On average, 92% of children born in 1940 grew up to earn more than their parents. In contrast, only 50% of children born in 1984 grew up to earn more than their parents."[14]

Consequently, the overall patterns of absolute mobility in the United States show a steady decline. Chetty writes, "children's prospects of earning more than their parents have faded over the past half-century in the United States. . . . Absolute income mobility has fallen across the entire income distribution, with the largest declines for families in the middle class."[15]

Conclusion

The United States has long prided itself on the idea that it represents a land of opportunity, where each person can achieve the American dream through their own hard work and diligence. We have celebrated across history the rags to riches stories of Horatio Alger and all who have climbed the ladder of success.

However, it turns out that an individual's economic position is determined to a much greater extent by the economic position of their parents in the United States than in many other countries. Furthermore, the dream of each generation doing better economically than the previous generation is becoming increasingly difficult to achieve.

One of the key reasons behind this has been the economic stagnation that has occurred over the past 50 years in the United States, combined with the rising levels of income and wealth inequality (see Chapter 18). For example, a large volume of research has found that since the early 1970s, the United States has been producing greater numbers of low-wage jobs (discussed in Chapter 6).[16] Approximately 40 percent of all jobs in the United States today are considered low-paying.[17] These jobs are frequently lacking in basic benefits and are increasingly part-time. Median wages for full-time male employees are actually lower today than they were in 1973.[18] Furthermore, the stability of jobs has become more precarious.[19] Likewise, the social safety net has been weakened considerably over time.[20] As a result, greater numbers of Americans are living one paycheck away from poverty. A recent study from the Federal Reserve found that 37 percent of Americans do not have enough savings put aside to protect them from a $400 emergency.[21]

In addition, as many others have noted, over the past few decades there appears to have been a significant shift of economic risk from employers and government onto the backs of individuals and families.[22] This, in turn, has made economic security an ever more difficult goal for Americans to attain.

At the same time, those at the very top have continued to prosper. In fact, virtually all of the economic gains over the past 50 years have been concentrated in the top 20 percent of the income distribution, and particularly the top 5 and 1 percent.[23] The result is that the distance between the rungs on the ladder of opportunity have been growing wider, making upward mobility more difficult. Over the past five decades, the divide between the top and bottom of the income distribution has been expanding. The distance between those at the 90th percentile of the income distribution and those at the 10th percentile currently stands at 13 to 1. This difference is much wider than that found in the other OECD countries.[24]

Even more extreme are the current patterns of wealth holdings in the United States. The top 1 percent of the U.S. population possess 46 percent of the entire financial wealth in the country, while the bottom 60 percent hold less than 1 percent of the wealth.[25] These patterns of wealth inequality have been widening over recent decades. In fact, the extent of income and wealth inequality now surpasses the extreme inequality found during the Gilded Age and the 1920s.[26]

The result of all this has been a society that has become more rigid in terms of its class structure. The American ideal of equality of opportunity is increasingly harder to achieve as income and wealth inequality widen. We are a society in which the rungs on the ladder of opportunity have grown further apart, resulting in greater numbers of Americans struggling and falling further behind.

An Expert Appraisal—Arlie Hochschild

Arlie Hochschild is Professor Emerita of Sociology at the University of California Berkeley. She is the author of numerous books, including her latest, *Strangers in Their Own Land: Anger and Mourning on the American Right.*

The "deep story" is the situation you find yourself in as it feels to you. If you take information out of the deep story, and moral beliefs out of the deep story, what is left is just how it feels to you. I believe that all of us have a deep story. There are deep stories on the liberal side, and deep stories on the conservative side. They are different deep stories, and my curiosity was about the right-wing deep story.

In that right-wing deep story, you are standing in line as in a pilgrimage. At the top of the hill in front of you is the American dream. You have been standing there a long time, your feet haven't moved, and you're tired. You feel a sense of deserving for that American dream. You feel that you have played by the rules, you've worked hard, you're middle-aged or older.

Then, in another moment of this deep story, it looks like people are cutting ahead of you in line. And you think, "Well who are they?" And they are African Americans who, through federally mandated affirmative action, finally have access to jobs that had been reserved for Whites. There are women cutting in line who, through federally mandated affirmative action, finally have access to jobs that have been reserved for men. And there are undocumented immigrants and refugees. You feel like you have been moved back in the line, and that something unfair has been done to you.

In another moment you have Barack Obama, who you believe should be impartially supervising the line, instead waving to the line cutters. He is sponsoring them, and pushing you back. You've been forgotten. And in the final moment of this right-wing deep story, somebody ahead of you in line, someone from say New York or Los Angeles, who has got higher education than you, this person ahead of you in line turns around and says, "You ill-educated backward redneck." And that is the last straw. You feel like a subgroup yourself, like an ignored minority group yourself. You feel that you have been stripped of honor, and in that state, you are looking for a leader to deliver you from this. So, that is the deep story.

The Playing Field Is Uneven

Historically, the belief that society represents a "level playing field" has been strongly held in the United States, and it continues to be popular to this day.[1] As Clifton Mark notes:

> *Meritocracy has become a leading social ideal. . . . The most common metaphor is the "even playing field" upon which players can rise to the position that fits their merit. . . . Under meritocracy, wealth and advantage are merit's rightful compensation, not the fortuitous windfall of external events. . . . Most people don't just think the world should be run meritocratically, they think it is meritocratic.[2]*

Yet, as Mark goes on to note, the reality of a U.S. meritocracy resting on a level playing field is highly doubtful.[3]

One way to quickly visualize the uneven playing field is with a simple analogy to the game of Monopoly. The objective of Monopoly is to acquire properties, build houses and hotels, collect rent, make money, and eventually put the other players out of business. The rules of the game are straightforward. Normally, each player is given $1,500 at the start of the game. The playing field is in effect level, with each player's outcomes determined by the roll of the dice and by the player's own skills and judgments.

This notion of a level playing field is largely the way that we like to imagine the economic race in America is run. Each individual's outcome is determined by the person's own skill and effort, and by taking advantage of what happens along the road of life. Our belief in equality of opportunity as a nation underlies this principle.

Now, let us imagine a modified game of Monopoly, in which the players start out with quite different advantages and disadvantages, much as they do in life. Player 1 begins with $5,000 and several Monopoly properties on which houses have already been built. Player 2 starts out with the standard $1,500 and no properties. Finally, player 3 begins the game with only $250.

The question becomes, "Who will be the winners and losers in this modified game of Monopoly?" Both luck and skill are still involved, and the rules of the game remain the same, but given the differing sets of resources and assets that each player begins with, these become much less important in predicting the game's outcome. Certainly, it is possible for player 1, with $5,000 to lose, and for player 3, with $250, to win, but that is unlikely given the unequal allocation of money at the start of the game. Moreover, while player 3 may win in any individual game, over the course of hundreds of games, the odds are that player 1 will win considerably more often, even if player 3 is much luckier and more skilled.

In addition, the ways in which each of the three individuals are able to play the game will vary considerably. Player 1 is able to take greater chances and risks. If player 1 makes several tactical mistakes, these probably will not matter much in the larger scheme of things. If player 3 makes one such mistake, it may very well result in disaster. Player 1 will also be easily able to purchase properties and houses that player 3 is largely locked out of, allowing the rich to get richer and the poor to get poorer. These assets, in turn, will generate further income later in the game for player 1 and in all likelihood will result in the bankrupting of players 2 and 3.

Consequently, given the initial advantages or disadvantages at the start of the game, the result is additional advantages or disadvantages as the games progresses. These, in turn, will then lead to further advantages or disadvantages, and so the process goes.

This analogy illustrates the concept that Americans are not beginning their lives at the same starting point. But it also illustrates the cumulative process that compounds advantages or disadvantages over time. Differences in parental incomes and resources exert a major influence over children's ability to acquire valuable education and experience. These differences in human capital will, in turn, strongly influence how well children compete in the labor market, and therefore help to determine the extent of their economic success during the course of their lives.

The Importance of Agency

If the playing field were truly level, then all Americans, regardless of their starting point in life, would possess agency. Agency refers to the ability to decide the life that one wants to live, and to be able to think and act autonomously in pursuit of that desired life. As Jim Cullen notes, true freedom depends on this agency— "all notions of freedom rest on a sense of agency, the idea that individuals have control over the course of their lives. Agency, in turn, lies at the very core of the American Dream, the bedrock premise upon which all else depends."[4]

What, then, is required for an individual to possess agency? True agency requires that individuals have their capabilities fully developed and that they have unobstructed access to important resources (economic, social, cultural, and so on) and opportunity pathways.[5] All of these components are essential. Capabilities and resources are of little use if one does not have access to opportunity pathways within which to utilize them. Likewise, it is difficult to make the most of opportunity pathways without the requisite capabilities and resources.

The likelihood that one will have their capabilities fully developed and the degree to which they have access to important resources and opportunity pathways vary widely by one's starting point in life. A large body of research clearly demonstrates that the families we are born into, the neighborhoods and communities we grow up in, the schools we attend, the peer networks we are embedded in, the structural arrangement of our country of birth, and a variety of other important social contexts and forces combine to profoundly influence how much agency we ultimately possess.

Of course, we do not choose the family we are born into or the community that we are raised in. Nor do we decide the quality of the K–12 schools we attend, or the peers and adults who we will live and learn among. We also have little say in the culture and structural arrangements that determine the rewards and/or punishments that will be associated with particular social positions in our society. As Raoul Martinez explains, all of this results not from our personal choices, but instead comes down to the lottery of our birth:

> We do not choose to exist. We do not choose the environment we will grow up in. We do not choose to be born Hindu, Christian or Muslim, into a war-zone or peaceful middle-class suburb, into starvation or luxury. We do not choose our parents, nor whether they'll be happy or miserable, knowledge-able or ignorant, healthy or sickly, attentive or neglectful. The knowledge we possess, the beliefs we hold, the tastes we develop, the traditions we adopt, the opportunities we enjoy, the work we do—the very lives we lead. . . . This is the lottery of birth.[6]

Let us examine a few key ways in which the "lottery of birth" distributes agency unequally, thus tilting the playing field against many Americans.

Unequal Families

The family one is born into is highly influential in determining whether their capabilities will be developed to the fullest extent, as well as the opportunities and resources that will be available to them.[7] As Richard Reeves and Kimberly Howard note, "Parenting quality is not randomly distributed across the population. . . . Almost half of all parents in the bottom income quintile fall into the category of weakest parents—and just three percent are among the strongest parents."[8] These differences have profound implications for life chances. Research suggests that approximately 40 percent of income-related differences in cognitive outcomes in early childhood can be explained by parenting.[9]

To take one powerful example of the impact of families, consider the research of Betty Hart and Todd Risley in their book, *Meaningful Differences in the Everyday Experience of Young American Children*. In that work, the authors conducted intensive research in the homes of 42 families in Kansas City over the course of more than 2 years. These families belonged to three different social classes: professional families, working-class families, and welfare-recipient families. The researchers were interested in the intellectual development and language acquisition of these children, and the role that the home environment played in their development. They found significant differences by social class in the children's development. By age 3 years, professional children had an average IQ score of 117 and average vocabulary size of 1,116 words. For welfare-recipient children, the IQ score average was 79, and their average vocabulary size was 525.[10] The higher the child's social class, the more words they were likely to hear spoken to them in the home, the more varied those words were, and the more encouragement they received. All of these differences in the home environment were strongly associated with the intellectual development and language acquisition of the children.[11] Hart and Risley's research made it clear that one's social position shapes the home environment in which they will be raised, and class-based differences in these environments were associated with highly uneven development among American children.

These early childhood inequalities can have a dramatic impact on one's life long after early childhood. As Greg Duncan and colleagues explain, "Income poverty has a strong association with a low level of preschool ability, which is associated with low test scores later in childhood as well as grade failure, school disengagement, and dropping out of school."[12]

The percentage of children born at the bottom of the income hierarchy who are meeting age-specific benchmarks at age 5 years (age-appropriate behavior and skills in prereading and math) is only 48 percent, compared with 78 percent for children born at the top. By age 29 years, they are still falling behind (based on benchmarks of living independently and either graduating from college or earning a decent income), and the gap has only increased (38 vs. 74 percent).[13]

Unequal Neighborhoods and Communities

Research suggests that the neighborhoods and communities in which we are raised also play a crucial role in determining our capabilities, resources, and opportunities.[14] Jonathan Rothwell and Douglas Massey, for instance, found that, "The effect of neighborhood income is 50 to 66 percent of the parental income effect, so that growing up in a poor neighborhood would wipe out much of the advantage of growing up in a wealthy household."[15] Unfortunately, neighborhoods and communities are not equal, and they have become increasingly less so in recent decades.[16]

Economist Raj Chetty and colleagues identified multiple variables related to place that are strongly associated (correlations of more than 0.50, with some higher than 0.60 and 0.70)[17] with one's likelihood of upward mobility. These variables included racial segregation, income inequality, school quality, and family structure and social capital of neighbors. According to Chetty, inequalities in these variables across communities largely explain why in "the Southeast and the Rust Belt—children in the bottom quintile have less than a 5 percent chance of reaching the top quintile. In other areas, such as the Great Plains and the West Coast, children in the bottom quintile have more than a 15 percent chance of reaching the top quintile."[18]

In addition, children raised in neighborhoods marked by high poverty are much more likely to encounter a variety of environmental health hazards. These include elevated exposure to various toxic pollutants, greater likelihood of being victimized by crime and violence, higher arrest rates, increased risk of substance abuse, greater exposure to sexually transmitted diseases, and so on.[19] All of these can detrimentally affect a child's health, which in turn can have a profound impact on that child's health and economic well-being as an adult. In an important study, Laura Dwyer-Lindgren and her colleagues found a life expectancy of up to 87 years in some of America's most affluent counties, while in some of its poorest counties, they report a life expectancy as low as 66 years, a gap of more than 20 years.[20]

Unequal Schools

Where children grow up typically determines where they go to school, and schools play a vital role in our life chances. School quality varies dramatically depending on the economic resources and assets that a community possesses. More than three decades ago, Jonathan Kozal referred to this situation as the "savage inequalities" of America.

Unfortunately, these inequalities are as real today, if not more so, than they were 30 years ago. A report by the Department of Education begins with the following statement, "While some young Americans—most of them white and affluent—are getting a truly world-class education, those who attend school in high poverty neighborhoods are getting an education that more closely approximates schools in developing countries."[21]

One reason for this is the way that public education is funded in this county. The United States is one of the very few industrialized countries where the bulk of funding for public schools comes from state and local tax dollars rather than from the federal government. In particular, the overall value of real estate in a school district is a key determinant of the amount of resources that district will have available. Consequently, children living in lower income neighborhoods tend to be enrolled in schools with far fewer resources and a lower quality of instruction than children living in well-to-do neighborhoods.

In their book, *The American Dream and the Public Schools*, Jennifer Hochschild and Nathan Scovronick note:

> *School district boundaries help to provide such an advantage when they follow neighborhood lines that separate wealthy children from those who are poor and often nonwhite; school financing schemes have this effect when they are based on local property value and thereby create or maintain a privileged competitive position for wealthier children at the expense of the others. Tracking provides advantages when the best teachers or the most resources are devoted to a high track disproportionately filled with wealthier students.*[22]

Research also indicates that since the mid-1970s, schools have actually become more segregated on the basis of race and income. As Erica Frankenberg and colleagues note, "Segregation for black students is rising in all parts of the U.S. Black students who account for 15% of enrollment, as they did in 1970, are in schools that average 47% black students."[23] Furthermore, Latino students are even more segregated. The authors found that "the segregation of Latino students is now the most severe of any group and typically involves a very high concentration of poverty."[24]

Schools that are predominately minority are also highly skewed in the direction of poverty and low income. Rather than reducing the differences and disadvantages that some children face, the structure of schooling in the United States further increases and exacerbates those differences. As Hochschild and Scovronick go on to state:

> *Public schools are essential to make the American dream work, but schools are also the arena in which many Americans first fail. Failure there almost certainly guarantees failure from then on. In the dream, failure results from lack of individual merit and effort; in reality, failure in school too closely tracks structures of racial and class inequality. Schools too often reinforce rather than contend against the intergenerational paradox at the heart of the American dream.*[25]

The intergenerational paradox that the authors refer to is that, "Inequalities in family wealth are a major cause of inequality in schooling, and inequalities of schooling do much to reinforce inequalities of wealth among families in the next generation—that is the intergenerational paradox." Indeed, research has shown that the amount of education and wealth of parents is highly correlated with the educational levels achieved by their children.

The cumulative advantages and disadvantages at the K–12 level become further extended into the likelihood of graduating from high school, and then completing a college degree. Children from wealthier families are often able to attend top-flight private universities, children from middle-class backgrounds may enroll at public universities, while children from lower-class backgrounds will probably not continue on to college at all, or if they do, are likely to attend a community or 2-year college. As Daniel McMurrer and Isabel Sawhill note, "Family background has a significant and increasing effect on who goes to college, where, and for how long. With the reward for going to college greater than ever, and family background now a stronger influence over who reaps those rewards, the United States is at risk of becoming more class stratified in coming decades."[26]

In summarizing the research on education, neighborhood, and income, Greg Duncan and Richard Marmame state, "As the incomes of affluent and poor American families have diverged over the past three decades, so too has the educational performance of the children in these families. Test score differences between rich and poor children are much larger now than thirty years ago, as are differences in rates of college attendance and college graduation."[27] Unfortunately, it appears that we are moving even further afield of a level playing surface when it comes to education.

Unequal Treatment of Groups

Beyond our unequal families, neighborhoods, communities, and schools, our membership in various social groups and the unequal manner in which these groups are treated by society matters a great deal as well. There are a myriad of important group memberships we could discuss—from gender to sexual orientation to disability and beyond—but we will limit our discussion to that of race.

While there are various disadvantaged racial and ethnic groups, let us consider the case of African Americans. The inequalities that the Black community experiences relative to Whites are too numerous to list here, in areas such as income and wealth, home ownership, education, employment, health and longevity, and incarceration, to name a few. These inequalities result from the variety of ways in which the field is tilted against African Americans.[28]

Inequalities both past and present ensure a lower socioeconomic status starting point and much worse social mobility for African Americans compared with Whites.[29] As Ta-Nehisi Coates explains, in America "the concentration of poverty has been paired with a concentration of melanin."[30] Seventy-eight percent of African Americans grow up in highly disadvantaged neighborhoods, compared with only 5 percent of Whites.[31] The schools that Whites and Blacks attend today are still segregated and unequal.[32] Environmental burdens also disproportionately threaten Black communities.[33] African Americans are treated unequally at every stage in the criminal justice process.[34] The list goes on and on; wherever one looks in American society, the playing field is not level.

In one of the more blatant examples, sociologist Devah Pager's employment audit experiments found that, despite identical qualifications, White job applicants were much more likely to receive positive employer responses (either a callback or job offer) compared with African Americans. This was the case even when Whites had a criminal record and identically credentialed African Americans did not (17 percent positive responses for Whites with a felony conviction compared with 13 percent for African Americans with a clean record).[35] Pager and colleagues concluded that, "Our findings add to a large research program demonstrating the continuing contribution of discrimination to racial inequality in the post-civil rights era."[36] The playing field is decidedly unequal for African Americans as well as for millions of other Americans who belong to disadvantaged social groups. And yet, despite the number of studies reporting findings similar to those found by Pager, a recent Gallup survey shows that 67 percent of Whites disagree that hiring discrimination against African Americans is a problem.[37]

Conclusion

The weight of the evidence quite clearly demonstrates that the United States does not represent a level playing field. Instead, high levels of inequality are built into the structure of our society due to the decisions that have been collectively made, and this inequality is getting worse.[38] This enormous inequality commits structural violence on different social groups, who carry a higher risk of hardship than other groups because of forces that are largely outside of their control. Structural violence refers to

> . . . *the avoidable limitations society places on groups of people that constrain them from achieving the quality of life that would have otherwise been possible. These limitations could be political, economic, religious, cultural, or legal in nature and usually originate in institutions that have authority over particular subjects. Because of its embedding within social structures, people tend to overlook them as ordinary difficulties that they encounter in the course of life. . . . Structural violence directly illustrates a power system wherein social structures or institutions cause harm to people in a way that results in maldevelopment or deprivation.*[39]

We decide as a country how much inequality we will have. We also decide what that inequality means in terms of the types of rewards and punishments that are associated with each social position and how severe the differences are. As Claude Fischer and his colleagues argue, "Inequality is not fated by nature, nor even by the 'invisible hand' of the market; it is a social construction, a result of our historical acts. Americans have created the extent and type of inequality we have, and Americans maintain it."[40]

The notion that American society operates as an even playing field, with meritocracy determining who does well and who does not, is a powerful yet fallacious myth. As we have shown, the playing field is decidedly uneven, benefiting some while penalizing others.

An Expert Appraisal—Stephen McNamee

Stephen McNamee is a professor of sociology at the University of North Carolina at Wilmington. He is the author (along with Robert Miller) of The Meritocracy Myth.

The default assumption among most Americans is that people get out of the system what they put into it. It is assumed that people achieve or do not achieve on the basis of individual merit. The United States is the most hyperindividualistic culture in the world, and we are particularly unique in that regard.

In thinking about why people get ahead, Americans identify innate talents, the right attitude, hard work, and playing by the rules as the dominant factors. The presumption in the United States is that these characteristics are directly associated with outcomes. The default explanation for most Americans is very individualistic and reductionist, not just for poverty but for virtually everything.

I argue in The Meritocracy Myth that this presumption is wildly overestimated. The weight of the evidence suggests that economic and structural factors are actually dominant. People are caught up in social forces based on the social location that they occupy within the larger social system.

Most Americans underestimate nonmerit factors in accounting for who ends up with what, the biggest of which is inheritance broadly defined, or where you start out in the first place. The privileges of starting ahead of others include nonmerit factors like social capital and cultural capital.[41] In addition, think about economic gifts from your parents. Most people would like to have their kids do well, but privileged parents are in a position to give them greater resources and make larger investments. Robert Putnam talks about the wealthy having "airbags" for their kids.

Lack of money will cause poverty every time, either people being born poor to begin with, or because of their circumstances and larger contextual factors. They do not have access to good education, or they do not have access to well-paying jobs. Maybe they are victims of automation or globalization or other forces beyond their control. They may have an illness or some kind of life event like divorce, loss of a wage earner, or other events that propels them into poverty.

Individualism is a really strong impulse that most Americans have, so it is an uphill battle to try to explain these things. You have to be convincing, compelling, and overwhelming with the evidence. It is relatively new that, in the last few years, Americans have talked about income and wealth inequality. I have been at this for 40 years, and some of us feel like we have been screaming in the wilderness and nobody has been listening. All of the sudden this has become a timely topic. The issue now is not that we have economic inequality but how much economic inequality can America tolerate without risking the legitimacy of the system as a whole.

Inequality Matters

There is a widespread myth, particularly among conservatives, that economic inequality is relatively unimportant. The reasons are twofold. First, as long as you are not poor, according to this logic, then why care about what anyone else has for any reason other than envy? Poverty can hurt you in various ways, it is argued, but how can inequality harm you? A second reason rests on the premise that as long as we have equality of opportunity, there is no need to worry about inequality of outcome. In other words, if everyone has a fair shot at getting ahead, then inequalities in income or wealth are tolerable. In fact, according to this argument, such inequalities may be desirable because they demonstrate the importance of meritocracy. Those with skills, talent, and motivation are rewarded, while those who are lacking will suffer. This is both desirable and fair.

In contrast, we argue that the wide inequality found in the United States is problematic for a number of reasons. Inequality has been shown to be associated with a range of troubling societal conditions, including lower life expectancy, worse health, reduced child well-being and academic performance, crime and incarceration, drug abuse, teenage birth rates, and lower levels of trust, to name but a few. High inequality can leave a country's social fabric "fraying at the edges."[1]

Let us begin looking at inequality by examining the extent of economic inequality in the United States (also discussed in Chapter 16), followed by the specific implications of this inequality for American society.

How Much Inequality Is There in the United States?

In the 1980s, the top 10 percent of Americans took home 37 percent of the income, compared with 18 percent for the bottom 50 percent. The most recent data available indicate that the top 10 percent's share has increased to

47 percent, while the bottom 50 percent's has fallen to 13 percent.[2] In a vivid illustration of this growing inequality, the bottom 90 percent now earns less in about a year than what the top 0.1 percent takes home in a day.[3]

Many countries perform much better. France, for instance, has a much more equitable income distribution, with the top 10 percent taking home less (33 percent in France compared with 47 percent in the United States), and the bottom 50 percent taking home more (23 percent compared with 13 percent).[4]

Researchers commonly use a measure called the Gini coefficient when comparing income inequality across countries (discussed in Chapters 1 and 15). It provides an overall gauge of how unequal a society is. The Gini coefficient ranges between 0 and 1, with 0 representing perfect income equality and 1 representing perfect inequality. The higher the value, the more unequal the income in that country. With respect to the income distribution within a country, a Gini coefficient of 0 would indicate that every household in that country was earning exactly the same amount with respect to income. A Gini coefficient of 1 would indicate that one household was earning all of the income in that country.

Table 18.1 displays the Gini coefficients across a broad grouping of OECD countries.[5] The Gini coefficients are shown before taxes and transfers are accounted for in the first column, and after taxes and transfers in the second column. In other words, we are looking at the extent of income inequality in column 1 before income taxes are taken out of household income and before income from various social programs are included in household income. Column 2 shows the Gini coefficients after these two factors are taken into account.

We can see in the first column of Table 18.1 that the United States is on the higher side with respect to income inequality, with a Gini coefficient of .505, but not at the very top. There are several countries either at that level or higher with respect to income inequality. In fact, most countries fall within a range of .445 to .520.

However, after taxes and transfer programs are factored into income, the United States stands at the very top with respect to income inequality. The Gini coefficient is reduced from .505 to .390 as a result of taxes and transfers. This is much less of a decline than that found in all of the other countries in Table 18.1. For example, in Finland the Gini coefficient is reduced from .512 to .266. Countries at the lower end of income inequality after taxes and transfers tend to be the Scandinavian and Benelux countries.

Along with worsening income inequality, wealth inequality in the United States has become more skewed over time as well.[6] Inequality in wealth is particularly important with respect to the intergenerational transmission of social position, according to William Chambliss and Daina Eglitis:

Wealth, unlike income, is built up over a lifetime and may be passed down to the next generations. It is used to create new opportunities rather than

TABLE 18.1 Gini Coefficients Among OECD Countries

Country	Gini coefficient (before taxes and transfers)	Gini coefficient (after taxes and transfers)
United States	.505	.390
Lithuania	.510	.374
United Kingdom	.506	.357
South Korea	.406	.355
Latvia	.481	.355
New Zealand	.462	.349
Israel	.444	.348
Japan	.504	.339
Italy	.516	.334
Spain	.507	.333
Luxemburg	.496	.327
Australia	.454	.325
Portugal	.517	.320
Greece	.528	.319
Canada	.438	.310
Estonia	.445	.309
Switzerland	.386	.296
Ireland	.535	.295
France	.519	.292
Germany	.500	.289
Hungary	.478	.289
Netherlands	.445	.285
Sweden	.434	.282
Poland	.447	.275
Austria	.485	.275
Finland	.512	.266
Belgium	.485	.263
Norway	.429	.262
Denmark	.447	.261
Iceland	.385	.257

Source: OECD data, 2020, https://data.oecd.org/inequality/income-inequality.htm#indicator-chart

merely to cover routine expenditures. Income buys shoes, coffee, and car repairs; wealth buys a high-quality education, business ventures . . . as well as financial security and creation of new wealth. Those who possess wealth have a decided edge at getting ahead in the stratification system.[7]

In the 1980s, the top 10 percent of Americans owned 61 percent of the financial wealth, while the bottom 50 percent owned only 2 percent. The most recent data available show that the top 10 percent now own almost three-fourths of the wealth (73 percent), while the bottom 50 percent's share has fallen to below zero (–0.1 percent).[8]

In addition, the Gini coefficient for wealth inequality in the United States is extremely skewed. Edward Wolff has calculated that in 2016, the Gini coefficient for net worth was .877, and .930 for financial wealth.[9] Recall that this coefficient cannot go higher than 1. These coefficients indicate that most of the wealth in this country is held by an extremely small number of individuals.

Beyond these measures of inequality, there are other signs that the United States has become more unequal. Deep poverty (typically measured as earning less than 50 percent of the official poverty thresholds) has increased since the 1970s, from 28 percent of the poor to approaching half (45 percent) today.[10] Male wages for high school graduates have declined since the 1970s, while those of college graduates have increased.[11] Neighborhoods are now more class-segregated than they were in the 1970s.[12] In the 1970s, less than 10 percent of students with low socioeconomic status (SES) completed college, compared with about 40 percent of high-SES students—a gap that has increased in recent years to approximately 70 percent for the top, but only 10 percent for the bottom.[13]

In addition, between 1980 and 2010, the gap in life expectancy (at age 50 years) between low-SES and high-SES Americans increased for both women (from almost 4 years to more than 13 years) and men (from 5 years to almost 13 years). Over this period of time, the life expectancy of low-SES Americans actually declined by about 4 years for women and 6 months for men. For high-SES Americans, life expectancy increased by about 5½ years for women and 7 years for men.[14]

In the 1970s, both college-educated and high school–educated women had marriage rates of more than 80 percent; that number dropped to less than 60 percent for high school–educated women in recent years, but stabilized at about 75 percent for college-educated women.[15] Sixty five percent of births occurring to women with 12 years or less of education are now outside of marriage, while the corresponding figure for college educated women is only 10 percent.[16] The gap in median age at first birth between high- and low-education mothers has also increased over time, from less than 5 years in the 1960s to more than 10 years today.[17]

All of this inequality is troubling for a variety of important reasons most notably because researchers have identified a number of detrimental outcomes as a result of such inequality. While each of these outcomes are important, we limit our discussion to two areas of concern—a lack of opportunity and violence.

Opportunity

Americans are typically much more concerned with equality of opportunity than equality of outcome, as economist Joseph Stiglitz notes:

Today, the United States has less equality of opportunity than almost any other advanced industrial country. Study after study has exposed the myth that America is the land of opportunity. This is especially tragic. While Americans may differ on the desirability of equality of outcomes, there is near-universal consensus that inequality of opportunity is indefensible. The Pew Research Center has found that some 90 percent of Americans believe that the government should do everything it can to ensure equality of opportunity.[18]

In another nationwide survey, Americans were asked, "What do you think is more important for this country: to reduce inequality in America or to ensure everyone has a fair chance of improving their economic standing?" Seventy-one percent chose a "fair chance," while only 21 percent chose "reduce inequality."[19]

However, what many have failed to grasp is that wide inequalities in outcomes can lead to a severe erosion of equality of opportunities. For example, the quality of K–12 education varies markedly depending on the income and wealth of parents (as discussed Chapter 17). Children whose parents are poor and non-White are likely to receive a substandard education in school districts strapped for resources, while children whose parents are wealthy and White will probably receive an excellent education either in a well-funded school district or an elite private school. As discussed in the prior chapter, these initial parental socioeconomic differences will have a profound influence on the types of opportunities that are available to their children. To argue that all children are exposed to the same opportunities is simply fantasy.

How might we measure the amount of opportunity available to Americans? One important way is by examining measures of social mobility as we began to explore in Chapter 16. Richard Wilkinson and Kate Pickett explain:

The possibility of social mobility is what we mean when we talk about equality of opportunity: the idea that anybody, by their own merits and hard work, can achieve a better social or economic position for themselves and their family. Unlike greater equality itself, equality of opportunity is valued across the political spectrum.[20]

Research suggests that higher inequality may be associated with worse intergenerational social mobility (measured by the intergenerational earnings elasticity [IGE], discussed in Chapter 16).[21] Consequently, in more unequal countries, it is harder to move out of your social class of birth in adulthood compared with more egalitarian countries.

In a 2012 speech, economist Alan Krueger (who was then an economic advisor to President Barack Obama) labeled the relationship between income inequality and intergenerational social mobility across countries the "Great Gatsby Curve."[22] Based on the work of economist Miles Corak, the Great Gatsby Curve demonstrates that highly unequal countries tend to have worse intergenerational social mobility (higher IGEs) than more egalitarian countries. In the study illustrated in Figure 18.1, Corak reported a strong correlation (0.59) between Gini coefficients and IGEs across countries. We can see in Figure 18.1 the tendency for countries with greater inequality to have less social mobility. One way to visualize this process is that as the rungs on the ladder of opportunity grow further apart, it becomes hard for individuals to climb up such a ladder.[23]

Economist Raj Chetty and his colleagues have identified a similar phenomenon across American communities, finding that "[commuting zones] with larger Gini coefficients have less upward mobility, consistent with the 'Great Gatsby curve' documented across countries."[24] Chetty found a strong negative correlation (–0.57) between Gini coefficients in communities and the likelihood of upward social mobility. This means that as the Gini coefficient increases (indicating an increase in income inequality), the likelihood of upward mobility of children from those areas decreases.[25]

Economist Bhashkar Mazumder has calculated the current IGE in the United States at 0.60 or higher (which indicates a very strong association).[26] He argues that available data "clearly challenge the ideal of America as a highly mobile society where individuals succeed or fail irrespective of their initial circumstances of birth."[27] In countries like Denmark and Finland, IGE

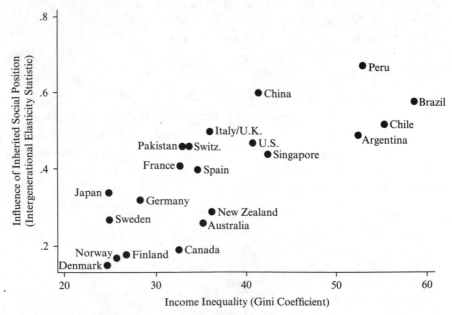

FIGURE 18.1 *The Great Gatsby Curve across 22 countries*

Note: Correlation = 0.59.

Source: Miles Corak, "Here Is the Source for the 'Great Gatsby Curve' in the Alan Krueger Speech at the Center for American Progress on January 12." Economics for Public Policy (January 12, 2012), https://milescorak.com/2012/01/12/here-is-the-source-for-the-great-gatsby-curve-in-the-alan-krueger-speech-at-the-center-for-american-progress/

values are regularly between 0.15 and 0.20 (considered weak assóciations) [28] suggesting that their greater equality relative to the United States has enhanced the availability of opportunities for their children. As Joseph Stiglitz states, "the life prospects of an American are more dependent on the income and education of [the individual's] parents than in almost any other advanced country for which there is data."[29] Or, as Richard Wilkinson is fond of saying, "If you want to live the American dream, you should move to Finland or Denmark."[30]

Violence

There is an abundance of evidence that poverty is associated with crime rates at both the individual and community levels.[31] In a review of 273 studies of the United States and a number of other countries by Lee Ellis and James McDonald, the authors found strong evidence of a relationship between criminal offending and low income, low occupational status, and low educational attainment.[32] Other studies have found associations between concentrated poverty in communities and crime rates. This relationship is likely due to some combination of related factors, including joblessness, neighborhood and community characteristics, school characteristics, peer networks, family structure, social bonds, self-control, and/or psychological strain.[33]

Researchers have estimated a correlation between poverty and homicide rates across American cities/metropolitan areas as high as 0.77.[34] According to the U.S. Department of Justice, Americans earning less than $10,000 per year are 4.9 times more likely to be victims of a serious violent crime (rape/sexual assault, robbery, or aggravated assault) compared with those earning $75,000 or more.[35] As Richard Wilkinson notes, "it is poor young men from disadvantaged neighborhoods who are most likely to be both victims and perpetrators of violence."[36]

Poverty is also associated with incarceration, as "the American prison system is bursting at the seams with people who have been shut out of the economy and who had neither a quality education nor access to good jobs."[37] A majority of incarcerated Americans do not have a high school degree and were earning less than $23,000 before incarceration. The median pre-incarceration income for American men who end up incarcerated is $19,650, compared with $41,250 for men who are not incarcerated.[38]

While a focus on poverty is clearly warranted, income inequality cannot be ignored, as researchers have also demonstrated a strong relationship (as high as 0.80) between inequality and homicide across countries.[39] According to psychologist Martin Daly, author of *Killing the Competition,* income inequality predicts homicide rates "better than any other variable."[40] Commenting on this relationship, Maia Szalavitz notes that, "The connection is so strong that, according to the World Bank, a simple measure of inequality predicts about half of the variance in murder rates between American states and between countries around the world."[41]

Daly and his colleagues found similar associations within countries. In their study, they demonstrated strong correlations between Gini coefficients in U.S. states/Canadian provinces and homicide rates (0.72 for the United States, 0.84 for Canada).[42] Beyond homicide, research also reveals associations between income inequality and property crimes, proportion who feel safe walking home, and level of confidence in police across countries.[43]

A number of studies have explored the causes of the relationship between inequality and homicide. Some have focused on the manner in which inequality negatively affects levels of trust and social capital, and how this may increase violence.[44]

Status competition, particularly among men, is another plausible explanation that may help to explain this correlation. Research suggests that for many men, being "masculine" means having status. The overwhelming majority of murders in the United States (where the gender of the perpetrator is known) are committed by men (88 percent).[45] These murders are often in response to "losing face" or a threat to one's status and/or reputation: feeling a sense of disrespect, embarrassment, humiliation, foolishness, and/or shame. Indeed, U.S. Federal Bureau of Investigation (FBI) data reveal that "just over half of murders in which the precipitating circumstances were known were set off by what is called the 'other argument'—not a robbery, a love triangle, drugs, domestic violence or money, but simply the sense that someone had been dissed."[46] Harvard psychiatrist James Gilligan explains that most violent acts are "attempts to ward off or eliminate the feeling of shame or humiliation," such as being abused by one's parents, cheated on by a romantic partner, or harassed by fellow schoolmates.[47]

The fact that threats to status and reputation are such important triggers of violence in men may help explain the connection between inequality and violence, linking our discussions of opportunity and violence. "If you foreclose [mainstream] opportunities for respect, status and personal advancement," explains Harold Pollack, co-director of the University of Chicago Crime Lab, "people will find other ways to pursue those things."[48] High inequality constrains opportunity, makes acquiring status and reputation more difficult, and makes the negative consequences of not having them more severe.

Conclusion and Looking Ahead

The level of inequality in the United States today has become concerning for many Americans. A recent survey from Gallup, for instance, found that

66 percent of Americans were either somewhat (23 percent) or very (43 percent) dissatisfied with the way that income and wealth are distributed in the United States (although 63 percent are still satisfied with the opportunity to get ahead by working hard in the United States).[49]

Clearly, inequality has taken a turn for the worse in the United States over the past 40 years. But if things can get much worse, then they can also get much better. The high level of inequality we are experiencing is not a naturally occurring phenomenon. The extent of inequality in our society, and the specific penalties and rewards associated with different social positions, are socially constructed and can therefore be socially dismantled.

In short, the level of inequality in America is not the result of inexorable laws of economics. It is "a matter of policies and politics," as Joseph Stiglitz argues, "None of this is inevitable. Some countries have made the choice to create more equitable economies."[50] There are important lessons to be learned from more egalitarian countries and their effective social policies. In such societies, there is still inequality, but the punishment for being at the bottom of the hierarchy is not as severe, and the rewards for being at the top are not as great. As a result, the severity of many of the social problems associated with high levels of economic inequality are significantly reduced.

The changes in thinking discussed throughout our chapters represent some of the key building blocks on which to challenge and ultimately replace the conventional understanding of American poverty. Unfortunately, the current narrative serves some people's interest quite well. For example, it provides politicians with a convenient target to attack and to argue for smaller government programs. Likewise, it provides us all with a justification for doing so little to address poverty.

As we have argued elsewhere, it is a key reason that the United States has such elevated rates of poverty compared with other OECD countries.[51] The United States has been an outlier with respect to its failure to adequately address a wide variety of social policy issues, from child care, to criminal justice, to health care. Poverty is prime example of this failure and the predictable result of extremely high numbers of poor people.

In the next section of this book, we provide an understanding into why the poverty myths and stereotypes persist despite strong evidence to the contrary. In addition, we provide a beginning policy blueprint for what a new agenda would look like to reduce the injustice of widespread poverty in America. Finally, we point to several ways in which each of us can make a difference in changing the traditional, destructive narrative of poverty that is so common to the United States.

An Expert Appraisal—Richard G. Wilkinson

Richard Wilkinson is Professor Emeritus of Social Epidemiology at the University of Nottingham. He is the author (along with Kate Pickett) of *The Spirit Level: Why Greater Equality Makes Societies Stronger.*

Our work in The Spirit Level looks at the scale of income differences between rich and poor in different rich developed societies. We found that those income differences closely correlated with things like the level of violence in societies, the overall life expectancy of populations, child well-being, measures of the strength of community life, levels of trust, the proportion of the population in prison, and so on. There are now two or three data sets showing that social mobility is lower in more unequal societies. Just a whole range of problems were worse in societies with bigger income differences between rich and poor.

That, of course, explains why the United States, which has very large income differences between rich and poor in the developed world, has among the lowest life expectancy amongst the rich developed countries, and the highest homicide rates, imprisonment rates, and obesity rates. There are a whole raft of these problems, which are more common the lower you go on the social ladder, and worse in societies with bigger income differences. The countries that do well and have smaller income differences, are the Scandinavian countries—Norway, Sweden, Denmark, and the Netherlands, as well as Japan.

I think one of the most fundamental impacts of inequality is the damage it does to social relations. Community life weakens in more unequal societies, and people trust each other less. The differences are actually quite large. In more unequal developed countries, levels of trust fall to about 15 or 20 percent of people who feel that they can trust most other people. Whereas in the more equal of the rich developed societies, it rises to 60 or 65 percent. It makes a huge difference.

If you go to the most unequal countries, countries like Mexico or South Africa, which have much higher income differences than the United States, you find that the houses are often barricaded. There are fences around everyone's yards, sometimes electric fences, and bars on all of the windows and doors. In South Africa, I have seen notices saying, "Armed Response."

What inequality does most fundamentally is make that transition from trust, community life, people's involvement with each other, to violence and fear and mistrust. It is a very, very clear pattern. Instead of a sense of a shared identity and shared well-being, you move to everyone being out for themselves. That is what I mean when I say that inequality is divisive and socially corrosive.

What is interesting is that people have intuitively recognized this since before the French Revolution. What is different is now you can actually see it in the data. We can compare amounts of inequality in different societies with these kinds of outcomes. It is no longer just a matter of private intuition, which it had been for the past few centuries; it is a publicly demonstrable truth.

We live closer to each other than ever before, and yet suffer so much from loneliness and from the breakdown of social cohesion. That is the real issue. We need to reduce inequality to tackle these problems. I think if Americans went to countries like Sweden and Norway, they would feel more rather than less free.

{ SECTION VI }

Pulling It Together

In the previous sections, we have examined a wide range of myths pertaining to the subject of poverty. In each case, the research evidence to support these myths has been sorely lacking. Rather, we have detailed a reality quite different than the common stereotypes, and in many ways, much more disturbing.

The question naturally arises, "If the myths are so wrong, why do they persist?" We address this question in our final section of the book. Here, we develop several arguments as to why the poverty myths continue despite overwhelming evidence to the contrary. Next, we will outline a policy agenda for confronting poverty based on the realities rather than the myths. Finally, we conclude *Poorly Understood* by suggesting some of the strategies that each of us might employ to change the narrative of poverty.

{ 19 }

Why Do the Myths Persist?

Reading through the chapters of this book, one must wonder why poverty myths persist despite so much evidence to the contrary. Not surprisingly, there is no simple or single agreed-on answer to this important question. In this chapter, we draw on research from the social sciences to identify several potential explanations for this tendency.

Specifically, we focus on two fundamental sets of factors that can help make sense of the persistence of poverty myths: (1) psychologically based factors and (2) sociologically based factors. For clarity, we present these as distinct explanations, but we regard them as complementary and co-occurring rather than competing, with each offering a unique take on the persistence of poverty myths. Perhaps, most important, we believe that identifying the roots of poverty myths—why they take hold and thrive—is pivotal to understanding not only their persistence but also our ability to dismantle them.

Social Psychological Understandings of Poverty Myths

A large body of social psychological research has sought to understand fundamental processes related to the phenomenon of stereotyping. Collectively, this scholarship has enhanced our knowledge of individual factors, widely shared cultural beliefs, cognitive processes, social dynamics, and contextual and/or environmental circumstances that contribute to the persistence of stereotypes. A unifying assumption is that stereotyping is a cognitive shortcut, albeit a problematic one, that helps us process the enormous amount of information that we encounter on a daily basis. Drawing broadly on research examining bias and attitude change, we highlight here some of the key psychological contributors that fuel the poverty myths despite ample evidence to the contrary.

Personality Traits

Personality characteristics and deeply held beliefs influence how we view the world as well our perceptions of poverty and economic inequality more specifically. Two personality characteristics are particularly associated with stereotyping—authoritarianism, which is characterized by a preference for order, tradition, and obedience to authority; and social dominance orientation, which is evidenced by a preference for group dominance and social hierarchies.[1] Both are strongly correlated with prejudice and political conservativism, and both contribute to intergroup bias. Emanating from these perspectives, it is common for low-income groups to be stereotyped as threatening to so-called middle-class values and the stability of more economically secure socioeconomic status (SES) groups.

Not surprisingly, people who score high on either of these orientations are more likely to endorse poverty myths than individuals who reject these beliefs. For example, stronger authoritarianism is associated with attributing poverty to individualistic causes, while lower levels of authoritarianism are correlated with more positive beliefs about people experiencing poverty.[2] Social dominance orientation also exerts a powerful influence. Individuals who endorse such a mindset are less likely to attribute poverty to structural causes and less likely to support government and nongovernmental efforts to reduce economic inequality.[3]

Broader societal conditions, such as actual or perceived worsening of economic trends, can heighten the propensity of these tendencies. For example, Edward Rickert found that participants who scored high in authoritarianism, and who perceived their standard of living as declining, expressed stronger support for restrictive entitlement programs and harsh social policies than participants who did not feel economically threatened.[4] These findings are a powerful reminder that even seemingly unmalleable characteristics and beliefs are influenced by social and economic conditions. And while unfavorable economic conditions could be sensitizing and reduce the endorsement of poverty myths, this is not necessarily the case.

Other Belief Systems

Of course, authoritarian and social dominance orientations are far from the only influential belief systems. Rather, they are facets of an interconnected web of beliefs that fuel poverty myths and make them resistant to change. Individualism, meritocratic beliefs, belief in a just world, and the Protestant Work Ethic also contribute to the persistence of stereotypes about people experiencing poverty.[5] These beliefs, which exert influence independently and through their correlations with each other, are considered legitimizing or system-justifying beliefs because of their role in upholding inequality. Their shared emphasis on defining poverty in terms of weak morals and personal shortcomings shifts responsibility for economic hardship from institutions to poor individuals and families, and dampens support for structural change.

A large body of research documents the relationship of these beliefs to poverty myths. Endorsement of individualism, just-world beliefs, meritocratic beliefs, and the Protestant Work Ethic are associated with negative stereotypes and internal attributions for poverty, whereas rejection of these beliefs predicts support for structural understandings of poverty.[6]

For example, research examining the prevalence and impact of meritocratic beliefs, notably the tendency to overestimate the likelihood of moving up the socioeconomic ladder, lends insight into the persistence of poverty myths and U.S. tolerance of staggering rates of economic inequality. Drawing on a large national survey, Shai Davidai and Thomas Gilovich found that respondents significantly underestimated the likelihood of a child born into the poorest 20 percent of the income distribution remaining there, and overestimated the likelihood of rising to the middle or higher quintiles.[7] Likewise, in another study, participants overestimated the odds of moving up the economic ladder, putting the likelihood of moving from the bottom to top income quintile at 1 in 6 when the likelihood is closer to 1 in 20.[8] Poverty myths thrive when class boundaries are perceived as permeable and scalable because economic hardship is therefore viewed as resulting from a lack of effort and ability rather than structural disadvantage.

The consequences of these beliefs are far reaching, feeding a closed, self-reinforcing feedback loop. By negating structural understandings of poverty and assigning responsibility for change to low-income people themselves, poverty myths remain unchallenged, while support for structural and institutional interventions that could reduce poverty is diminished. In the absence of strong safety net programs and policies to reduce rising economic inequality, it becomes increasingly difficult to build the political momentum to secure their passage and the powerful impact they could have on poverty.

System Justification

Many of the same beliefs that social scientists have identified as justifying inequality are also foundational cultural values. This undoubtedly contributes to the persistence of poverty myths. For instance, individualism and meritocracy are key tenets of American ideology, and to question these fundamental values is to question messages about mobility and opportunity that we have been inundated with since childhood. Critically interrogating these messages can be difficult and psychologically threatening. In many respects, it is "easier" to believe that the world is a fair place in which people who experience poverty "deserve it" and that economic security and other advantages are the result of

hard work rather than systemic advantage. To think otherwise opens up potentially difficult questions about one's own position and privilege as well as the
recognition that experiencing poverty is more likely than experiencing wealth.
Put simply, confronting injustice can be psychological aversive.[9]

Research examining system justification—the tendency of individuals
to "exaggerate their system's virtues, downplay its vices, and see the societal
status quo as more fair and desirable than it actually is,"[10] helps explain how
legitimizing beliefs and poverty myths help people cope with this pain and de-
fend unjust systems even when they are not skewed in our favor. By increasing
satisfaction with the status quo, system justification has a palliative function
that increases positive affect and decreases negative emotions. A study by Cheryl
Wakslak and her colleagues vividly illustrates this point.[11] When participants
were primed with common rags-to-riches stories, they reported less negative
affect and moral outrage than respondents in the control condition. Reduced
moral outrage, in turn, resulted in lower support for soup kitchens, job training
programs, crisis hotlines, and mentoring programs.[12]

System justification theory is particularly useful in making sense of support
for poverty myths among low-income groups, who arguably have the most to
lose by their endorsement. For example, belief in meritocracy, individualism,
and poverty myths may serve as important self-protective functions, allowing
low-income individuals to maintain optimism about their ability to move out
of poverty and maintain the belief that the world is a just place.[13] Conversely,
recognizing structural sources of inequality can have negative psychological
consequences. For example, Kristin Mickelson and Emily Hazlett found that
low-income mothers' endorsement of structural attributions for poverty was
associated with higher levels of depression and anxiety.[14] Because structural
sources of poverty may be perceived as stable and outside of our personal control, they may contribute to feelings of unpredictability and helplessness.[15]

Beyond maintaining harmful stereotypes, system-justifying beliefs also reduce the likelihood of collective action (discussed under the sociological section
as well). Danny Osborne and Chris Sibley found that system-justifying beliefs
dampened the effects of individual and group relative deprivation, resulting
in reduced distress and dissatisfaction with one's own standard of living, less
perceived discrimination against one's own ethnic group, and reduced support
for protest activities on behalf of one's group.[16] Collectively, these responses act
as powerful obstacles to challenging poverty myths.

Fundamental Cognitive Processes and Biases

Implicit Bias: Insidious and Unconscious

Although it is often assumed that we are aware of our biases and that stereotyping
is under our conscious control, research examining cognitive processes tells a far
more complex story. Studies indicate that as soon as we identify an individual as

belonging to a particular group, stereotypic associations are activated quickly, even among people who may be relatively unbiased.[17] Adults, for instance, have been found to strongly associate outgroups with negative characteristics and ingroups with positive characteristics.[18] Learned over a lifetime of socialization, these implicit stereotypes may be outside of our conscious control. Even when individuals claim that low-income people have similar academic abilities, they may still associate greater competence with financially secure groups without being consciously aware of this relationship. Commenting on the perniciousness of implicit stereotypes, Susan Fiske and Courtney Tablante observe, "the immediate, spontaneous, not-always-conscious-nature of these biases makes them more insidious because they are typically unexamined."[19]

Suzanne Horwitz and John Dovidio's research on implicit and explicit attitudes toward the wealthy highlights the importance of examining unconscious biases.[20] Across three related studies, they found that participants, most of whom identified as middle class, implicitly favored the rich over the middle class but did not explicitly express this preference.[21] Importantly, implicit biases are not benign. Implicit pro-rich attitudes were found to predict leniency toward a wealthy driver who was described as causing a car accident, while explicit attitudes did not.[22] Collectively, these findings make clear that interventions and trainings that seek to reduce stereotypes must address both explicit and implicit stereotypes. This is particularly important among groups with high-stakes decision-making power such as judges, law enforcement, employers, caseworkers, and health care professionals.[23]

Confirmation Bias: Affirming What We Already Believe

Confirmation bias—the tendency to search for, pay attention to, and remember information that confirms preexisting beliefs and dismiss contradictory evidence—also contributes to the persistence of poverty myths. Confirmation bias "locks" stereotypes in place by closing us off to alternative information. Contradictory evidence, if noticed, is likely to be forgotten or misremembered, fueling an "echo chamber" in which we only "see" and "hear" what we already believe.

A classic study by John Darley and Paget Gross illustrates how social class labels create expectations for performance and how information is misconstrued to uphold common stereotypes.[24] Participants received socioeconomic information about a hypothetical child who was portrayed as being from either a high- or low-SES family and then watched an identical videotape of her taking an exam. Although the child's test performance did not vary, participants who believed that she came from a higher SES background rated her academic abilities as being above grade level, while those who believed that she was from a lower SES family evaluated her skills as being below grade level.[25] Tellingly, both groups perceived her videotaped test performance differently and in ways that supported their conflicting assessments. These findings make clear that simply presenting information that refutes poverty myths is unlikely to be sufficient to sway strong believers, and that more creative strategies are needed to interrupt confirmatory biases.

The Fundamental Attribution Error: Individual Over Structural

On any given day, we make countless attributions to explain the behaviors of family members, friends, coworkers, and others whom we encounter. We also make causal attributions for societal events and other aspects of the social world, including why some people are poor and others are rich. Among the most basic distinctions is the split between internal (e.g., dispositional, personal) and external (e.g., situational, environmental) attributions. While internal or individualistic attributions for poverty focus on the role of individuals in creating their economic situation (e.g., laziness, lack of effort, lack of frugality), structural explanations for poverty emphasize institutional and societal sources of economic hardship (e.g., discrimination, low wages). Many of the myths that we have discussed throughout this book are integral to internal attributions for poverty, making them largely synonymous with poverty stereotypes.

Research on attributions identifies not only content but also tendencies, biases, and patterns in causal explanations. The fundamental attribution error, or "the tendency for attributers to underestimate the impact of situational factors and to overestimate the role of dispositional factors," is a common bias, particularly in Western societies.[26] Consistent with this bias, individualistic attributions for poverty tend to enjoy stronger support in the United States than structural explanations.[27] Many explanations for this general bias have been advanced, including cross-cultural differences in individualism and interdependence in Western versus Eastern nations and the possibility that a greater cognitive load is associated with situational than individualistic attributions.[28] Regardless of the root cause, overestimating the importance of internal attributions for poverty serves to reflect and reinforce poverty myths, which contributes to their dominance in U.S. culture.

Sociological Understanding of Poverty Myths

Fifty years ago, the sociologist Herbert Gans wrote a provocative essay detailing the economic, social, cultural, and political functions of poverty.[29] Gans argued that in order for poverty to exist and persist, it must be serving a function or purpose within American society. He went on to describe more than a dozen potential functions that poverty could be fulfilling. For example, it ensures that there is a labor pool willing to work at low-wage, dead-end jobs, which are undesirable but necessary.

In thinking about why the myths of poverty persist, we can ask a similar sociological question—who benefits from the existence of these myths? Furthermore, what functions might these myths play for the wider society?

With respect to the question of who benefits, several groups immediately come to mind. Most obvious are political actors. Politicians of various stripes have used the myth of the welfare freeloader to score political points with their constituents over the decades. A classic example of this was the case of Bill Clinton during his 1992 campaign in the Democratic presidential nomination race. Clinton was running well behind the frontrunners, when he began emphasizing that he would "end welfare as we know it." Internal polling showed that this resonated with voters in the early primary states, and indeed he began to rise in popularity as he increasingly used this issue to demonstrate that he represented what he called a "new Democrat." Clinton clearly exploited the myth of the undeserving welfare recipient to his advantage in appealing to more conservative voters. This was an important element in his winning the nomination and attaining the presidency.[30]

Likewise, Ronald Reagan was notorious in his use of the "welfare queen" and the "strapping young buck" myths to attract voters who had become disillusioned with the Democratic Party. Reagan was able to use this messaging (along with others) to pull blue-collar Democrats into the Republican fold. The myths of poverty and welfare recipients clearly helped to facilitate Reagan's rise to the executive office.[31]

These are but two examples of politicians who have strategically used various poverty myths to further their political careers. The myth of the lazy poor living off welfare has been utilized repeatedly by politicians to appeal to voters, and to garner their support in the ballot box. It has also been used as a code word for "Black" in particular, again appealing to a certain segment of the population.[32]

A second group that has clearly benefited from the myths of poverty has been the affluent. The myth that poverty is the result of individual inadequacies rather than structural failings provides a convenient justification for the status quo of rising inequality. According to this myth, those at the top have earned it, while those at the bottom have deserved it (as discussed in Chapters 6 and 12). Consequently, no policy change is needed to redistribute some of the enormous gains in wealth over the past decades. The myths of poverty allow and justify the greater accumulation of income and assets for those with much to begin with.

One could also argue that the myth of poverty being the result of individual failure has discouraged low-income groups from forming alliances to advocate for their shared interest. This, in turn, weakens the position of lower income workers and their unions, which in turn facilitates the desire of big business over the past 50 years to seriously diminish the labor union movement in this country.[33] The stigma of poverty, fueled by myths and stereotypes, works against people acknowledging their low-income status, which then weakens any sense of a collective interest. As Frances Fox Piven and Lorraine Minnite write:

No matter their hardship, before people can mobilize for defiant collective action, they have to develop a proud and angry identity. They have to go from being hurt and ashamed to being angry and indignant. In the 1930s, many of the jobless tried to hide their travails; hangdog unemployed workers swung empty lunch boxes as they strode down the street so the neighbors would not know. But many of the unemployed also harbored other ideas, half-formed perhaps, about who was to blame for their plight. When those ideas were evoked they could be rallied to rise up with others in anger over their condition.[34]

Again, the argument is that the myths of poverty persist partially because specific groups within society are benefiting from their perpetuation.

This is not to say that the process is always a consciously deliberate one. For example, it is unlikely that big business sits around a conference table to discuss how the myths of poverty can be used to weaken union activity. Nevertheless, the persistence of poverty myths helps to undercut a collective impetus to organize, which in turn dovetails with one component of the long-term stated agenda of corporate America.

It is also important to recognize that each of these groups—politicians, the wealthy, corporate America—yields considerable power. It is therefore not just a question of various groups benefiting from the myths, but of who in particular benefits, and to what extent they are able to shape the narrative. Each of these groups, in various ways, is able to influence the discussion around poverty and welfare.

On a broader level, we can also ask what functions the poverty myths serve for American society as a whole. In answering this question, we would argue that the myths ironically serve to legitimize the status of America as exceptional.[35] The ideology of the United States has been steeped in the concept of the American dream. The American dream represents the idea that everyone can achieve economic success through their own hard work and talent. America is viewed as a land of abundant opportunities, with everyone having an equal chance to climb the ladder of success.[36]

On the other hand, poverty represents the American nightmare. Given the ideology of the American dream, how then do we explain the fact that many Americans are living in poverty? We do so through the poverty myths that have been described throughout this book—that those in poverty have simply not worked hard enough, have made poor decisions in their lives, have not acquired enough skills, or any number of such explanations. The implication is that there is something wrong with the individual, rather than the system. The alternative would be to question the very structure of American society. Consequently, the poverty myths provide for a ready explanation to the fact that some Americans do not achieve economic success in a land of plenty. This is quite consistent with the system justification research discussed earlier in the psychological section.

To acknowledge that poverty is simply endemic to America as a whole is to challenge the very core of the nation's ideals and creed. Such a task is not taken on lightly. Rather, the cognitively easier approach is to explain those in poverty as outliers and exceptions to the rule.

Moving Forward

Although our discussion has focused on the persistence of poverty myths and how resistant these stereotypes are to change, we also believe that it is possible to shift the dominant narrative. We see the evidence that we have presented in this book as offering a road forward, albeit a challenging one.

A multifaceted attack on poverty myths is necessary, and raising awareness of the fallacies of common stereotypes about economic hardship, as we have sought to do in writing this book, is just one step in a far broader movement. Summoning a newfound willingness to interrogate the role of individualism and meritocracy in shaping our attitudes toward each other and the distribution of resources is likely to prove especially difficult. Doing so will undoubtedly require taking on the winner-take-all approach to "success" that is so much a part of contemporary U.S. society. Economic inequality, itself, decreases social cohesion, increases competition and the odds of conflict, encourages "us" versus "them" stereotypes, and deepens political polarization. This makes clear the mutually reinforcing nature of ideological and material disparities and the need for initiatives capable of interrupting this dynamic.[37]

However, as we note in our final chapter, change can and does occur. In particular, ideologies and mindsets can be altered. To take but one example, the paradigm surrounding the physical environment has changed dramatically over the past several decades. Before the 1970s, the environment was routinely viewed as a resource to be used and exploited. Today, the environment is increasingly understood as something that must be nurtured and protected. Many other examples could be given to illustrate the fact that fundamental changes in belief systems can and do occur.

Furthermore, changing the paradigm toward one based on fact and reality moves us closer to effectively addressing and alleviating poverty. To cure a patient's illness, the doctor must be able to make a correct diagnosis. After an accurate diagnosis has been made, the patient can begin down the road to recovery. We take up what that road might look like in our next chapter.

{ 20 }

Reshaping Social Policy

A major reason that poverty in the United States has been historically high is that our social and economic policies aimed at alleviating poverty have been largely ineffective or nonexistent. And a key reason for why they have been ineffective or nonexistent is because they have been based on the many myths that we have discussed throughout this book. The relevant analogy would be that of a doctor who has misdiagnosed the patient. No matter how high a dosage of the wrongly prescribed medicine, it is unlikely to be effective, and in fact may prove to be harmful. Such has been the case with poverty.

Our policies have been primarily aimed at attempting to "improve" individuals such that they can either make their way out of poverty or are able to avoid poverty in the first place. As we have argued throughout the chapters, from this perspective, the causes of poverty are viewed as lying within the individual. Specifically, that there is some kind of individual failing that needs to be corrected. Therefore, the solutions to poverty must lie with reforming or improving individuals, or simply letting them work through their shortcomings on their own.

This tactic has taken several different forms. One approach has been referred to as the "tough love" approach. This strategy is closely associated with various welfare reform measures over the years. It has included a variety of incentives and disincentives, carrots and sticks, to entice individuals to "do the right thing." Particular behaviors are disincentivized, such as having children, while other behaviors are incentivized, such as locating a job.

A second major approach aimed at improving individuals is through job training and skill development programs. The goal of these programs is to make poverty-prone individuals more competitive in the labor market. These programs are targeted at improving the human capital of individuals such that they are able to locate and secure better paying jobs.

Closely associated with these human capital strategies has been an emphasis on either graduation from high school or getting a 2- or 4-year college degree. Again, the idea is to make individuals more competitive in the labor market and therefore reduce their risk of poverty.

A third major policy approach has been one of benign, or not so benign, neglect. This is premised on the belief that government programs do more harm than good and, therefore, that social policy should be kept to a minimum in the lives of the populace. Indeed, the social safety net in the United States has often been referred to as the "reluctant welfare state."

In each of these approaches, the focus is on the shortcomings of the individual rather than the shortcomings of the social structure. As discussed in Chapter 7, the emphasis in U.S. social policy has been on improving those who are playing the game, rather than restructuring the game itself. Like a large-scale version of musical chairs with 10 players but only eight chairs, we can improve each individual's skills and abilities to play the game, but two people are still going to lose given the structure of the game. The rules follow that of a zero-sum scenario—one person's chances of doing well can be improved only at the expense of someone else.

Our argument is that social policy must be focused an altering the game itself. This involves structural changes such that greater numbers of individuals and families are able to support themselves economically. What might some of these strategies be? Although many effective policies and initiatives exist, we limit our discussion to three: (1) ensuring the availability of jobs that will economically support a household; (2) providing an effective social safety net that also incorporates key social and public goods; and (3) building lower income individual and community assets. Each are discussed next.

Ensuring the Availability of Decent-Paying Jobs

Essential to any overall strategy to reduce poverty within both the United States and other countries are policies that will increase the availability of jobs that can support a family above the poverty line. As Bradley Schiller argues, "Jobs—in abundance and of good quality—are the most needed and most permanent solution to the poverty problem."[1]

The problem of not enough jobs has played itself out somewhat differently within an American versus a European context. Within the United States, the economy over the past 40 years has done quite well in terms of creating new jobs. The problem has been that many of these jobs are low paying and/or lacking in basic benefits such as health care. The result is that although unemployment rates have been relatively low in the United States (often averaging between 4 and 6 percent), working full-time does not ensure that a family will be lifted out of poverty or near-poverty. For example, Timothy Smeeding and colleagues found that 25 percent of all American full-time workers could be classified as being in low-wage work (defined as earning less than 65 percent of the national median for full-time jobs).[2] This was by far the highest percentage of the developed countries analyzed, with the overall average falling at 12 percent.

In contrast, European economies have been more sluggish in terms of creating new jobs over the past 40 years, resulting in unemployment rates much higher than in the United States. In addition, workers have remained out of work for longer periods of time. However, for those who are employed, employees are generally paid more and have greater benefits than their American counterparts, resulting in substantially lower rates of poverty.[3]

What, then, can be done to address the related problems of jobs that do not pay enough to support a family, and not enough jobs in the first place? Two broad initiatives would appear essential. The first is transforming the existing job base so that it is better able to support families. The second is the creation of enough jobs to employ all who are in need of work.

Within the context of the United States, one might begin with the following benchmark: Individuals who are employed full-time throughout the year (defined as working 40 hours per week over a 50-week period) should be able to generate earnings that will enable them to lift a family of three above the near-poverty threshold (150 percent of the poverty line). Such a family might include a married couple with one child, a one-parent household with two children, or a three-generation household of mother, grandmother, and son. The 2019 near-poverty threshold for a family of three in the United States was set at $30,503. Consequently, in order to lift such a family above the poverty line, an individual needs to be earning approximately $15.25 an hour. It is interesting that this calculation is nearly identical to the benchmark used for the Fight for $15 movement.

There are two specific ways of accomplishing this. One is to raise the minimum wage to a level that will support a family above the near-poverty line ($15 an hour), and then index it to inflation so that it will continue to lift such a family over the poverty line in the future. A second approach is to provide a tax credit (such as the Earned Income Tax Credit [EITC]) that supplements workers' wages so that their total income for the year lifts them above the near-poverty line.

The minimum wage in the United States went into effect in October 1938 at an initial level of $0.25 an hour. The basic concept was that no employee should fall below a certain wage floor. There was an underlying value that workers should receive a fair wage for a fair day's work. However, unlike Social Security, the minimum wage has never been indexed to inflation; changes in the minimum wage must come through congressional legislation. Years go by before Congress acts to adjust the minimum wage upward, causing it to lag behind the rising cost of living. The current minimum wage in the United States stands at $7.25 an hour, a rate that went into effect in July 2009. An individual working full-time at the minimum wage during the year (50 weeks at 40 hours per week) would earn a total of $14,500, far short of the $30,503 needed to lift a family of three above the near-poverty line.

As noted, to lift such a family above the near-poverty line, an individual needs to be earning at least $15 per hour. Consequently, what is needed is to raise the minimum wage to $15 per hour, and then index it each year to the rate of inflation in order to hold its purchasing power. The phase-in period to raise the minimum wage to $15 per hour might take place over several years in order to spread out the increase. Indeed, many states currently have a minimum wage much higher than the federal minimum wage.

The positive impact of tying the minimum wage to the near-poverty level for a family of three and indexing it to the rate of inflation would be substantial. First, it would establish a reasonable floor below which no full-time worker would fall. Second, it would allow such a worker to support a family of three above the near-poverty line. Third, it would reinforce the value that Americans have consistently attached to work. Fourth, it would remove the political wrangling from the minimum wage debate. Fifth, it would address in a limited way the increasing inequities between CEOs who earn 300 times what their average paid workers earn.

A second approach for supplementing and raising the earnings of low-income workers is through the tax structure, specifically through the use of tax credits. The primary example of such a credit in the United States is the EITC.[4] The EITC was enacted in 1975 and underwent a significant expansion during the 1990s. It currently represents the largest cash antipoverty program in the United States and is frequently considered one of the more innovative American economic policy ideas.

The program is designed to provide a refundable tax credit to low-income workers, with the vast majority going to households with children. In 2018, a family with one child could qualify for the EITC if its earned income was below $40,320 (or $46,010 for married couples), while a family with three or more children could qualify if its household income was under $49,194 (or $54,884 for married couples). The maximum credit for a one-child family was $3,461; the benefit rose to $6,431 for a family with three or more children. The credit is normally received in a lump-sum payment as part of an overall tax refund for the previous year. Since it is a refundable credit, families receive the payment even if they do not owe any taxes.

The goals of the EITC are to deliver economic relief at the low end of the earnings distribution and to furnish a strong work incentive. An individual cannot qualify for the EITC without earned income, and the impact is particularly strong at the lower levels. For example, for a head of household with one child that was earning $7.50 an hour (and total earnings that were under $10,000), the EITC would effectively raise the individual's wage by an additional $3.00 an hour to $10.50 an hour.

The program thus provides a significant supplement to low earners as well as an incentive to work. In 2018, it was estimated that 28 million Americans benefited from the EITC, and along with the Child Tax Credit, it pulled approximately 10.6 million individuals above the poverty line who otherwise would have fallen into poverty.[5] For families that remain in poverty, the EITC has helped to reduce the distance between their household income and the poverty line. It has also enabled families to purchase particular resources that can improve their economic and social mobility (i.e., school tuition) or to meet daily expenses.[6]

To make the EITC even more effective, its benefits should be expanded so that they provide greater assistance to low-income workers without children. The vast majority of the EITC benefits go to families with children. Yet, there is no compelling reason that such benefits should not also be provided for individuals without children. Further research also needs to be done in order to examine the feasibility of receiving the EITC throughout the year, rather than as lump sum during the tax season (although many families do prefer this way of receiving the EITC). Third, some households that qualify for the EITC fail to claim and take advantage of the tax credit. Better educating tax filers about the benefits of the EITC appears warranted. Finally, state EITC programs should be encouraged as an additional antipoverty component on top of the federal EITC benefits.

The policy of an expanded EITC, in conjunction with the raising and indexing of the minimum wage to the level of a living wage, would substantially help working women and men in the United States who, despite their efforts, are unable to get themselves and their families out of poverty or near-poverty. In addition, such policies begin to address (although in a very limited way) the increasing inequalities and perceived unfairness of American income distribution and wage structure.

In terms of the problem of producing enough jobs, in many ways this is a much more difficult task than supplementing and raising the wages of existing jobs. Nevertheless, it is essential that a sufficient number of jobs be available to meet the demands of the existing labor pool.

Various labor demand policies have the potential to generate a more robust rate of job growth. Several approaches can be taken. First, economic policy should seek in a broad way to stimulate job growth. This would include fiscal policies such as increasing government expenditures, enhancing tax incentives for investment, or enacting consumer tax cuts. The strategy of investing in a "Green New Deal" could be one specific area of such investment. Monetary policy can also provide a stimulus by making access to credit easier and cheaper.[7]

A second approach is to provide targeted wage subsidies to employers in order to stimulate job creation. Although the details of such programs can vary considerably, the basic concept is that an employer receives a monetary subsidy for creating a position and/or hiring an individual (often from a targeted population) that the employer might not have hired without such an incentive. This approach could be aimed at businesses and industries that are potential employers of individuals from lower income or lower skill backgrounds.

A third strategy for creating jobs is through public service employment.[8] As David Ellwood and Elisabeth Welty note in their review of the effectiveness of public service employment programs, if done carefully and judiciously, they can help increase employment without displacing other workers, and they can produce genuinely valuable output.[9] Such an approach appears particularly pertinent for those out of work for long periods of time.

Taken as a whole, an overall strategy for reducing poverty must begin with a set of policies that will increase the availability of jobs that can economically support families above the poverty threshold. To a large extent, poverty is the result of not having a job, or of having a job that is not able to viably support a family.

Providing an Effective Social Safety Net and Access to Key Social Goods

A second general strategy for reducing poverty is the existence of an effective social safety net along with providing access to key social and public goods, such as health care, a quality education, child care, and affordable housing. No matter how strong economic growth may be, individuals and families will invariably fall between the cracks. Whether through the loss of a job, a sudden disability, or some other unanticipated event, there are times and situations in people's lives when a social safety net is needed. In OECD countries, this has taken the form of various programs and policies encompassed under the social welfare state.

The economist Hyman Minsky pointed out that free-market economies are prone to periods of instability, such as periodic recessions and economic downturns.[10] Safety net programs help to serve as automatic stabilizers for the economy during these periods. That is, they grow during times of need and diminish during more prosperous times. For example, as rates of unemployment rise, more individuals draw on unemployment insurance to weather the temporary economic problems caused by a lack of jobs. As economic conditions improve, more people are able to find jobs and so no longer need unemployment insurance. In this fashion, safety net programs help to automatically stabilize the instability inherent within the economy.

A social safety net is therefore important in assisting individuals and families during times of need and in alleviating the economic instability associated with recessionary periods. As discussed in Chapters 9 and 13, one of the reasons that the United States' rate of poverty is so high, and the Scandinavian nations' rates are so low, is a result of differences in the extent and depth of their social safety nets. Compared with other Western industrialized countries, the United States devotes far fewer resources to programs aimed at assisting the economically vulnerable.[11] In fact, the United States allocates a smaller proportion of its GDP to social welfare programs than virtually any other industrialized country.[12] As Charles Noble writes, "The U.S. welfare state is striking precisely because it is so limited in scope and ambition."[13]

In contrast, most European countries provide a wide range of universal social and insurance programs that largely prevent families from falling into poverty. These include substantial family or children's allowances, which are designed to transfer cash assistance to families with children. Unemployment assistance is far more generous in these countries than in the United States, often providing support for more than a year following the loss of a job. Furthermore, health coverage is routinely provided, along with considerable support for child care.

The result of these social policy differences is that they substantially reduce the extent of poverty in Europe and Canada, while U.S. social policy exerts only a small impact on poverty reduction. As Rebecca Blank notes, "the national choice in the United States to provide relatively less generous transfers to low-income families has meant higher relative poverty rates in the country. While low-income families in the United States work more than in many other countries, they are not able to make up for lower governmental income support relative to their European counterparts."[14]

Consequently, a key reason behind why the United States has such high levels of poverty is the nature and scope of its social safety net. The United States provides substantially less support to its social safety net than other countries, resulting in poverty rates that are currently among the highest in the industrialized world. Lane Kenworthy argues:

The United States has done less well by its poor than a number of other affluent nations. The reason is straightforward. Like their counterparts abroad, America's least well-off have been hit hard by shifts in the economy since the 1970s, but whereas some countries have ensured that government supports rise as the economy grows, the United States hasn't.[15]

An alternative policy strategy that approaches a social safety net in a substantially different manner than the previously mentioned policies is what is known as a universal basic income. The concept itself has been proposed at various times across the past few centuries. In fact, Thomas Paine, the author of *Common Sense* in 1776, was an early proponent of a guaranteed income for all Americans.

The basic structure would be that every citizen in the United States is guaranteed a set amount of income from the government. This income would be received on a monthly or bimonthly basis. Everyone would be entitled to this income, regardless of whether they were employed or not. Advocates argue that such an approach is a straightforward and effective way of addressing poverty: Since poverty is a lack of income, providing a guaranteed minimal income can substantially reduce poverty directly.[16] In addition, the argument is made that this represents a possible solution to a future in which automation and artificial intelligence are likely to dominate the workplace. On the other hand, opponents point out the potential work disincentives embedded in such a program.

The United States seriously considered the idea of a guaranteed income in the early 1970s when President Richard Nixon proposed to Congress a variant of this idea. Currently, several countries have been exploring the feasibility of such a policy, most notably Finland and Switzerland. In addition, the idea has been gaining some traction within the progressive wing of the Democratic Party. For example, Democratic candidate Andrew Yang made it the focal point of his 2020 bid for the presidency. Yang proposed giving all U.S. citizens over the age of 18 a guaranteed payment of $1,000 per month, or $12,000 for the year. He argued that such assistance would dramatically cut the rate of poverty.

There have been a number of experiments and trials that have sought to examine the feasibility and effects of a universal basic income. What these studies have generally found is that increasing the amount of income to poverty-stricken families makes a significant difference in the well-being of children and parents. As Jeff Madrick writes, recent research

> . . . *has increasingly shown that low income itself is key, and arguably the major cause of the debilitating outcomes in cognition, emotional stability, and health for poor children. The countless studies reinforcing this claim are an important breakthrough. . . . Now we know that there is growing evidence that universal cash transfers, money itself, can solve or mitigate many problems.*[17]

Consequently, programs that direct additional income to such families see significant gains in the physical and mental well-being of children and adults.

The concept of a child cash allowance is a similar idea.[18] Throughout most European countries, families with children younger than 18 years receive a monthly cash payment. This applies to all children, regardless of their circumstances. The idea behind this policy is that parents with young children are in need of additional economic help in raising their children, and that such assistance also allows parents to spend more time with their children.

Beyond providing a social safety net, it is critical that governments make available easy and affordable access to several key social and public goods. In particular, a quality education, health care, affordable housing, and child care are vital in building and maintaining healthy and productive citizens and families. Each of these deserves a chapter in its own right.

The other OECD countries provide far greater access and coverage to health care, affordable housing, and child care than does the United States (although it is also true that the social welfare states in many of these countries have been under increasing retrenchment pressure).[19] All of them provide some form of national health care. In addition, many provide accessible, affordable, and good-quality child care and subsidized housing. European countries also do not tend to display the wide fluctuations in educational quality that American children are subjected to at the primary and secondary levels.

The result is that these policies have the effect of mitigating the harshness of poverty and economic vulnerability.[20] In addition, there is a belief that there are certain social and public goods that all individuals have a right to, and that making such resources accessible results in more productive citizens and societies in both the short term and the long run. As stated in the European Union Council's communication to the Nice European Council:

> [T]he European social model, with its developed systems of social pro-
> tection, must underpin the transformation to the knowledge economy.
> People are Europe's main asset and should be the focal point of the Union's
> policies. Investing in people and developing an active and dynamic welfare
> state will be crucial both to Europe's place in the knowledge economy and
> for ensuring that the emergence of this new economy does not compound the
> existing social problems of unemployment, social exclusion and poverty.[21]

Providing easy and affordable access to these vital social and public goods is essential to any overall strategy of alleviating poverty.

Building Assets

Social policies are frequently designed to alleviate the current conditions of poverty. Indeed, the strategies of creating work and providing a social safety net are each aimed at improving the current economic conditions of individuals and families. This is understandable, given that poverty affects children and adults in the here and now.

Yet, approaches to poverty alleviation must also pay attention to longer-term processes and solutions. In particular, the accumulation of assets is crucial, both across the individual life course and within the communities in which families reside. The acquisition of such assets allows families to function more effectively and, for our purposes, to reduce their risk of poverty. These assets enable households to ride out periods of economic vulnerability. They also allow for the growth and strengthening of individual and family development. Assets build a stake in the future that income by itself often cannot provide.[22] Unfortunately, the opportunities to acquire such assets have often been in short supply for lower income families.

This has been particularly the case for African Americans. Although the income gap between Whites and Blacks is approximately 1.3 to 1, the wealth gap currently stands at 10 to 1.[23] There has been a long history of denying African Americans the means to building their assets. From the broken promise of "40 acres and a mule," to the continuing practice of redlining and predatory lending, the ability to build wealth and pass it on to the next generation has been extremely difficult for Blacks.[24] This has also been the case for Latinos and Native Americans for many of the same reasons.

Fortunately, there are evolving initiatives designed to increase the asset holdings of these and other low-income households. The rising tide of children's development accounts (CDAs) is one such policy. These accounts are designed to build the savings of children such that they can be used for educational or other expenses when they turn 18 years old. They are generally started with an initial deposit by the government, and then later deposits by parents are frequently matched by state governments. These programs are found in a majority of U.S. states as well as in a number of other countries.[25] An example of a country that has invested heavily in the concept of asset building has been that of Singapore, with its Central Provident Fund (CPF). Introduced in 1955, the CPF is a mandatory pension fund in which its members are able to use their savings for housing, medical expenses, and education.[26]

The idea of economic reparations is another asset-building tool to be considered. As William Darity and Kristen Mullen argue, the case for reparations to U.S. Black descendants of slavery is a strong one.[27] Such a policy would begin to address the historical and ongoing wrongs that have been committed to African American. The monetary reparations might be structured in a way that could be used to build Black Americans' assets, including attaining a higher education, providing a down payment on a home, or starting a small business.

Just as individuals thrive with the acquisition and development of assets, so too do communities. Poor neighborhoods are often characterized by their lack of strong community assets, such as quality schools, decent housing, adequate infrastructure, economic opportunities, and available jobs. These, in turn, affect the life chances of residents in such communities.[28]

Strengthening the major institutions found within lower income communities is vital because they have the power to improve the quality of life, foster the accumulation of human capital, and increase the overall opportunities for community residents. Among such institutions are schools, businesses and industries, lending establishments, community centers, and so on. A wide range of strategies can be used to strengthen these institutions to meet the needs of the community. Creating greater equity in funding across school districts, attracting businesses in lower income communities, and opening up the lending practices of banks and savings and loans to people in economically depressed areas all would provide substantial benefits.[29]

Some of the techniques and policies for arriving at such goals would include community development strategies, grassroots organizing techniques, neighborhood movements such as the rise of community development corporations, and tax incentive policies targeted at businesses that choose to locate in a specified impoverished area. Strengthening the resources and assets of economically vulnerable communities is vital, in conjunction with individual and family asset building, to an overall poverty reduction strategy.

Conclusion

In some ways, finding the solutions to poverty is far easier than finding the political will to engage in such policies. As we have discussed throughout the book, the United States has been steeped in various myths that have encouraged a general apathy toward addressing the problem. These myths have allowed us to remain comfortable despite extremely high rates of poverty. They have reinforced the status quo of widespread poverty and inequality.

Yet, how do we as individuals and as a society begin to change the mythology and resulting lack of urgency? These are difficult but highly pertinent questions. As Dr. Martin Luther King Jr. observed, the arc of the moral universe is long, but it bends toward justice. The question for us to explore is how to begin bending that arc sooner rather than later. We take up these questions in our final chapter.

Creating the Change

A final set of questions for us to explore in this book is how we as a society, and how we as individuals, can create the kinds of social change that will allow us to effectively understand and alleviate poverty. These are questions to which we do not pretend to have the definitive answers. However, what we can provide are some thoughts and suggestions on ways in which we might begin the process of changing both the mindset surrounding poverty and our approach toward addressing poverty.

We should start by noting that during the past 10 years, there has been growing awareness and concern regarding the issue of economic inequality broadly defined. Beginning with the Occupy Wall Street movement in 2011 and 2012, considerable discussion has taken place around the concept of the 1 and 99 percent. This rising tide of inequality discourse has also washed into mainstream political debates across the country. Presidential candidates on the progressive side of the aisle routinely discuss the alarming trend of growing income and wealth inequality in the United States.

The Black Lives Matter movement has cast a further spotlight on racial inequality in the United States, while the Fight for $15 struggle has been garnering support for lifting the wages of fast-food workers. In addition, cities and states around the country have been raising their minimum wages in recognition of the need to assist those in low-paying jobs. All of these changes encouraged Stephen McNamee to write at the end of Chapter 17, "It is relatively new that, in the last few years, Americans have talked about income and wealth inequality. I have been at this for 40 years, and some of us feel like we have been screaming in the wilderness and nobody has been listening. All of the sudden this has become a timely topic."

So, the good news with respect to changing the country's understanding of poverty and inequality is that we have made a solid start in the past 10 years. There is a growing recognition that poverty and inequality are problems rooted at the structural or policy level, rather than solely at the individual level. As such, there is a push to consider more fundamental change in our policy approaches to solving poverty. Nevertheless, there are many miles to go before such a realization becomes a consensus. How might we move further in such a direction?

Raising Awareness and Connections

One key factor to shifting the status quo is for more people to feel a personal connection to the issue of poverty. This has been true for many, if not most, social movements in the past. To take but one example, the rise and growing support of the environmental movement over the past 50 years has been based on the realization that we all have a personal stake in the health and well-being of the planet. Furthermore, we have come to recognize that in one way or another, we all impact and are affected by the environment. It has become painfully clear that each of us has a serious stake in halting both the acceleration of climate change and the degradation of our planet.

Support for other social movements has also hinged on feelings of personal connection and urgency to an issue. That connection may be through one's sense of justice, or through one's sense of self-interest. In either case, individuals generally must feel some connection to a social problem in order to be motivated enough to become involved.

Such is the case with poverty. As we discussed in Chapters 2 and 11, too often the attitude regarding poverty has been, "I don't see how it affects me, so why be concerned?" Yet, as we have hopefully demonstrated throughout this book, poverty is an issue that, in one way or another, affects us all. In addition, more Americans are feeling a sense of economic insecurity, and yet may not be aware of the source of this insecurity. Consequently, there is a need to raise an awareness regarding the connections that each of us have to the issue. How might we accomplish this?

To begin, we should note that given our current political climate and age of "alternative facts" and "fake news," the idea of moving research evidence into the hands of a wider audience has taken on an added importance. There is a growing need to base our understanding of social issues on well-supported and documented research evidence. Yet, too often in higher education we wind up talking only to our fellow academics. This must change. Now, more than ever, there is a need to lift our research into the public arena.

This idea has a long history behind it. For example, the land grant universities were established in 1862 with the mission of translating academic research into practical applications at the state level. The 1914 federal initiative of building cooperative extension networks was designed to further extend the land grant universities' knowledge and research to the broader constituencies of practitioners and nonacademics.

The discipline of sociology in particular has begun to think seriously about this issue. In his 2004 American Sociological Association's Presidential Address, Michael Burawoy called for elevating the visibility of public sociology in the field. He explained the concept and impetus by noting, "We have spent a century building professional knowledge, translating common sense into science, so that now, we are more than ready to embark on a systematic back-translation, taking knowledge back to those from whom it came, making public issues out of private troubles, and thus regenerating sociology's moral fiber. Herein lies the promise and challenge of public sociology."[1]

How might we extend this idea further with respect to poverty? Can we begin to actively awaken our fellow citizens to what sociologist C. Wright Mills described as understanding one's personal troubles within the context of the sociological imagination? That would mean providing the public with the knowledge that the issues and problems facing them often have a societal context and that, rather than individual failure, many of these issues are the result of structural failings. Such knowledge can begin to shift the paradigm from one of status quo to active change. In addition, can we begin to facilitate individuals' understanding of their personal connection to the issue?

One example of an attempt to accomplish this has been the recent development of a poverty risk calculator and website. As discussed in Chapter 2, Mark Rank and Thomas Hirschl have been engaged in a long line of research examining the lifetime risk of experiencing poverty. This has resulted in a substantial body of empirical findings and research. Yet, as Rank describes it, the question was, "How might this research be made accessible to a much larger audience?"[2] What if one could take this body of research and develop a tool that would allow individuals to estimate their own personal risk of poverty in the next 5, 10, or 15 years? The prototypes that immediately came to mind were the heart disease calculators found across the Internet. Based on longitudinal data from the Framingham Heart Study, these calculators allow individuals to input basic health and background information, which is then used to determine their risk of a heart attack in the next 10 years. Why not develop such a tool to predict the risk of poverty?

After literally hundreds of hours of programming and designing, there is now such a tool and website. The website is called "Confronting Poverty: Tools for Understanding Economic Hardship and Risk," and the tool itself is a poverty risk calculator. It represents a radical extension of the concept of public research in several ways. First, the poverty risk calculator allows users to engage first hand with the research. It is one thing to report research findings to a wider audience; it is quite another to enable individuals to use that research to directly inform their own lives. The poverty risk calculator allows individuals to enter their background information on five dimensions (age, race, gender, education, and marital status). Based on that information, they are then given a 5-, 10-, and 15-year probability of experiencing at least 1 year of poverty during these time periods. Individuals can also calculate their odds of experiencing near-poverty (below 150 percent of the official poverty line), poverty (below 100 percent of the poverty line), and extreme poverty (below 50 percent of the poverty line). Placing this research directly into the hands of the wider public can serve as a potentially empowering and enlightening experience.

Second, because the risk of poverty for so many Americans is significant (as we saw in Chapter 2), it allows them to begin to see poverty as both a public and systemic issue. This lies at the heart of what is known as the sociological imagination. The systemic nature of poverty is revealed through the factor of time. Because one is able to display longitudinal data graphically, the risk of poverty becomes apparent. While the probability of poverty may be low during any single year, across multiple years the risk can rise substantially, revealing the prevalent nature of U.S. poverty. Seeing this firsthand allows users to begin to recognize the systemic nature of poverty.

To further assist in this understanding, Rank and Hirschl have developed an accompanying discussion guide that explores various aspects of poverty and inequality. This is designed to raise awareness around the underlying causes and solutions to poverty. It can be used in either a group or individual setting.

Third, the calculator is designed so that individuals can easily compare their profile with other profiles to examine how the risk of poverty varies by different characteristics. The impact of each of these variables is profound, and one can readily see how poverty is affected by, for example, race or gender. This allows individuals to observe in real time the impact that these key sociological dimensions have on life chances.

Finally, the website with its discussion guide and additional research components is designed to encourage individuals to begin to take action toward alleviating poverty. The poverty risk calculator allows people to see into their future. However, that future is not a fait accompli. Individuals can begin to take both personal and collective/political action in order to reduce the extent of poverty in this country. The poverty risk calculator represents a wakeup call. It is a challenge and a warning that we must do better. Poverty is an issue that affects us all, and as such, we each have a responsibility to work toward its reduction. Interacting with the website creates a personal connection with the issue of poverty, which in turn can create the motivation to become a change agent.

To date, the website has received hundreds of thousands of visitors from more than 200 countries around the globe. Its use has also entered into a number of different settings, including high school classrooms, university courses, community and civic agencies, and many more.

This represents but one example of bringing research evidence into the public arena in order to reshape general perceptions to align better with the actual realities rather than the myths of poverty. We might think of many other creative ways in which to bring evidence to bear. For example, social media provides a particularly powerful outlet for getting the word out regarding social issues and problems. The Me Too movement is a prime example of how social media has been used effectively to spread awareness, experiences, and action toward sexual harassment and assault.

Another striking example of the power of social media were the uprisings known as the Arab Spring. A series of protests and rebellions spread across North Africa and the Middle East demanding governmental reforms. The role of social media was crucial to disseminating the news of successful efforts and facilitating the ability of people to organize and stage rallies against these regimes.

The Black Lives Matter movement is yet another example of the power of social media to bring together millions in the United States and around the world to protest and press for action against the police atrocities occurring within the Black population. The posting of the horrific deaths of George Floyd and others has served to galvanize a movement aimed at overturning racial injustice and inequity.

Beyond being active on social media, there are many other ways for us to begin to take action in confronting poverty. For example, we can continue to learn about the dynamics of poverty and share this newfound knowledge with others. We can get involved in our community with those organizations that are assisting low-income families. We can mobilize a group of our friends and acquaintances to begin to consider the ways in which they might stand up to poverty and injustice. We can make our voices heard to legislators and policymakers in our community, state capital, and Washington DC. We can vote.

In short, there are many ways in which each of us can work toward being proactive in creating a positive change. Such change can begin with conversations in our daily lives. The well-known phrase, "Think globally, act locally" epitomizes the idea that when thinking about widespread change, it is helpful to put it into the context of our local environment.

Change Does Occur, Sometimes Quickly

Yet it can often feel as if social change is glacial—that nothing really happens over the course of decades, that the problems of yesterday are the problems of today, and the problems of tomorrow. And, in fact, it is true that significant change often does take a considerable amount of time.

However, it is also true that social and policy change can occur over relatively short periods of time. For example, the mid-1930s saw a dramatic change in the role of the federal government providing long-term economic protections to its citizens. Among the array of programs begun during this time period were the Social Security and Unemployment Insurance Programs. As a result of the catastrophic economic conditions of the Great Depression, President Franklin Roosevelt was able to sign into law many of his New Deal initiatives.

Likewise, during the 1960s, President Johnson was able to legislate many of his Great Society and War on Poverty programs in a very short period of time. These included major civil rights legislation along with the Medicare and Medicaid programs.

We could point to other examples as well. Laying the groundwork for social change often involves years of determination and hard work, but it is also possible to see rapid change over fairly short periods of time given the right conditions.

We feel that it is quite possible we are entering such a time with respect to poverty and inequality. Of course, it is difficult to predict the future, but we see hopeful signs that fundamental change could be on the horizon. As we noted earlier, there is a growing awareness surrounding the issues of inequality and poverty. There is also an increasing sense of injustice with respect to the schism between the haves and have-nots, with the have-nots becoming more plentiful and more vulnerable. These realizations have been brought to the fore through the organizing efforts of many grassroots groups around the country.

In Mark Rank's book, *Chasing the American Dream*, a gathering of rural, upstate New Yorkers were brainstorming about how positive change can come about on a national level. After much discussion, one of the focus group members had the floor:

> *So what do you do that lets you go beyond the local level? And I can't give precise answers to that, but I can give a generic answer. And that is, organization. I think the history of the country and the world show that in any society at anytime there is a struggle between those who want to dominate politically, socially, economically, and control everything. And those who want to live their lives in a broader, comfortable way, but they don't feel the need to own vast amounts. They just want enough. And some call that class struggle. And the only thing that has ever won, the larger numbers of people win against the small group that controls the money and the power has been organization.*
>
> *And Mary made a comment a little while ago, that she'll be dust before we see major social change. And I think that's a mistake. Again, I think if you look at history, what I see is that social change has come very rapidly when it's come. And usually to everyone's surprise. People are always trying to organize, and every once in awhile, something clicks and it all happens. And I can't explain what it's going to take to make it click, all I can say is that you keep trying to organize. But you look at—Jim Crow was around for a hundred years, and it collapsed in about five. The Soviet Union was around for 70 or 80 years and it fell apart in months. And I think there's a very real possibility that things like that can happen. And I don't know when they'll*

happen, or what's going to trigger them, and what's going to make it work.
But when it happens it'll surprise you, and it'll be fast.[3]

This is particularly the case when individuals effectively organize themselves in groups devoted to specific issues of concern. Such groups can be found in a wide array of settings, including local communities, religious congregations, student groups, national organizations, and so on. Many examples exist of grassroots organizations that are working on issues with the potential to increase opportunities at the structural level, including groups focusing on living-wage campaigns, child and health care legislation, affordable housing, and asset-building initiatives.

At the same time, what is needed is a national focus on the issues of poverty and economic inequality. These are topics that underlie and pull together many of the concerns that various groups are attempting to redress. Building coalitions across racial and gender lines, socioeconomic classes, community boundaries, and various interest groups is essential for developing a strong political focus on the problem of poverty. As we have seen throughout this book, poverty is not an issue of *them*, but rather an issue of *us*. It is a problem that will affect all Americans in one way or another. Understanding this and acting politically on such information is critical. As Paul Rogat Loeb observes:

> *The lesson here is not to stop challenging injustices that arise from people's particular identities and backgrounds. But to promote human dignity, we need to build coalitions that are as broad as possible. In addition to the important task of staking out rights for specific marginalized groups, we also need to organize around issues that affect everyone, such as the unprecedented gap between rich and poor, the corrupting influence of unaccountable wealth, the threats to our environment, and the general sense of powerlessness that pervades America today.*[4]

More than 130 years ago, the damaging effects of American poverty were documented in Jacob Riis' landmark 1890 book, *How the Other Half Lives*. Riis detailed in both words and photographs the impoverished conditions of tenement families in an area known as "the Bend" in New York City. He wrote about the difficulty of eliminating the wretched conditions of those living in that neighborhood. There were times when it appeared very little was being accomplished. Yet, as Riis observed regarding such feelings of discouragement:

> *When nothing seems to help, I go and look at a stonecutter hammering away at his rock perhaps a hundred times without as much as a crack showing in it. Yet at the hundred and first blow it will split in two, and I know it was not that blow that did it—but all that had gone before.*[5]

This relates back to what our focus group member was discussing in terms of rapid change occurring after years of the status quo. Often, we may feel as if little is being accomplished, when in fact we have been laying the foundation for a profound shift to occur.

Final Thought

We began this book by noting that there are few subjects with as many myths, stereotypes, and misperceptions surrounding them as poverty in America. Throughout these pages we have sought to set the record straight. We have looked at who actually experiences poverty, why poverty exists, the costs of poverty, what the facts are regarding the social safety net, and the realities of the wider context of inequality in American society.

We encourage you, our readers, to use this information as a valuable tool in creating the kinds of change we have been discussing in this chapter. Diagnosing the scope and cause of a problem is a first step toward addressing that problem. A second step is using that diagnosis to shift the prevailing status quo mentality to one of social action. A third step is building the momentum to leverage a change in how we address the problem.

Ultimately, such change begins with each of us. As Margaret Mead once poignantly remarked, "Never doubt that a small group of committed citizens can change the world. Indeed, it is the only thing that ever has." As we look into the future, let us create a community and a country that are transformed by the knowledge that poverty can and must be eradicated, once and for all.

Further Readings and Resources

Listed here are additional readings and resources to help you explore in greater detail the subject matter of each chapter.

Chapter 2

BOOKS AND ARTICLES

Mark Robert Rank, *One Nation, Underprivileged: Why American Poverty Affects Us All* (New York: Oxford University Press, 2004).

> Examines the characteristics and nature of American poverty, why poverty is a concern for all Americans, and how to create a fundamental change in America in order to address and reduce poverty. Lifetime risk of poverty and welfare use are analyzed in detail.

Mark R. Rank and Thomas A. Hirschl, "The Likelihood of Experiencing Relative Poverty Across the Life Course," *PLOS ONE* 10 (2015): e01333513.

> Analysis of the lifetime risk of experiencing relative poverty during adulthood.

Caroline Ratcliffe, "Child Poverty and Adult Success," Low-Income Working Families Brief (Washington, DC: The Urban Institute, 2015).

> Brief overview of the dynamics of child poverty and its effects on life outcomes.

WEBSITES

Mark Robert Rank and Thomas A. Hirschl, "Confronting Poverty: Tools for Understanding Economic Hardship and Risk" (2021), https://confrontingpoverty.org/.

Website that allows individuals to assess their future risk of poverty through a poverty risk calculator. Also contains information and links to various topics regarding poverty.

U.S. Census Bureau (2021), https://www.census.gov/topics/income-poverty/poverty.html.

U.S. Census Bureau website that measures and estimates the extent of poverty in the United States.

MEDIA

Mark Rank, "A Radically New Understanding of American Poverty and Inequality" (2020).

TED-style talk discussing the logic behind the life course research on poverty.

Chapter 3

BOOKS AND ARTICLES

Cynthia M. Duncan, *Worlds Apart: Poverty and Politics in Rural America* (New Haven, CT: Yale University Press, 2014).

Examines rural poverty in New England, Appalachia, and the Mississippi Delta through in-depth interviews conducted with poor families.

Paul A. Jargowsky, "Concentration of Poverty in the New Millennium: Changes in Prevalence, Composition, and Location of High Poverty Neighborhoods," A Report by The Century Foundation and Rutgers Center for Urban Research and Education (2015).

Analysis and overview of the trends and prevalence of high-poverty neighborhoods using 20 years of Census data. Shows that the majority of individuals in poverty do not live in high-poverty neighborhoods.

Daniel T. Lichter and Kai A. Schafft, "People and Places Left Behind: Rural Poverty in the New Century," in David Brady and Linda M. Burton eds., *The Oxford Handbook of the Social Science of Poverty* (New York: Oxford University Press, 2016), pp. 317–340.

Reviews the key features of contemporary rural poverty, both in the United States and globally.

Elizabeth Kneebone and Alan Berube, *Confronting Suburban Poverty in America* (Washington, DC: Brookings Institution Press, 2013).

Authors examine the rising prevalence of poverty in suburban areas of the United States. Demonstrates that more poor Americans now live in the suburbs than in the city.

Mary Pattillo and John N. Robinson, "Poor Neighborhoods in the Metropolis," in David Brady and Linda M. Burton eds., *The Oxford Handbook of the Social Science of Poverty* (New York: Oxford University Press, 2016), pp. 341–368.

Argues for broadening the scope of neighborhood poverty studies from central cities to entire metropolitan regions.

William Julius Wilson, "Urban Poverty, Race, and Space," in David Brady and Linda M. Burton eds., *The Oxford Handbook of the Social Science of Poverty* (New York: Oxford University Press, 2016), pp. 394–413.

Reviews the political, economic, and cultural forces that have led to high concentrations of poverty in Black inner-city neighborhoods.

WEBSITE

Washington Post Residential Mapping Program (2018) https://www.washingtonpost.com/graphics/2018/national/segregation-us-cities/.

Interactive program from the *Washington Post* for mapping residential segregation across the United States.

MEDIA

Pulitzer Center, "Geography of Poverty: A Journey Through Forgotten America" (2015).

A photographic look at the experience of poverty across different regions of the United States.

Chapter 4

BOOKS AND ARTICLES

Stephanie Riegg Cellini, Signe-Mary McKernan, and Caroline Ratcliffe, "The Dynamics of Poverty in the United States: A Review of Data, Methods and Findings," *Journal of Policy Analysis and Management* 27 (2008): 577–605.

Review of the empirical literature with respect to the likelihood of individuals experiencing poverty, the length of poverty spells, and the events associated with entering and exiting poverty.

Shelley K. Irving and Tracy A. Loveless, "Dynamics of Economic Well-Being: Participation in Government Programs, 2009–2012: Who Gets Assistance?" U.S. Census Bureau (2015) (https://www.census.gov/content/dam/Census/library/publications/2015/demo/p70-141.pdf).

Complementing the poverty spell research, this analysis examines welfare spells in the major means-tested programs in the United States.

Mark R. Rank, "Alleviating Poverty," in Mark Robert Rank ed., *Towards a Livable Life: A 21st Century Agenda for Social Work* (New York: Oxford University Press, 2020).

Explores the dynamics and patterns of poverty.

Daniel A. Sandoval, Mark R. Rank, and Thomas A. Hirschl, "The Increasing Risk of Poverty Across the American Life Course," *Demography* 46 (2009): 717–737.

Uses a life course analysis to show that the long-term risk of poverty has been rising since the 1970s.

MEDIA

On the Media, "Busted: America's Poverty Myths" (2017).

On the Media and WNYC audio series on the myths and realities of American poverty.

Chapter 5

BOOKS AND ARTICLES

Martin Gilens, *Why Americans Hate Welfare: Race, Media, and the Politics of Antipoverty Policy* (Chicago: University of Chicago Press, 1999).

Argues that Americans' negative views about welfare are largely shaped by media representations of welfare recipients as Black and undeserving.

Steven M. Gillon, *Separate and Unequal: The Kerner Commission and the Unraveling of American Liberalism* (New York: Basic Books, 2018).

Historical analysis of the politics behind the writing of the Kerner Commission report, and its powerful conclusion that "Our nation is moving toward two societies, one black and one white—separate and unequal."

Arlie Russell Hochschild, *Strangers in Their Own Land: Anger and Mourning on the American Right* (New York: The New Press, 2016).

Provides an understanding into the mindset of conservative working-class residents of the Louisiana bayou country. Insightful analysis through interviews and participant observation.

Felicia Kornbluh and Gwendolyn Mink, *Ensuring Poverty: Welfare Reform in Feminist Perspective* (Philadelphia: University of Pennsylvania Press, 2019).

This book approaches poverty and welfare policies through a feminist lens, offering insight into why female-headed households with children experience high rates of poverty. Importantly, the authors highlight efforts by social justice feminists to reduce poverty and promote equality for mothers, particularly mothers of color.

Bas W. Van Doorn, "Pre- and Post-Welfare Reform Media Portrayals of Poverty in the United States: The Continuing Importance of Race and Ethnicity," *Politics & Policy* 43 (2015): 142–162.

Analyzes racial and ethnic patterns in media coverage of poverty in the United States, specifically focusing on African Americans and Hispanics.

Rachel Wetts and Robb Willer, "Privilege on the Precipice: Perceived Racial Status Threats Lead White Americans to Oppose Welfare," *Social Forces* 97 (2018): 793–822.

Focuses on the role of perceived threats to racial standing in shaping Whites' views of welfare policy.

WEBSITE

General Social Survey Data Explorer (2021), https://gssdataexplorer.norc.org/.

Allows for the graphing by various demographic characteristics a range of attitudinal questions over the past five decades. In particular, one can plot attitudinal data on whether federal spending on poverty and welfare programs is too high or too low, along with whether more should be spent addressing issues related to race.

Chapter 6

BOOKS AND ARTICLES

Jennie E. Brand, "The Far-Reaching Impact of Job Loss and Unemployment," *Annual Review of Sociology* 41 (2015): 359–375.

Details the various negative consequences on individuals and families resulting from job loss and unemployment.

Lawrence M. Eppard, Mark Robert Rank, and Heather E. Bullock, *Rugged Individualism and the Misunderstanding of American Inequality* (Bethlehem, PA: Lehigh University Press, 2020).

Using various sources of data, this book looks at how the ideology of rugged individualism shapes the way that inequality is understood within the American context.

Amy Goldstein, *Janesville: An American Story* (New York: Simon and Schuster, 2017).

Powerful case study of what happens to workers when the main industry in a town closes its factory doors.

Arne L. Kalleberg, *Good Jobs, Bad Jobs: The Rise of Polarized and Precarious Employment Systems in the United States, 1970s to 2000s* (New York: Russell Sage Foundation, 2011).

Discusses the changing nature of the labor market, including the rise of low-paying jobs.

Lawrence Mishel, Josh Bivens, Elise Gould, and Heidi Shierholz, *The State of Working America* (12th ed.) (Ithaca, NY: Cornell University Press, 2012).

This book is an essential resource for data on jobs, wages, income and wealth inequality, poverty, and intergenerational mobility in the United States. Includes survey results of low-wage workers in the United States. Demonstrates that the working poor have a strong work ethic and believe that hard work is rewarded.

David K. Shipler, *The Working Poor: Invisible in America* (New York: Knopf, 2004).

Journalistic accounting into the lives and problems of approximately 20 low-income workers from around the country. Based on these interviews, Shipler argues that poverty is a complex combination of structural problems and individual bad choices.

WEBSITE

Bureau of Labor Statistics (2021), https://www.bls.gov/.

Allows one to explore the latest data on employment, underemployment, and unemployment. Also contains a variety of useful data tools.

MEDIA

Roger Weisberg, "Waging a Living: Working Overtime in Pursuit of the Elusive American Dream" (2005), https://www.youtube.com/watch?v=OXHzJVY1nOU.

Point of View documentary film that explore the working lives of four different individuals. Poignantly reveals the struggles and fortitude of those trying to survive and work themselves out of poverty.

Oxfam America, "Hard Work, Hard Lives: Survey Exposes Harsh Reality Faced by Low-Wage Workers in the US" (2014), https://www.oxfamamerica.org/static/media/files/low-wage-worker-report-oxfam-america.pdf.

Report based on a national survey that found "America's working poor have a strong work ethic, put in long hours, and believe that hard work can pay off."

Chapter 7

BOOKS AND ARTICLES

David Brady, "Theories and the Causes of Poverty," *Annual Review of Sociology* 45 (2019): 155–175.

> Concise review of various perspectives that have been used to understand poverty, including behavioral, structural, and political theories.

Mark Robert Rank, *Rethinking American Poverty: A Theory of Structural Vulnerability* (New York: Oxford University Press, forthcoming).

> Develops an approach for understanding poverty known as structural vulnerability.

Mark R. Rank, "Rethinking American Poverty," *Contexts* 10 (2011): 16–21.

> Accessible short article presenting the musical chairs analogy as a tool for understanding poverty.

Eric Olin Wright, "A Class Analysis of Poverty." In *Interrogating Inequality: Essays on Class Analysis, Socialism and Marxism* (London: Verso, 1994), pp. 32–50.

> Argues for the importance of a class analysis in understanding poverty; that is, there are specific groups of privilege that have a strong material interest in maintaining poverty.

WEBSITES

Stanford Center on Poverty and Inequality (2021), https://inequality.stanford.edu/.

> Website that provides many resources dealing with the causes of poverty and inequality.

Institute for Research on Poverty, University of Wisconsin (2021), https://www.irp.wisc.edu/.

> Website that contains a variety of research focusing on poverty and inequality.

Chapter 8

BOOKS AND ARTICLES

David Brady, Ryan M. Finnegan, and Sabine Hübgen, "Rethinking the Risks of Poverty: A Framework for Analyzing Prevalences and Penalties," *American Journal of Sociology* 123 (2017): 740–786.

> In this article, the authors analyze the prevalence of single motherhood, young headship, unemployment, and low educational attainment across wealthy countries. They

confirm that the United States is actually below average on these characteristics compared with other wealthy countries, supporting the notion that they are a poor explanation for high poverty in the United States—rather, it is the way countries penalize these characteristics that matters for poverty.

Kathryn Edin, Maria J. Kefalas, and Joanna Reed, "A Peek Inside the Black Box: What Marriage Means for Poor Unmarried Parents," *Journal of Marriage and Family* 66 (2004): 1007–1014.

> Provides an important qualitative exploration into the choices available to poor American parents, and the crucial ways in which their precarity impacts their decisions about marriage.

Laurie C. Maldonado and Rense Nieuwenhuis, "Single-Parent Family Poverty in 24 OECD Countries: A Focus on Market and Redistribution Strategies" (2015), https://osf.io/preprints/socarxiv/w9htc/.

> An excellent analysis of pretax/pretransfer and post-tax/post-transfer single-parent poverty rates among wealthy countries. It demonstrates that while pretax/pretransfer poverty may be somewhat unavoidable, even in wealthy countries, post-tax/post-transfer poverty can be quite low if governments commit themselves to achieving this through effective policy.

Frank Schilback, Heather Schofield, and Dendhil Mullainathan, "The Psychological Lives of the Poor," *American Economic Review* 106 (2016): 435–440.

> Discusses the idea of poverty limiting an individual's ability to use what the authors refer to as bandwidth. The result is impaired decision-making.

Bruce Western and Becky Petit, "Incarceration and Social Inequality," *Daedalus* 139 (2010): 8–19.

> The authors provide an excellent explanation of the connection between race, education, and incarceration rates in the United States, including the way that this relationship has changed over time.

MEDIA

The Line (2012), https://www.youtube.com/watch?v=zZxjb4gB93A.

> Documentary film that explores the human dimensions of poverty, including the fact that decision-making is much more constrained and difficult for those in poverty.

Chapter 9

BOOKS AND ARTICLES

Alberto Alesina and Edward L. Glaeser, *Fighting Poverty in the US and Europe: A World of Difference* (New York: Oxford University Press, 2004).

Comparison of the differing approaches taken in the United States and Europe to addressing poverty. Details why such differences exists, and what the consequences are.

Martha J. Bailey and Sheldon Danziger eds., *Legacies of the War on Poverty* (New York: Russell Sage Publications, 2013).

Edited book providing a detailed examination of both the successes and failures of the War on Poverty.

Robert Haveman, Rebecca Blank, Timothy Smeeding, and G. Wallace, "The War on Poverty: Measurement, Trends, and Policy," *Journal of Policy Analysis and Management* 34 (2015): 593–638.

Examines the impact of antipoverty programs over a 50-year period. Demonstrates that such programs have reduced poverty, particularly for elderly, disabled, and Black individuals.

Alice O'Connor, *Poverty Knowledge: Social Science, Social Policy, and the Poor in Twentieth-Century U.S. History* (Princeton, NJ: Princeton University Press, 2001).

Argues that poverty research over the past 100 years in the United States has shifted from an understanding of the structural causes of poverty to an overemphasis on individual behavior and personal characteristics as the reasons for poverty.

U.S. Census Bureau, "The Supplemental Poverty Measure: 2019," P60-272 (Washington, DC: U.S. Government Printing Office, 2020).

Provides an analysis of how much poverty is reduced as a result of various government programs such as Social Security or the Earned Income Tax Credit.

MEDIA

Yes! Solutions Journalism, "Poverty Is Not Inevitable: What We Can Do Now to Turn Things Around" (2014).

Article discussing many ways in which to reduce poverty.

Chapter 10

BOOKS AND ARTICLES

David Brady, *Rich Democracies, Poor People: How Politics Explain Poverty* (New York: Oxford University Press, 2009).

The author demonstrates that the extent of poverty across countries is largely the result of variations in social policies and programs. Countries with lower rates of poverty do so through a more proactive social welfare state.

Matthew Desmond, *Evicted: Poverty and Profit in the American City* (New York: Penguin Random House, 2016).

Pulitzer Prize–winning book that follows eight families in Milwaukee struggling to survive in poverty and maintain their homes.

Francesco Duina, *Broke and Patriotic: Why Poor Americans Love Their Country* (Stanford, CA: Stanford University Press, 2018).

Explores the puzzle of why those in poverty display high levels of patriotism. In-depth interviews reveal that those in poverty reflect mainstream values.

Lane Kenworthy, *Social Democratic Capitalism* (New York: Oxford University Press, 2020).

Examines the impact of the social welfare state on a variety of outcome measures including poverty and inequality.

Jonathan Morduch and Rachel Schneider, *The Financial Diaries: How American Families Cope in a World of Uncertainty* (Princeton, NJ: Princeton University Press, 2017).

Innovative study that follows 235 low- and middle-income families through their financial diaries over the course of a year.

WEBSITE

Amy K. Glasmeier, "MIT Living Wage Calculator" (2021), http://livingwage.mit.edu/.

Groundbreaking website that allows users to estimate how much income is needed in order to achieve a living wage across all regions of the United States. Analysis can be broken down to the state, county, and metropolitan level.

MEDIA

BBC, *Poor America*, Panorama Documentary (2012).

Short documentary produced by the BBC looking at the dire circumstance of poverty in America.

Chapter 11

BOOKS AND ARTICLES

Gary W. Evans, "The Environment of Childhood Poverty," *American Psychologist* 59 (2004): 77–92.

> A thorough and succinct review of the various environmental inequities experienced by children in poverty. These include family unrest, air and water pollution, neighborhood violence, and inadequate schools.

Linda Giannarelli, Kye Lippold, Sarah Minton, and Laura Wheaton, "Reducing Child Poverty in the US: Costs and Impacts of Policies Proposed by the Children's Defense Fund," Urban Institute Research Report (January 2015).

> Analyzes the cost of reducing childhood poverty through various social policies proposed by the Children's Defense Fund. Concludes that childhood poverty could be reduced by approximately 60 percent at an overall federal cost of $77 billion.

Harry J. Holzer, Diane Whitmore Schanzenbach, Greg J. Duncan, and Jens Ludwig, "The Economic Costs of Childhood Poverty in the United States," *Journal of Children and Poverty* 14 (2008): 41–61.

> The authors estimate that the overall annual cost of childhood poverty in the United States is approximately $500 billion, or nearly 4 percent of GDP. This is caused by poverty resulting in reduced worker productivity, greater health care expenditures, and higher rates of crime.

Jeff Madrick, *Invisible Americans: The Tragic Cost of Child Poverty* (New York: Alfred A. Knopf, 2020).

> Examines the various costs of childhood poverty. Argues for a universal cash allowance as an effective way of reducing poverty.

Michael McLaughlin and Mark R. Rank, "Estimating the Economic Cost of Childhood Poverty in the United States," *Social Work Research* 42 (2018): 73–82.

> Calculates the overall economic cost of childhood poverty in the United States. Various costs are calculated, including lower economic productivity, criminal justice costs, and increased health care expenditures.

MEDIA

Unnatural Causes: Is Inequality Making Us Sick? California Newsreel (2008).

> Seven part series that explores the negative health impacts of inequality and poverty on individuals, families, and communities.

Chapter 12

BOOKS AND ARTICLES

Matthew Desmond and Bruce Western, "Poverty in America: New Directions and Debates," *Annual Review of Sociology* 44 (2018): 305–318.

> Reviews the field of poverty studies, with a section discussing the relationship between poverty and justice.

Herbert J. Gans, *The War Against the Poor: The Underclass and Antipoverty Policy* (New York: Basic Books, 1995).

> Explores the various reasons behind why the myth of the undeserving poor persists.

Hugh H. Heclo, "Values Underpinning Poverty Programs for Children," *The Future of Children* 7 (1997):141–148.

> Examines the public attitudes toward children, poverty, and government. Argues that Americans believe helping children in economic need is a top policy priority, but that there is also a strong emphasis placed on the importance of parents fulfilling their responsibility to their children through hard work and effort.

Michael B. Katz, *The Undeserving Poor: America's Enduring Confrontation With Poverty* (New York: Oxford University Press, 2013).

> Groundbreaking book exploring the dynamic of the undeserving versus the deserving poor across American history.

National Conference of Catholic Bishops, *Economic Justice for All: Pastoral Letter on Catholic Social Teaching and the U.S. Economy* (Washington, DC: United States Catholic Conference, 1986).

> Official statement by the Catholic Church regarding the moral imperative to address issues of poverty and economic justice. Combines social science research with theological understandings.

Mark R. Rank, "Why Poverty and Inequality Undermine Justice in America" in Michael Reisch ed., *Routledge International Handbook of Social Justice* (New York: Routledge Press, 2014), pp. 436–447.

> Analysis of how justice is defined in American society, and why poverty and inequality undermine this conception of justice.

Cass R. Sunstein, *The Second Bill of Rights: FDR's Unfinished Revolution and Why We Need It More Than Ever* (New York: Basic Books, 2004).

> Examines and analyzes President Roosevelt's introduction of a second bill of rights in his State of the Union address in 1944. Introduced the idea that freedom from want should be considered a basic human right. Although the second bill of rights was never instituted in the United States, it had a major influence on the development of the Universal Declaration of Human Rights, finalized in 1948.

MEDIA

Frontline, *Poor Kids* (2017).

> Documentary film examining hunger among America's children. In-depth exploration of the struggles of several children in poverty.

Dan Ariely, TED Talk (2015).

> Psychologist Dan Ariely provides insights into the psychological perceptions of inequality.

Chapter 13

BOOKS AND ARTICLES

Kathryn J. Edin and H. Luke Shaefer, *$2.00 a Day: Living on Almost Nothing in America* (Boston: Houghton Mifflin Harcourt, 2015).

> This award winning book powerfully documents the growing number of U.S. families who live on less than $2.00 a day in four sites across the United States: Chicago, Illinois; Cleveland, Ohio, Johnson City, Tennessee; and rural towns in the Mississippi Delta. Weaving together interviews with poor families and larger demographic trends (e.g., wage erosion, weak safety net programs), the authors powerfully show how low-income individuals and families struggle to make ends meet.

Christopher Howard, *The Hidden Welfare State: Tax Expenditures and Social Policy in the United States* (Princeton, NJ: Princeton University Press, 1999).

> Classic analysis of the range of tax expenditures and benefits that largely aid the middle and upper classes.

Suzanne Mettler, *The Government-Citizen Disconnect* (New York, NY: Russell Sage Foundation, 2018).

This book examines Americans' complex relationship with the federal government. Although many U.S. residents benefit from social programs, there is also deep suspicion of and dislike for the federal government. In this compelling book, Mettler explores the consequences of these paradoxical beliefs.

Monica Prasad, *Starving the Beast: Ronald Reagan and the Tax Cut Revolution* (New York: Russell Sage Foundation 2018).

Provides a historical analysis behind the conservative emphasis on tax cuts and a minimal welfare state.

Joe Soss, Richard C. Fording, and Sanford F. Schram, *Disciplining the Poor: Neoliberal Paternalism and the Persistent Power of Race* (Chicago, IL: University of Chicago, 2011).

This insightful book examines the functions of antipoverty programs, arguing that "poverty governance" is about controlling and disciplining people experiencing poverty rather than ending poverty, per se. Throughout their analysis, they consider the impact of race on U.S. welfare policies.

WEBSITE

OECD data website (2021), https://data.oecd.org/inequality/poverty-gap.htm.

Extremely valuable interactive website that allows users to examine how approximately 37 OECD countries differ with respect to various measures of poverty and inequality.

MEDIA

The Economist, "Why Is There Still Poverty in America?" (2019). https://www.youtube.com/watch?v=5i45h76ioHY

Short video that explores poverty in the United States and the lack of a strong safety net.

Chapter 14

BOOKS AND ARTICLES

Jason DeParle, *American Dream: Three Women, Ten Kids, and a Nation's Drive to End Welfare* (New York: Viking, 2004).

Insightful accounting of three women, their family history, and their encounters with the welfare system and the changes resulting from the 1996 passage of welfare reform.

Sharon Hays, *Flat Broke With Children: Women in the Age of Welfare Reform* (New York: Oxford University Press, 2003).

Qualitative analysis that examines how welfare recipients have fared following the passage of welfare reform changes in 1996.

Josh Levin, *The Queen: The Forgotten Life Behind an American Myth* (New York: Little, Brown and Company, 2019).

Explores the real life of Linda Taylor who came to represent the epitome of the stereotypical welfare queen.

Robert A. Mofitt, "The Deserving Poor, the Family, and the US Welfare System," *Demography* 52 (2015): 729–749.

Analysis of what has happened since the 1960s to welfare spending. Argues that it has shifted from single parent families with children to elderly people and those with disabilities.

Mark Robert Rank, *Living on the Edge: The Realities of Welfare in America* (New York: Columbia University Press, 1994).

Quantitative and qualitative analysis of various aspects of living on welfare. Argues that welfare recipients largely reflect mainstream American attitudes and values, and that recipients are often receiving welfare on a short-term basis as a result of job loss, family disruption, or medical problems.

MEDIA

DW Documentary, "How Poor People Survive in the USA" (2019).

German public broadcast documentary on the struggles of trying to survive in poverty in the United States. Illustrates how difficult it is to get by on the safety net.

Chapter 15

BOOKS AND ARTICLES

Sasha Abramsky, *The American Way of Poverty: How the Other Half Still Lives* (New York: Nation Books, 2013).

Intended as a 50-year follow-up to Michael Harrington's classic book, *The Other America*. Looks at contemporary poverty from the perspective of injustice rather than individual blame. Second half of book provides a range of policy strategies that can reduce poverty.

Lawrence M. Eppard, Noam Chomsky, Mark Robert Rank, and David Brady, "On Culture, Politics, and Poverty," *Contexts* 16 (2017): 8–11.

This article contains an engaging conversation between prominent social thinkers about the political and cultural forces responsible for the significant variation in economic deprivation across wealthy countries.

Lane Kenworthy, *Social Democratic America* (New York: Oxford University Press, 2014).

Argues for a much more robust safety net and social programs than are currently found in the United States. Uses comparative data to make the case that such policies can be effective in reducing poverty.

Laura Lein, Sandra K. Danziger, H. Luke Shaefer, and Amanda Tillotson, "Social Policy, Transfers, Programs, and Assistance," in David Brady and Linda M. Burton eds., *The Oxford Handbook of the Social Science of Poverty* (New York: Oxford University Press, 2016), pp. 733–750.

Reviews the key features of cash transfer programs, public provision on child and medical care, and public housing programs.

WEBSITE

Luxembourg Income Study homepage (2021), https://www.lisdatacenter.org/.

Contains a variety of working papers addressing the impact that government programs have on reducing poverty across a wide range of OECD countries.

Chapter 16

BOOKS AND ARTICLES

Raj Chetty, David Grusky, Maximillian Hell, Nathaniel Hendren, Robert Manduca, and Jimmy Narang, "The Fading American Dream: Trends in Absolute Income Mobility Since 1940," *Science* 356 (2017): 398–406.

Groundbreaking article that empirically demonstrates with big data the difficulties of more recent birth cohorts to attain an income greater than their parents.

Marie Connoly, Miles Corak, and Catherine Haeck, "Intergenerational Mobility Between and Within Canada and the United States," NBER Working Paper Series, Working Paper 25735 (Cambridge, MA: National Bureau of Economic Research, 2019).

Compares Canada with the United States in terms of the amount and patterns of intergenerational income mobility.

Thomas A. DiPrete, "The Impact of Inequality on Intergenerational Mobility," *Annual Review of Sociology* 46 (2020): 1–29.

> Reviews the impact that economic inequality has on both relative and absolute intergenerational mobility.

Federal Reserve Bank of St. Louis and the Board of Governors of the Federal Reserve System, *Economic Mobility: Research and Ideas on Strengthening Families, Communities, and the Economy* (St. Louis: Federal Reserve Bank of St. Louis, 2017).

> Edited book exploring various aspects of inequality and economic mobility in the United States. Includes chapters on income, wealth, and educational mobility.

Mark R. Rank, "Reducing Cumulative Inequality," in Mark Robert Rank ed., *Toward a Livable Life: A 21st Century Agenda for Social Work* (New York: Oxford University Press, 2020).

> Details the process of cumulative advantage and disadvantage across the life course. Author argues that this process undermines the core American value of equality of opportunity.

Mark Robert Rank, Thomas A. Hirschl, and Kirk A. Foster, *Chasing the American Dream: Understanding What Shapes Our Fortunes* (New York: Oxford University Press, 2014).

> Looks at what is meant by the American dream, the pathways taken to achieve it, the barriers that lie in the way, and what can be done to reshape American society such that everyone is able to live a fulfilling life.

Richard V. Reeves, *Dream Hoarders: How the American Upper Middle Class Is Leaving Everyone Else in the Dust, Why That is a Problem, and What to Do About It* (Washington, DC: Brookings Institution Press, 2017).

> Argues that the top 20 percent of the income distribution has seen virtually all of the economic gains over the past 30 years, and that as a result, America has become much more stratified by class.

WEBSITE

Opportunity Atlas website (2021), https://www.opportunityatlas.org/.

> Interactive website that allows users to examine how much intergenerational economic mobility exists at the Census tract level. Looks at the impact of parents' socioeconomic status, the neighborhood one was raised in, race, and gender on children's earnings as adults.

Chapter 17

BOOKS AND ARTICLES

Heather Bullock, *Women and Poverty: Psychology, Public Policy, and Social Justice* (Malden, MA: Wiley Blackwell, 2013).

> Bullock's interdisciplinary analysis explores the social and structural factors that contribute to and legitimize inequalities, with a specific focus on women's poverty, as well as possible policy solutions.

Thurston Domina, Andrew Penner, and Emily Penner, "Categorical Inequality: Schools as Sorting Machines," *Annual Review of Sociology* 43 (2017): 311–330.

> Reviews the research demonstrating that schools sort students into unequal categories, which then result in later life inequalities.

Stephen J. McNamee, *The Meritocracy Myth* (4th ed.) (Lanham, MD: Rowman & Littlefield, 2018).

> Provides an excellent overview of the problems with meritocratic beliefs. McNamee explores the equally important nonmerit factors that help to transmit social inequality across generations, including parental resources (economic, cultural, and social), education, racism and sexism, and just plain luck, among others.

Robert D. Putnam, *Our Kids: The American Dream in Crisis* (New York: Simon & Schuster, 2015).

> Explores the growing opportunity gap between American children from different social class backgrounds in our age of inequality, and the impact that this is having on the declining availability of the American dream.

Tavis Smiley and Cornel West, *The Rich and the Rest of Us: A Poverty Manifesto* (New York: SmileyBooks, 2012).

> Smiley and West argue that the time has come to address the civil rights struggle of this century—growing inequality and dwindling opportunity in the United States. The authors argue that anything less than an approach that focuses on systemic causes and solutions will be inadequate.

Joseph E. Stiglitz, *The Great Divide: Unequal Societies and What We Can Do About Them* (New York: W. W. Norton, 2015).

> In this book, Stiglitz explains that we do not need to be defeatist in the face of growing inequality and declining opportunity. Better policies can indeed restore the American dream for millions and produce a healthier economy, more egalitarian society, and fairer democracy.

WEBSITES

Income Calculator (2018), https://www.pewresearch.org/fact-tank/2018/09/06/are-you-in-the-american-middle-class/.

> This calculator allows users to identify which income tier they are in, compared with both the people in their own metropolitan area and with the entire U.S. population. Additionally, it allows users to compare themselves to people who are similar to them in terms of age, education, marital status, and race/ethnicity.

Life Expectancy Map (2018), https://qz.com/1462111/map-what-story-does-your-neighborhoods-life-expectancy-tell/.

> Interactive map from Quartz, utilizing Centers for Disease Control and Prevention (CDC) data, lets users explore the manner in which life expectancy varies from neighborhood to neighborhood in the United States. Additionally, users can compare a particular neighborhood's life expectancy to that of the county, state, and country.

EPA's Environmental Justice Screening and Mapping Tool (2019), https://ejscreen.epa.gov/mapper/.

> This interactive tool from the U.S. Environmental Protection Agency (EPA) allows users to identify the degree of exposure to environmental burdens experienced by Americans living in different areas of the country. This tool also allows users to map demographic characteristics side by side with these burdens, clearly illustrating which social groups face the highest and lowest risks.

Chapter 18

BOOKS AND ARTICLES

Anne Case and Angus Deaton, *Deaths of Despair and the Future of Capitalism* (Princeton, NJ: Princeton University Press, 2020).

> Looks at the relationship between the rise of deaths of despair over the past 20 years (suicide, drug overdose, and alcoholism) and the collapse of economic opportunities in the United States.

Raj Chetty, Nathaniel Hendren, Patrick Kline, and Emmanuel Saez, "Where Is the Land of Opportunity? The Geography of Intergenerational Mobility in the United States," NBER Working Paper Series, Working Paper 19843 (Cambridge, MA: National Bureau of Economic Research, 2014), https://www.nber.org/papers/w19843.

> Using administrative records of more than 40 million children and their parents, the authors were able to identify the crucial role that segregation, inequality, low school quality, low social capital, and family instability play in constraining upward mobility

in many areas of the United States. This is one of the most important studies of social inequality conducted in recent decades.

Miles Corak, "Inequality from Generation to Generation: The United States in Comparison," IZA Discussion Paper No. 9929 (2016), http://ftp.iza.org/dp9929.pdf.

In this paper, Corak compares intergenerational mobility in the United States to other wealthy countries, with a particular focus on Canada. Corak's "Great Gatsby Curve" is included in this paper.

Martin Daly, *Killing the Competition: Economic Inequality and Homicide* (New York: Routledge, 2016).

This book explores the best predictor of homicide rates: income inequality. It also explores the likely cause of this relationship: the fact that growing inequality increases competitive interactions between men.

Richard Wilkinson and Kate Pickett, *The Spirit Level: Why Greater Equality Makes Societies Stronger* (New York: Bloomsbury Press, 2010).

Wilkinson and Pickett demonstrate how a wide variety of social phenomena—including child well-being, imprisonment, mental health, obesity, social mobility, teenage birth rates, and trust—are strongly correlated with income inequality across countries. The book also goes beyond identifying the problems with income inequality, offering ways to promote more equal societies as well.

WEBSITE

World Inequality Database (2021), https://wid.world/country/usa/.

This website is an invaluable tool allowing users to examine the changes over time in income and wealth inequality across a number of countries, as well as to compare inequality between countries.

MEDIA

Robert Reich, "Inequality for All" (2013). https://www.youtube.com/watch?v=YCbAyk8aRxI

Documentary exploring the growing inequality in the United States and the negative impacts on the American economy, workforce, population, and democracy. Economist Robert Reich leads the way throughout, making the complex information assessable through his personable approach, humor, easy-to-understand explanations, and real-world examples.

Richard Wilkinson, "How Economic Inequality Harms Societies," TED Talk (2011). https://www.ted.com/talks/richard_wilkinson_how_economic_inequality_harms_societies

TED Talk by epidemiologist Richard Wilkinson presenting data on how economic inequality detrimentally impacts societies.

Chapter 19

Frances Fox Piven and Lorraine C. Minnite, "Poor People's Politics," in David Brady and Linda M. Burton eds., *The Oxford Handbook of the Social Science of Poverty* (New York: Oxford University Press, 2016), pp. 751–773.

Discusses the role of political action by those in poverty to influence public policy.

Herbert Gans, "The Benefits of Poverty," *Challenge* 55 (2012): 114–125.

Argues poverty exists because it serves a number of intended and unintended benefits for society as a whole, and particularly for those in the upper classes.

Lawrence E. Mitchell, *Stacked Deck: A Story of Selfishness in America* (Philadelphia, PA: Temple University Press, 1998).

Explores how individualism and selfishness result in the status quo of high poverty and inequality being maintained.

Alice O'Conner, "Poverty Knowledge and the History of Poverty Research," in David Brady and Linda M. Burton eds., *The Oxford Handbook of the Social Science of Poverty* (New York: Oxford University Press, 2016), pp. 169–192.

Presents the case that poverty research in recent times has reinforced the overall mainstream ideology in America. The result has been a noticeable lack of challenge and confrontation to the status quo of widespread poverty.

WEBSITE

Poverty Next Door (2021), https://blogs.msn.com/povertynextdoor/.

Project developed by Microsoft News and Spotlight on Poverty and Opportunity to confront the stereotypes and misconceptions surrounding who experiences poverty in the United States.

Chapter 20

Maria Cancian and Daniel R. Meyer, "Reforming Policy for Single-Parent Families to Reduce Child Poverty," *Russell Sage Foundation Journal of the Social Sciences* 4 (2018): 91–112.

Argues for the importance of child support as a key strategy in reducing poverty among single-parent families. Proposes a revamping of the child support system, including a public guarantee of a minimum amount of support per child.

William A. Darity and A. Kirsten Mullen, *From Here to Equality: Reparations for Black Americans in the Twenty-First Century* (Chapel Hill, NC: University of North Carolina Press, 2020).

Focuses on the importance of economic reparations for U.S. descendants of slavery. Given the historical patterns of slavery, discrimination, and inequality, such a policy is essential for beginning to build the assets of Black Americans.

National Academies of Sciences, Engineering, and Medicine, *A Roadmap to Reducing Child Poverty* (Washington, DC: National Academies Press, 2019).

Looks at the linkages between child poverty and child well-being, demonstrating the significant negative effects. Develops a set of policy and program recommendations to cut child poverty in half within 10 years.

Mark Robert Rank, *Toward a Livable Life: A 21st Century Agenda for Social Work* (New York: Oxford University Press, 2020).

Edited book that looks at a variety of challenges facing society in the future and details a range of solutions to these problems.

Mark Robert Rank, *Confronting Poverty: Understanding Economic Hardship in the United States* (Thousand Oaks, CA: Sage Publications, 2021).

Explores the patterns, dynamics, and consequences of poverty, and details a variety of anti-poverty programs.

H. Luke Schaefer, Sophie Collyer, Greg Duncan, Kathryn Edin, Irwin Garfinkel, David Harris, Timothy M. Smeeding, Jane Waldfogel, Christopher Wimer, and Hirokazu Yoshikawa, "A Universal Child Allowance: A Plan to Reduce Poverty and Income Instability Among Children in the United States," *The Russell Sage Foundation Journal of the Social Sciences* 4 (2018): 22–42.

Estimates that the introduction of a universal child allowance could reduce childhood poverty in the United States by approximately 40 percent.

MEDIA

Sebastian Johnson, "The Case for Basic Income" (2017). https://www.youtube.com/watch?v=H3YbZs-tu-I

TEDx Talk on the idea behind a guaranteed income by Sebastian Johnson.

{ NOTES }

Chapter 1

1. Mark Robert Rank, Thomas A. Hirschl, and Kirk A. Foster, *Chasing the American Dream: Understanding What Shapes Our Fortunes* (New York: Oxford University Press, 2014).

2. David Brady and Markus Jantti, "Economic Performance, Poverty, and Inequality in Rich Countries," in David Brady and Linda M. Burton eds., *The Oxford Handbook of the Social Sciences of Poverty* (New York: Oxford University Press, 2016), pp. 555–573.

3. U.S. Census Bureau, *Income and Poverty in the United States: 2019* (Report Number P60-270) (Washington DC: U.S. Government Printing Office, 2020).

4. Timothy Smeeding, "Poverty Measurement," in David Brady and Linda M. Burton eds., *The Oxford Handbook of the Social Sciences of Poverty* (New York: Oxford University Press, 2016), pp. 21–46.

5. Stephen P. Jenkins and Philippe Van Kerm, "The Measurement of Economic Inequality," in Wiemer Salverda, Brian Nolan, and Timothy M. Smeeding eds., *The Oxford Handbook of Economic Inequality* (New York: Oxford University Press, 2009), pp. 40–67.

6. James B. Davies, "Wealth and Economic Inequality," in Wiemer Salverda, Brian Nolan, and Timothy M. Smeeding eds., *The Oxford Handbook of Economic Inequality* (New York: Oxford University Press, 2009), pp. 127–149.

7. Sharon Hays, *Flat Broke With Children: Women in the Age of Welfare Reform* (New York: Oxford University Press, 2003); H. Luke Shaefer, Kathryn Edin, Vince Fusaro, and Pingui Wu, "The Decline of Cash Assistance and the Well-Being of Poor Households and Children," *Social Forces* 98 (2020): 1000–1025.

8. Andrea Brandolini and Timothy M. Smeeding, "Income Inequality in Richer and OECD Countries," in Wiemer Salverda, Brian Nolan, and Timothy M. Smeeding eds., *The Oxford Handbook of Economic Inequality* (New York: Oxford University Press, 2009), pp. 71–100.

9. Jenkins and Van Kerm 2009.

10. Miles Corak, "Chasing the Same Dream, Climbing Different Ladders: Economic Mobility in the United States and Canada" (Economic Mobility Project, the Pew Charitable Trusts, 2010); Miles Corak, "Inequality from Generation to Generation: The United States in Comparison" (Unpublished paper, Graduate School of Public and International Affairs, University of Ottawa, 2011); Marie Connoly, Miles Corak, and Catherine Haeck, "Intergenerational Mobility Between and Within Canada and the United States" NBER Working Paper Series, Working Paper 25735 (Cambridge, MA: National Bureau of Economic Research, 2019).

Chapter 2

1. Matthew O. Hunt and Heather E. Bullock, "Ideologies and Beliefs About Poverty," in David Brady and Linda M. Burton eds., *The Oxford Handbook of the Social Sciences of Poverty* (New York: Oxford University Press, 2016), pp. 93–116.

2. Alice O'Connor, *Poverty Knowledge: Social Science, Social Policy, and the Poor in Twentieth-Century U.S. History* (Princeton, NJ: Princeton University Press, 2001); Alice O'Connor, "Poverty Knowledge and the History of Poverty Research," in David Brady and Linda M. Burton eds., *The Oxford Handbook of the Social Sciences of Poverty* (New York: Oxford University Press, 2016), pp. 169–192.

3. Fabian T. Pfeffer, Paula Fomby, and Noura Insolera, "The Longitudinal Revolution: Sociological Research at the 50-Year Milestone of the Panel Study of Income Dynamics," *Annual Review of Sociology* 46 (2020): 1–26.

4. Mark Robert Rank, *One Nation, Underprivileged: Why American Poverty Affects Us All* (New York: Oxford University Press, 2004).

5. Mark R. Rank and Thomas A. Hirschl, "The Likelihood of Experiencing Relative Poverty Across the Life Course," *PLoS One* 10 (2015): E01333513.

6. Mark Robert Rank, Thomas A. Hirschl, and Kirk A. Foster, *Chasing the American Dream: Understanding What Shapes Our Fortunes* (New York: Oxford University Press, 2014).

7. Mark R. Rank, "Alleviating Poverty," in Mark Robert Rank ed., *Towards a Livable Life: A 21st Century Agenda for Social Work* (New York: Oxford University Press, 2020), pp. 45–69.

8. Mark R. Rank and Thomas A. Hirschl, "The Economic Risk of Childhood in America," *Journal of Marriage and the Family* 61 (1999): 1058–1067.

9. Mark R. Rank and Thomas A. Hirschl, "Estimating the Proportion of Americans Ever Experiencing Poverty During Their Elderly Years," *Journal of Gerontology: Social Sciences* 54B (1999): S184–S193.

10. Hunt and Bullock 2016.

11. Martin Gilens, *Why Americans Hate Welfare: Race, Media, and the Politics of Antipoverty Policy* (Chicago: University of Chicago Press, 1999), pp. 2–3.

12. Josh Levin, *The Queen: The Forgotten Life Behind an American Myth* (New York: Little, Brown and Company, 2019).

13. Rank 2020.

14. Mark R. Rank and Thomas A. Hirschl, "Estimating the Risk of Food Stamp Use and Impoverishment During Childhood," *Archives of Pediatrics and Adolescent Medicine* 163 (2009): 994–999.

15. John Rawls, *A Theory of Justice* (Cambridge, MA: Harvard University Press, 1971).

16. C. Wright Mills, *The Sociological Imagination* (New York: Oxford University Press, 1959), p. 9.

Chapter 3

1. Josh Levin, *The Queen: The Forgotten Life Behind an American Myth* (New York: Little Brown and Company, 2019); Jill Quadagno, *The Color of Welfare: How Racism Undermined the War on Poverty* (New York: Oxford University Press, 1994).

2. Paul A. Jargowsky, "Concentration of Poverty in the New Millennium: Changes in Prevalence, Composition, and Location of High Poverty Neighborhoods," A Report by the

Century Foundation and Rutgers Center for Urban Research and Education (2013), p. 15. https://production-tcf.imgix.net/app/uploads/2013/12/18013623/Concentration_of_Poverty_in_the_New_Millennium-9.pdf

3. Douglas S. Massey, "Segregation and the Perpetuation of Disadvantage," in David Brady and Linda M. Burton eds., *The Oxford Handbook of the Social Sciences of Poverty* (New York: Oxford University Press, 2016), pp. 369–393; Sean F. Reardon and Kendra Bischoff, "Income Inequality and Income Segregation," *American Journal of Sociology* 116 (2011): 1092–1153.

4. William Julius Wilson, *The Truly Disadvantaged: The Inner City, the Underclass, and Public Policy* (Chicago: University of Chicago Press, 1989); William Julius Wilson, *More Than Just Race: Being Black and Poor in the Inner City* (New York: W. W. Norton, 2009).

5. U.S. Census Bureau, *Geography Program, Glossary, 2019.* https://www.census.gov/programs-surveys/geography/about/glossary.html

6. U.S. Census Bureau 2020.

7. Jargowsky 2013.

8. Jargowsky 2013, pp. 11–13.

9. Katrin B. Anacker, *The New American Suburb: Poverty, Race and the Economic Crisis* (Burlington, VT: Ashgate Publishing, 2015); Karyn Lacy, ' The New Sociology of Suburbs: A Research Agenda for Analysis of Emerging Trends," *Annual Review of Sociology* 42 (2016): 369–384.

10. Elizabeth Kneebone and Alan Berube, *Confronting Suburban Poverty in America* (Washington, DC: Brookings Institution Press, 2013).

11. Kneebone and Berube 2013, p. 3.

12. Lauren Gurley, "Who's Afraid of Rural Poverty? The Story Behind America's Invisible Poor," *American Journal of Economics and Sociology* 75 (2016): 589–604.

13. Daniel T. Lichter and Kai A. Schafft, "People and Places Left Behind: Rural Poverty in the New Century," in David Brady and Linda M. Burton eds., *The Oxford Handbook of the Social Sciences of Poverty* (New York: Oxford University Press, 2016), pp. 317–340.

14. Cynthia M. Duncan, *Worlds Apart: Poverty and Politics in Rural America* (New Haven, CT: Yale University Press, 2014).

15. Linda Labao, Minyu Zhou, Mark Partridge, and Michael Betz, "Poverty, Place, and Coal Employment Across Appalachia and the United States in a New Economic Era," *Rural Sociology* 81 (2016): 343–386.

16. Cynthia M. Duncan, "Persistent Poverty in Appalachia: Scarce Work and Rigid Stratification," in Cynthia M. Duncan ed., *Rural Poverty in America* (New York: Auburn House, 1992), p. 120.

17. Angela Hattery and Earl Smith, "Social Stratification in the New/Old South: The Influences of Racial Segregation and Social Class in the Deep South," *Journal of Poverty* 11 (2007): 55–81; Heather O'Connell, Katherine J. Curtis, and Jack DeWaard, "Population Change and the Persistence of the Legacy of Slavery," Paper presented at the Rural Poverty Research Conference, March 21–22, 2018, Washington, DC.

18. Joan Moore and Raquel Pinderhughes, *In the Barrios: Latinos and the Underclass Debate* (New York: Russell Sage Foundation, 1993); Joan B. Anderson, "The U.S.–Mexico Border: A Half Century of Change," *Social Science Journal* 40 (2003): 535–554.

19. U.S. Census Bureau, "American Indian and Alaska Native Heritage Month: November 2019," Profile America Fact for Features, CB19-FF.11; James J. Davis,

Vincent J. Roscigno, and George Wilson, "American Indian Poverty in the Contemporary United States," *Sociological Forum* 31 (2015) 138–148; Whitney K. Mauer, "Indian Country Poverty: Place-Based Poverty on American Indian Territories, 2006–10," *Rural Sociology* 82 (2016): 473–498.

20. Philip Martin, Michale Fix, and J. Edward Taylor, *The New Rural Poverty: Agriculture and Immigration in California* (Washington, DC: The Urban Institute Press, 2006).

21. Lichter and Schafft 2016.

22. Vanessa Fabbre, Eleni Gaveras, Anna Shabsin, Janelle Gibson, and Mark R. Rank, "Confronting Stigma, Discrimination, and Social Exclusion," in Mark Robert Rank ed., *Towards a Livable Life: A 21st Century Agenda for Social Work* (New York: Oxford University Press, 2020), pp. 70–93.

Chapter 4

1. Ruby K. Payne, *A Framework for Understanding Poverty—A Cognitive Approach* (6th ed.) (New York: aha! Process, 2019).

2. Fabian T. Pfeffer, Paula Fomby, and Noura Insolera, "The Longitudinal Revolution: Sociological Research at the 50-Year Milestone of the Panel Study of Income Dynamics," *Annual Review of Sociology* 46 (2020): 1–26.

3. Ann Huff Stevens, "Climbing Out of Poverty, Falling Back In: Measuring the Persistence of Poverty Over Multiple Spells," *Journal of Human Resources* 34 (1999), p. 568.

4. Mary Jo Bane and David T. Ellwood, "Slipping Into and Out of Poverty: The Dynamics of Spells," *Journal of Human Resources* 21 (1986), p. 12.

5. U.S. Census Bureau, *Dynamics of Economic Well-Being: Poverty 2009–2011*, Current Population Reports, P70-137 (Washington, DC: U.S. Government Printing Office, 2014).

6. See Stephanie Riegg Cellini, Signe-Mary McKernan, Caroline Ratcliffe, "The Dynamics of Poverty in the United States: A Review of Data, Methods, and Findings," *Journal of Policy Analysis and Management* 27 (2008): 577–605; Ann Huff Stevens, "The Dynamics of Poverty Spells: Updating Bane and Ellwood," *American Economic Review* 84 (1994): 34–37; Ann Huff Stevens, "Climbing Out of Poverty, Falling Back in: Measuring the Persistence of Poverty Over Multiple Spells," *Journal of Human Resources* 34 (1999): 557–588; Signe-Mary McKernan, Caroline Ratcliffe, and Stephanie R. Cellini, "Transitioning in and Out of Poverty," The Urban Institute, September 2009; Ann Huff Stevens, "Transitions Into and Out of Poverty in the United States," UC-Davis Center for Poverty Research, https://poverty. ucdavis.edu/policy-brief/transitions-out-poverty-united-states.

7. Cellini et al. 2008; Stevens 1994, 1999; McKernan et al. 2009. See also Stevens, https:// poverty.ucdavis.edu/policy-brief/transitions-out-poverty-united-states.

8. Bane and Ellwood, 1986, p. 12.

9. Bane and Ellwood, 1986, p. 11.

10. Cellini et al. 2008; Stevens 1994, 1999; McKernan et al. 2009. See also Stevens, https:// poverty.ucdavis.edu/policy-brief/transitions-out-poverty-united-states.

11. Shelley K. Irving and Tracy A. Loveless, *Dynamics of Economic Well-Being: Participation in Government Programs, 2009–2012: Who Gets Assistance?* Current Population Reports, P70-141 (Washington, DC: U.S. Census Bureau, 2015).

12. Irving and Loveless 2015.

13. U.S. Department of Health and Human Services, "Welfare Indicators and Risk Factors: Thirteenth Report to Congress," pp. II-25–II-30. https://aspe.hhs.gov/report/welfare-indicators-and-risk-factors-thirteenth-report-congress

14. Mark R. Rank, Hong-Sik Yoon, and Thomas A. Hirschl, "American Poverty as a Structural Failing: Evidence and Arguments," *Journal of Sociology and Social Welfare* 30 (December 2003), p. 20.

15. Mark Robert Rank, Thomas A. Hirschl, and Kirk A. Foster, *Chasing the American Dream: Understanding What Shapes Our Fortunes* (New York: Oxford University Press, 2014), p. 37.

16. Rank, Hirschl, and Foster 2014, p. 37.

17. Rank, Hirschl, and Foster 2014, p. 37.

18. Rank, Hirschl, and Foster 2014, p. 38.

19. Rank, Hirschl, and Foster 2014, p. 37.

20. Federal Reserve Bank, "Report on the Economic Well-Being of U.S. Households in 2019" (Washington DC: Board of Governors of the Federal Reserve System, 2020).

21. Laurie C. Maldonado and Rense Nieuwenhuis, "Single-Parent Family Poverty in 24 OECD Countries: A Focus on Market and Redistribution Strategies" (Luxembourg Income Study Research Brief, 2015).

22. David Brady, Ryan M. Finnegan, and Sabine Hübgen, "Rethinking the Risks of Poverty: A Framework for Analyzing Prevalences and Penalties," *American Journal of Sociology* 123 (November 2017), p. 753.

23. For 25-64 year olds, latest data available (2015 for Finland, 2016 for United States). See OECD.Stat, https://stats.oecd.org/.

24. For 25–64 year-olds. See OECD.Stat, https://stats.oecd.org/.

25. Based on relative poverty measures reported by the OECD for 25- to 64-year-olds. Belgium reports a 6 percent poverty rate for high school graduates compared with 26 percent reported in the United States. See OECD.Stat, https://stats.oecd.org/.

Chapter 5

1. Thomas M. Shapiro, *Toxic Inequality: How America's Wealth Gap Destroys Mobility, Deepens the Racial Divide, and Threatens Our Future* (New York: Basic Books, 2017).

2. Ryan Sit, "Trump Thinks Only Black People Are on Welfare, but Really, White Americans Receive the Most Benefits," *Newsweek* (January 12, 2018).

3. U.S. Department of Agriculture, *Characteristics of Supplemental Nutrition Assistance Program Households: Fiscal Year 2017* (February 26, 2019).

4. Kaiser Family Foundation, *Distribution of Nonelderly with Medicaid by Race/Ethnicity.* https://www.kff.org/medicaid/state-indicator/distribution-by-raceethnicity-4/?currentTimefr ame=0&sortModel=%7B%22colId%22:%22Location%22,%22sort%22:%22asc%22%7D

5. U.S. Department of Health and Human Services, *Characteristics and Financial Circumstances of TANF Recipients: Fiscal Year (FY) 2018* (August 26, 2019).

6. Travis L. Dixon, "A Dangerous Distortion of Our Families: Representations of Families, by Race in News and Opinion Media," *Family Story and Color of Change* (December 2017). https://colorofchange.org/dangerousdistortion/

7. Dixon 2017.

8. Martin Gilens, "Race and Poverty in America: Public Misperceptions and the American News Media," *Public Opinion Quarterly* 60 (1996): 515–541.

9. Bas W. van Doorn, "Pre- and Post-Welfare Reform Media Portrayals of Poverty in the United States: The Continuing Importance of Race and Ethnicity," *Politics & Policy* 43 (2015): 142–162.

10. Maura Kelly, "Regulating the Reproduction and Mothering of Poor Women: The Controlling Image of the Welfare Mother in Television News Coverage of Welfare Reform," *Journal of Poverty* 14 (2010): 76–96.

11. van Doorn 2015.

12. Gilens 1996, p. 521.

13. Gilens 1996; van Doorn 2015.

14. Gilens 1996.

15. Christopher Howard, Amirio Freeman, April Wilson, and Eboni Brown, "The Polls—Trends: Poverty," *Public Opinion Quarterly* 81 (2017): 769–789; Gilens 1996.

16. Howard, Freeman, Wilson, and Brown 2017.

17. Howard, Freeman, Wilson, and Brown 2017.

18. Arthur Delaney and A. Edwards-Levy, *Americans Are Mistaken About Who Gets Welfare* (February 5, 2018). https://www.huffpost.com/entry/americans-welfare-perceptions-survey_n_5a7880cde4b0d3df1d13f60b

19. Franklin D. Gilliam, "The 'Welfare Queen' Experiment," *Nieman Reports* (Summer 1999).

20. Jazmin L. Brown-Iannuzzi, Ron Dotsch, Erin Cooley, and B. Keith Payne. "The Relationship between Mental Representations of Welfare Recipients and Attitudes toward Welfare," *Psychological Science* 28 (2017): 92–103.

21. Brown-Iannuzzi, Dotsch, Cooley, and Payne 2017.

22. Rachel Wetts and Robb Willer, "Privilege on the Precipice: Perceived Racial Status Threats Lead White Americans to Oppose Welfare," *Social Forces* 97 (2018): 793–822.

23. Alberto Alesina and Edward L. Glaeser, *Fighting Poverty in the US and Europe: A World of Difference* (New York: Oxford University Press, 2004), p. 218.

24. Alesina and Glaeser 2004.

25. Robert Dalleck, *Lone Star Rising: Lyndon Johnson and His Time, 1908–1960* (New York: Oxford University Press, 1991), p. 584.

Chapter 6

1. Lawrence Eppard, Mark Robert Rank, and Heather E. Bullock, *Rugged Individualism and the Misunderstanding of American Inequality* (Bethlehem, PA: Lehigh University Press, 2020).

2. Shari Davidai, "Why Do Americans Believe in Economic Mobility? Economic Inequality, External Attributions of Wealth and Poverty, and the Belief in Economic Mobility," *Journal of Experimental Psychology* 79 (2018): 138–148.

3. Mark Robert Rank, *One Nation, Underprivileged: Why American Poverty Affects Us All* (New York: Oxford University Press, 2004).

4. Mark Robert Rank, Thomas A. Hirschl, and Kirk A. Foster, *Chasing the American Dream: Understanding What Shapes Our Fortunes* (New York: Oxford University Press, 2014).

5. Rank, Hirschl, and Foster 2014, p. 103.

6. Rank, Hirschl, and Foster 2014, p. 104.

7. Elliot Liebow, *Tally's Corner: A Study of Negro Streetcorner Men* (Boston: Little, Brown, 1967), p. 63.

8. Rank, Hirschl, and Foster 2014.

9. Martin Ross and Nicole Bateman, "Meeting the Low-Wage Workforce," Metropolitan Policy Program at Brookings, Brookings Institution, November 2019.

10. U.S. Bureau of Labor Statistics, "Employment Situation Summary—September 2020," https://www.bls.gov/news.release/empsit.nr0.htm

11. Elise Gould, "Poor People Work: A Majority of Poor People Who Can Work Do," Economic Policy Institute, Economic Snapshot, May 19, 2015.

12. Jerome Gautie and Sophie Ponthieux, "Employment and the Working Poor," in David Brady and Linda M. Burton eds., *The Oxford Handbook of the Social Sciences of Poverty* (New York: Oxford University Press, 2016), pp. 486–504.

13. Rank, Hirschl, and Foster 2014.

14. Mark R. Rank, "Why Poverty and Inequality Undermine Justice in America," in Michael Reisch ed., *Routledge International Handbook of Social Justice* (New York: Routledge Press, 2014), pp. 436–447.

15. Michael Harrington, *The Other America: Poverty in the United States* (Baltimore, MD: Random House, 1963), p. 23.

Chapter 7

1. Teresa Sommer et al., "A Two-Generation Human Capital Approach to Antipoverty Policy," *Russell Sage Foundation Journal of the Social Sciences*, 4 (2018): 118–143.

2. Gary S. Becker, *Human Capital: A Theoretical and Empirical Analysis, With Special Reference to Education* (Chicago: University of Chicago Press, 1994).

3. David B. Bills, Valentina Di Stasio, and Klarita Gerxhani, "The Demand Side of Hiring: Employers in the Labor Market," *Annual Review of Sociology*, 43 (2017): 291–310.

4. Lynn A. Karoly, "Investing in the Future: Reducing Poverty Through Human Capital Investments," in Sheldon H. Danziger and Robert H. Haveman eds., *Understanding Poverty* (New York: Russell Sage Foundation, 2001), pp. 314–356.

5. U.S. Census Bureau, *Income and Poverty in the United States: 2018* (Report Number P60-266) (Washington DC: U.S. Government Printing Office, 2019).

6. U.S. Census Bureau 2019.

7. Arne L. Kalleberg, *Good Jobs, Bad Jobs: The Rise of Polarized and Precarious Employment Systems in the United States, 1970s to 2000s* (New York: Russell Sage Foundation, 2011).

8. Martha Ross and Nicole Bateman, "Meeting the Low-Wage Workforce," Metropolitan Policy Programs at Brookings, Brookings Institution, November 2019.

9. Federal Reserve Bank of St. Louis, FRED Economic Research (2020).

10. U.S. Bureau of Labor Statistics, "Work Experience of the Population (Annual) News Release" (December 14, 2018). https://www.bls.gov/news.release/archives/work_12142018.htm

11. Lane Kenworthy, *Social Democratic Capitalism* (New York: Oxford University Press, 2020).

12. Mark Robert Rank, *One Nation, Underprivileged: Why American Poverty Affects Us All* (New York: Oxford University Press, 2004).

13. Rank 2004.

14. Bradley R. Schiller, *The Economics of Poverty and Discrimination* (Upper Saddle River, NJ: Prentice Hall, 2008); John Iceland, *Poverty in America: A Handbook* (Berkeley, CA: University of California Press, 2013).

15. David Brady, Agnes Blome, and Hanna Kleider, "How Politics and Institutions Shape Poverty and Inequality," in David Brady and Linda M. Burton eds., *The Oxford Handbook of the Social Sciences of Poverty* (New York: Oxford University Press, 2016); Kenworthy 2020, pp. 117–140; Laura Tach and Kathryn Edin, "The Social Safety Net After Welfare Reform: Recent Developments and Consequences for Household Dynamics," *Annual Review of Sociology* 43 (2017): 541–561.

16. Mark R. Rank and James Herbert Williams, "A Life Course Approach to Understanding Poverty Among Older American Adults," *Families in Society*, 91 (2010): 337–341.

17. Janet C. Gornick and Natascia Boeri, "Gender and Poverty," in David Brady and Linda M. Burton eds, *The Oxford Handbook of the Social Sciences of Poverty* (New York: Oxford University Press, 2016), pp. 221–256; H. Luke Shaefer, Kathryn Edin, Vince Fusaro, and Pingui Wu, "The Decline of Cash Assistance and the Well-Being of Poor Households With Children," *Social Forces* 98 (2020): 1000–1025.

18. Alberto Alesina and Edward L. Glaeser, *Fighting Poverty in the US and Europe: A World of Difference* (New York: Oxford University Press, 2004); Xixia Cai and Timothy Smeeding, "Deep and Extreme Poverty in Rich and Poor Nations: Lesson From Atkinson for the Fight Against Child Poverty" (LIS Working Paper Series, No. 780, 2019). https://ideas.repec.org/p/lis/liswps/780.html

19. Richard Easterlin, *Birth and Fortune: The Impact of Numbers on Personal Welfare* (Chicago: University of Chicago Press, 1987).

20. Patrick Sharkey, *Stuck in Place: Urban Neighborhoods and the End of Progress Toward Racial Equality* (Chicago: University of Chicago Press, 2013); Fredrik Andersson, John C. Haltiwanger, Mark J. Kutzbach, Henryo Pollackoski, and Daniel H. Weinberg, "Job Displacement and the Duration of Joblessness: The Role of Spatial Mismatch," *Review of Economics and Statistics* 100 (2018): 203–218.

21. Thomas J. Cottle, *Hardest Times: The Trauma of Long Term Unemployment* (Westport, CT: Praeger, 2001), p. 216.

22. Mark Robert Rank, Thomas A. Hirschl, and Kirk A. Foster, *Chasing the American Dream: Understanding What Shapes Our Fortunes* (New York: Oxford University Press, 2014), p. 69.

Chapter 8

1. Isabel V. Sawhill, "The Behavioral Aspects of Poverty," *Public Interest* 153 (2003): 79–93, p. 83.

2. Sawhill 2003.

3. Matthew Desmond, "Americans Want to Believe Jobs Are the Solution to Poverty. They're Not," *New York Times* (September 11, 2018). Desmond notes that, "A 2013 study by the sociologist Ofer Sharone found that unemployed workers in the United States blame themselves, while unemployed workers in Israel blame the hiring system."

4. Elise Gould, "Poor People Work: A Majority of Poor People Who Can Work Do" (Washington, DC: Economic Policy Institute, May 19, 2015).

5. Jordan Weissman, "Why the Poor Don't Work, According to the Poor," *Atlantic* (September 23, 2013).

6. Jay Shambaugh, Lauren Bauer, and Audrey Breitwieser, "Who Is Poor in the United States? A Hamilton Project Annual Report" (Washington, DC: The Brookings Institution, October 12, 2017). https://www.brookings.edu/research/who-is-poor-in-the-united-states-a-hamilton-project-annual-report/

7. Arne L. Kalleberg, *Good Jobs, Bad Jobs: The Rise of Polarized and Precarious Employment Systems in the United States, 1970s to 2000s* (New York: Russell Sage Foundation, 2011).

8. Timothy M. Smeeding, Lee Rainwater, and Gary Burtless, "U.S. Poverty in a Cross-National Context," in S. H. Danziger and R. H. Haveman eds., *Understanding Poverty* (Cambridge, MA: Harvard University Press, 2001), pp. 162–189.

9. Kathryn Edin, Maria J. Kefalas, and Joanna Reed, "A Peek Inside the Black Box: What Marriage Means for Poor Unmarried Parents," *Journal of Marriage and Family* 66 (2004): 1014.

10. Olga Khazan, "The Luxury of Waiting for Marriage to Have Kids," *Atlantic* (June 17, 2014).

11. Khazan 2014.

12. Lawrence Mishel, Josh Bivens, Elise Gould, and Heidi Shierholz, *The State of Working America* (12th ed.) (Ithaca, NY: Cornell University Press, 2012). See also Ariel J. Binder and John Bound, "The Declining Labor Market Prospects of Less-Educated Men," NBER Working Paper Series, Working Paper 25577 (Cambridge, MA: National Bureau of Economic Research, February 2019).

13. Sandra Black, Jason Furman, Emma Rackstraw, and Nirupama Rao, "The Long-Term Decline in U.S. Prime-Age Male Labour Force Participation," *VOX CEPR Policy Portal* (July 2016). See also Adam Harris, "Where Have All the Men Without College Degrees Gone?" *Atlantic* (March 9, 2019).

14. "Economically insecure" is defined as below the 150% poverty threshold. Analysis was conducted using the IPUMS online data analysis tool: https://usa.ipums.org/usa/sda/.

15. Bruce Western and Becky Petit, "Incarceration and Social Inequality," *Daedalus* 139 (2010): 8–19.

16. See Pamela J. Smock, Wendy D. Manning, and Meredith Porter, "Everything's There Except Money: How Money Shapes Decisions to Marry Among Cohabitors," *Journal of Marriage and Family* 67 (2005): 680–696. See also Kathryn Edin, Maria J. Kefalas, and Joanna Reed, "A Peek Inside the Black Box: What Marriage Means for Poor Unmarried Parents," *Journal of Marriage and Family* 66 (2004): 1007–1014.

17. Ariel J. Binder and John Bound, "The Declining Labor Market Prospects of Less-Educated Men," NBER Working Paper Series, Working Paper 25377 (Cambridge, MA: National Bureau of Economic Research, February 2019), p. 46.

18. Elizabeth Wildsmith, Jennifer Manlove, and Elizabeth Cook, "Dramatic Increase in the Proportion of Births Outside of Marriage in the United States from 1990 to 2016," *Child Trends* (August 8, 2018).

19. Mark R. Rank, "Fertility Among Women on Welfare: Incidence and Determinants," *American Sociological Review* 54 (1989): 296–304.

20. Scott Myers-Lipton, *Social Solutions to Poverty: America's Struggle to Build a Just Society* (Boulder, CO: Paradigm Publishers, 2006), p. 243.

21. National Academies of Sciences, Engineering, and Medicine, *A Roadmap to Reducing Child Poverty* (Washington, DC: National Academies Press, 2019).

22. Frank Schilback, Heather Schofield, and Sendhil Mullainathan, "The Psychological Lives of the Poor," *American Economic Review* 106 (2016): 435–440, p. 435.

23. Schilback, Schofield, and Mullainathan 2016, p. 438.

Chapter 9

1. *Harper Collins Study Bible* (New York: HarperCollins Publishers, 1989).

2. C-Span, *Joint Session of Congress* (January 25, 1988).

3. Monica Prasad, *Starving the Beast: Ronald Reagan and the Tax Cut Revolution* (New York: Russell Sage Foundation, 2018).

4. Charles Murray, *Losing Ground: American Social Policy 1950–1980* (New York: Basic Books, 1984); Lawrence Mead, *Beyond Entitlement: The Social Obligations of Citizenship* (New York: Free Press, 1986).

5. Alexis de Tocqueville, "Momoir on Pauperism," *Public Interest* 70 (1983): 102–120.

6. *Harper Collins Study Bible*, 1989.

7. Lyndon B. Johnson, "President Lyndon B. Johnson's Annual Message to the Congress on the State of the Union, January 8, 1964," Public Papers of the Presidents of the United States: Lyndon B. Johnson, 1965, Volume I (Washington, DC: U.S. Government Printing Office, 1965), entry 27, pp. 71–74.

8. Martha J. Bailey and Sheldon Danziger, *Legacies of the War on Poverty* (New York: Russell Sage Publications, 2013).

9. Alice O'Connor, "Poverty Knowledge and the History of Poverty Research," in David Brady and Linda M. Burton eds., *The Oxford Handbook of the Social Sciences of Poverty* (New York: Oxford University Press, 2016), pp. 169–192.

10. O'Connor 2016; Bailey and Danziger 2013.

11. U.S. Census Bureau, *Income and Poverty in the United States: 2018* (Report Number P60-266) (Washington DC: U.S. Government Printing Office, 2019).

12. Michael B. Katz, *The Undeserving Poor: America's Enduring Confrontation with Poverty* (New York: Oxford University Press, 2013).

13. Katz 2013.

14. Katz 2013.

15. Kathleen Romig, "Social Security Lifts More Americans Above Poverty Than Any Other Program" (Washington, DC: Center on Budget and Policy Priorities, 2018).

16. U.S. Census Bureau 2019.

17. Lauri C. Maldonado, "Single-Parent Family Poverty in 24 OECD Countries: A Focus on Market and Redistribution Strategies," LIS Center Research Brief (October 19, 2015).

18. David Brady, Ryan M. Finnigan, and Sabine Hubgen, "Rethinking the Risks of Poverty: A Framework for Analyzing Prevalences and Penalties," *American Journal of Sociology* 123 (2017): 740–786.

19. Tan Weiping, "Chinese Approach to the Eradication of Poverty: Taking Targeted Measures to Lift People Out of Poverty" A Speech at the Expert Panel on the Implementation of the Third UN Decade for the Eradication of Poverty (2018–2027); Tan Weiping, Deputy Director-General, IPRCC (Addis Ababa, April 18, 2018).

20. World Poverty Clock, "Venezuela: South America's Poverty Outlier" (2019). https://worlddata.io/blog/venezuela-south-america-poverty-outlier

Chapter 10

1. Rachel Sheffield and Robert Rector, "Air Conditioning, Cable TV, and an Xbox: What Is Poverty in the United States Today?" (Backgrounder Executive Summary, no. 2575, The Heritage Foundation, 2011), p. 14.

2. See also Robert Rector and Jamie Hall, "How Poor, Really, Are America's Poor?" *Daily Signal* (March 5, 2020).

3. U.S. Census Bureau, *Income and Poverty in the United States: 2019* (Report Number P60-270) (Washington DC: U.S. Government Printing Office, 2020).

4. U.S. Census Bureau 2020.

5. Amy K. Glasmeier, "MIT Living Wage Calculator Website" (2020) http://livingwage.mit.edu/.

6. U.S. Census Bureau 2020.

7. "Americans Say Family of Four Needs Nearly $60K to 'Get By,'" *Gallup Poll* (2013).

8. U.S. Census Bureau 2020.

9. U.S. Census Bureau 2020.

10. Howard Glennerster, "United States Poverty Studies and Poverty Measurement: The Past Twenty-Five Years," *Social Service Review* (2002): 83–107, p. 90.

11. United Nations Development Programme, Human Development Reports, "Illuminating Inequalities" (2019). http://hdr.undp.org/sites/default/files/mpi_2019_publication.pdf

12. Weimer Salverda, Brian Nolan, and Timothy M. Smeeding, *The Oxford Handbook of Economic Inequality* (New York: Oxford University Press, 2009).

13. Xixia Cai and Timothy Smeeding, "Deep and Extreme Poverty in Rich and Poor Nations: Lessons From Atkinson for the Fight Against Child Poverty" (LIS Working Paper Series, No. 780, 2019); Lane Kenworthy, *Social Democratic Capitalism* (New York: Oxford University Press, 2019).

14. OECD data website, https://data.oecd.org/inequality/poverty-gap.htm.

15. OECD data website, https://data.oecd.org/inequality/poverty-gap.htm.

16. Carlotta Balestra and Richard Tonkin, "Inequalities in Household Wealth Across OECD Countries: Evidence From the OECD Wealth Distribution Database," (OECD Statistics Working Papers, 2018/01); Pasquale Tridico, "The Determinants of Income Inequality in OECD Countries," *Cambridge Journal of Economics* 42 (2018): 1009–1042.

17. Cai and Smeeding 2019, p. 19.

18. Stephanie Riegg Cellini, Signe-Mary McKernan, and Caroline Ratcliffe, "The Dynamics of Poverty in the United States: A Review of Data, Methods and Findings," *Journal of Policy Analysis and Management* (2008): 577–605.

19. David K. Shipler, *The Working Poor: Invisible in America* (New York: Alfred A. Knopf, 2004).

20. Mark Robert Rank, Thomas A Hirschl, and Kirk A. Foster, *Chasing the American Dream: Understanding What Shapes Our Fortunes* (New York: Oxford University Press, 2014), p. 44.

21. Amartya Sen, *Development as Freedom* (New York: Alfred A. Knopf, 1999).

22. Emily Underwood, "Can Disparities Be Deadly?" *Science* 344 (2014): 829–831.

23. Richard Wilkinson and Kate Pickett, *The Spirit Level: Why Greater Equality Makes Societies Stronger* (New York: Bloomsbury Press, 2010); Leonard Beeghley, *The Structure of Social Stratification in the United States* (New York: Routledge, 2007).

24. Wilkinson and Pickett 2010; Mark Robert Rank, *Confronting Poverty: A Primer for Understanding Economic Hardship in the United States* (Thousand Oaks, CA: Sage Publications, 2021).

25. Vanessa D. Fabbre, Eleni Gaveras, Anna Goldfarb Shabsin, Janelle Gibson, and Mark R. Rank, "Confronting Stigma, Discrimination, and Social Exclusion," in Mark Robert Rank ed., *Toward a Livable Life: A 21st Century Agenda for Social Work* (New York: Oxford University Press, 2020), pp. 70–93.

26. Matthew O. Hunt and Heather E. Bullock, "Ideologies and Beliefs About Poverty," in David Brady and Linda M. Burton eds., *The Oxford Handbook of the Social Science of Poverty* (New York: Oxford University Press, 2016), pp. 93–116.

27. Mark Robert Rank, *Living on the Edge: The Realities of Welfare in America* (New York: Columbia University Press, 1994).

28. Francesco Duira, *Broke and Patriotic: Why Poor American Love Their Country* (Stanford, CA: Stanford University Press, 2018), p. 70.

29. Duira 2018, p. 156.

Chapter 11

1. Mark Robert Rank, *One Nation, Underprivileged: Why American Poverty Affects Us All* (New York: Oxford University Press, 2016).

2. Ronald J. Angel, "Social Class, Poverty, and the Unequal Burden of Illness," in David Brady and Linda M. Burton eds., *The Oxford Handbook of the Social Science of Poverty* (New York: Oxford University Press, 2016), pp. 660–683; Darrell L. Hudon, Sarah Gehlert, and Shanta Pandey, "Tackling the Root Social Determinants of Ill Health," in Mark Robert Rank ed., *Toward a Livable Life: A 21st Century Agenda for Social Work* (New York: Oxford University Press, 2020), pp. 16–44.

3. Council on Community Pediatrics, "Poverty and Child Health in the United States," *Pediatrics* 137 (2016): e20160339.

4. Bruce Jesse Biddle, *Social Class, Poverty, and Education: Policy and Practice* (New York: Routledge, 2013); Jeanne Brooks-Gunn, Greg Duncan, and Lawrence Aber, *Neighborhood Poverty: Context and Consequences for Children* (New York: Russell Sage Foundation, 1997); Esther K. Chung, "Screening for Social Determinants of Health Among Children and Families Living in Poverty: A Guide for Clinicians," *Current Problems in Pediatric and Adolescent Health Care* 46 (2016): 135–153; Ajay Chaudry and Christopher Wimer, "Poverty Is Not Just an Indicator: The Relationship Between Income, Poverty, and Child Well-Being," *Academic Pediatrics* 16 (2016): S23–S29; Michelle Hughes and Whitney Tucker, "Poverty as an Adverse Childhood Experience," *North Carolina Medical Journal* 79 (2018): 124–126.

5. Children's Defense Fund, *Wasting America's Future: The Children's Defense Fund Report on the Costs of Child Poverty* (Boston: Beacon Press, 1994), p. 99.

6. Alexis de Tocqueville, *Democracy in America*, Vol. 2 (New York: Knopf, 1994, originally published 1840), p. 525.

7. Michael McLaughlin and Mark R. Rank, "Estimating the Economic Cost of Childhood Poverty in the United States," *Social Work Research* 42 (2018): 73–83.

8. Martin Ravallion, *The Economics of Poverty* (New York: Oxford University Press, 2016).

9. Congressional Budget Office, *Monthly Budget Review: Summary for Fiscal Year 2015* (Washington, DC: Author, 2015).

10. Linda Giannarelli, Kye Lippold, Sarah Minton, and Laura Wheaton, "Reducing Child Poverty in the US: Costs and Impacts of Policies Proposed by the Children's Defense Fund," *Urban Institute Research Report* (January 2015).

11. H. Luke Schaefer, Sophie Collyer, Greg Duncan, Kathryn Edin, Irwin Garfinkel, David Harris, Timothy M. Smeeding, Jane Waldfogel, Christopher Wimer, and Hirokazu Yoshikawa, "A Universal Child Allowance: A Plan to Reduce Poverty and Income Instability Among Children in the United States," *Russell Sage Foundation Journal of the Social Sciences* 4 (2018): 22–42.

12. U.S. Census Bureau, "Income Deficit or Surplus of Families and Unrelated Individuals by Poverty Status" (POV-28, 2016). https://www.census.gov/data/tables/2016/demo/cps/pov-28.html

13. Jason M. Fletcher and Barbara L. Wolfe, "Education and Labor Market Consequences of Teenage Childbearing: Evidence Using the Timing of Pregnancy Outcomes and Community Fixed Effects," *Journal of Human Resources* 44 (2009): 303–305.

14. U.S. Census Bureau, "Income and Poverty in the United States: 2019," Report Number P60-270 (2020). https://www.census.gov/content/dam/Census/library/publications/2020/demo/p60-270.pdf

15. Arthur M. Okun, *Equality and Efficiency: The Big Tradeoff* (Washington DC: The Brookings Institution, 1975), p. 2.

16. Lane Kenworthy, *Social Democratic Capitalism* (New York: Oxford University Press, 2019).

17. Monica Prasad, *Starving the Beast: Ronald Reagan and the Tax Cut Revolution* (New York: Russell Sage Foundation, 2018), p. 219.

18. Anthony B. Atkinson, *Inequality: What Can Be Done?* (Cambridge, MA: Harvard University Press, 2015); Barry Z. Cynamon and Steven M. Fazzari, "Rising Inequality and Stagnation in the US Economy," *European Journal of Economics and Economic Policies: Intervention* 12 (2015): 170–182.

19. Joseph E. Stiglitz, *The Price of Inequality: How Today's Divided Society Endangers Our Future* (New York: W. W. Norton, 2012).

Chapter 12

1. Yascha Mounk, *The Age of Responsibility: Luck, Choice, and the Welfare State* (Cambridge, MA: Harvard University Press, 2017); Lawrence M. Eppard, Mark Robert Rank, and Heather E. Bullock, *Rugged Individualism and the Misunderstanding of American Inequality* (Bethlehem, PA: Lehigh University Press, 2020); Peter Edelman, *Not a Crime to Be Poor* (New York: Farrar, Strauss and Giroux, 2017).

2. John Kenneth Galbraith, *A View From the Stands: Of People, Politics, Military Power and the Arts* (Boston, MA: Houghton Mifflin, 1986), p. 35.

3. Galbraith 1986, p. 36.

4. Michael B. Katz, *In the Shadow of the Poorhouse: A Social History of Welfare in America* (New York: Basic Books, 1996); Michael B. Katz, *The Undeserving Poor: America's Enduring Confrontation With Poverty* (New York: Oxford University Press, 2013).

5. Mark R. Rank, "Why Poverty and Inequality Undermine Justice in America," in Michael Reisch ed., *Routledge International Handbook of Social Justice* (New York: Routledge Press, 2016), pp. 436–447.

6. Elise Gould, "Poor People Work: A Majority of Poor People Who Can Work Do" (Economic Policy Institute, Economic Snapshot, May 19, 2015).

7. Arne L. Kalleberg, *Good Jobs, Bad Jobs: The Rise of Polarized and Precarious Employment Systems in the United States, 1970s to 2000s* (New York: Russell Sage Foundation, 2011).

8. Judith Goode and Jeff Maskovsky, *The New Poverty Studies: The Ethnography of Power, Politics, and Impoverished People in the United States* (New York: New York University Press, 2001); Oxfam America, "Hard Work, Hard Lives: Survey Exposes Harsh Reality Faced by Low-Wage Workers in the US" (2014). https://s3.amazonaws.com/oxfam-us/www/static/oa4/low-wage-worker-report-oxfam-america.pdf; Francesco Duina, *Broke and Patriotic: Why Poor Americans Love Their Country* (Stanford, CA: Stanford University Press, 2018).

9. Lyndon B. Johnson, "The President's Inaugural Address, January 20, 1965" in *Public Papers of the Presidents of the United States: Lyndon B. Johnson, 1965* (Vol. I, entry 27) (Washington DC: U.S. Government Printing Office, 1965), pp. 71–74.

10. Paul A. Samuelson, *Economics: An Introductory Analysis* (New York: McGraw-Hill, 1948); Paul A. Samuelson and William D. Nordhaus, *Economics* (17th ed.) (New York: McGraw-Hill, 2001)

11. Lawrence Mishel and Julia Wolfe, "CEO Compensation has Grown 940% since 1978," *Economic Policy Report* (August 14, 2019).

12. Edward N. Wolff, "Household Wealth Trends in the United States, 1962 to 2016: Has Middle Class Wealth Recovered?" NBER Working Paper Series, Working Paper 24085 (Cambridge, MA: National Bureau of Economic Research, 2017).

13. Martin Luther King, *Where Do We Go From Here: Chaos or Community?* (New York: Harper and Row, 1967), pp. 187–188.

Chapter 13

1. Amina Dunn, *Partisans Are Divided Over the Fairness of the U.S. Economy—and Why People Are Rich or Poor* (Pew Research Center, October 4, 2018).

2. Dunn 2018; Emily Ekins, *What Americans Think About Poverty, Wealth, and Work* (Washington, DC: Cato Institute, 2019).

3. Robert Greenstein, Richard Kogan, and Emily Horton, *Low-Income Programs Not Driving Nation's Long-Term Fiscal Problem: Programs Outside Health Projected to Decline Relative to Economy* (Washington, DC: Center on Budget and Policy Priorities, June 26, 2018).

4. Greenstein, Kogan, and Horton 2018.

5. Greenstein, Kogan, and Horton 2018.

6. Greenstein, Kogan, and Horton 2018.

7. *Policy Basics: Where Do Our Federal Tax Dollars Go?* (Washington, DC: Center on Budget and Policy Priorities, April 9, 2020).

8. *Policy Basics: Where Do Our Federal Tax Dollars Go?* (Washington, DC: Center on Budget and Policy Priorities, April 9, 2020).

9. Elise Gould and Hilary Wething, *U.S. Poverty Rates Higher, Safety Net Weaker Than in Peer Countries* (Washington, DC: Economic Policy Institute, July 24, 2012).

10. Hilary W. Hoynes and Diane Whitmore Schanzenbach, "Safety Net Investments in Children," NBER Working Paper Series, Working Paper 24594 (Cambridge, MA: National Bureau of Economic Research, 2018).

11. Hoynes and Schanzenbach 2018.

12. Personal Responsibility and Work Reconciliation Act of 1996. Pub. L. No. 104–193, 110 Stat. 2105 (1997); Laura Tach and Kathryn Edin, "The Social Safety Net After Welfare Reform: Recent Developments and Consequences for Household Dynamics," *Annual Review of Sociology* 43 (2017): 541–561.

13. *Chart Book: Temporary Assistance for Needy Families* (Washington, DC: Center on Budget and Policy Priorities, August 21, 2019).

14. *Chart Book: Economic Security and Health Insurance Programs Reduce Poverty and Provide Access to Needed Care* (Washington, DC: Center on Budget and Policy Priorities, March 21, 2018).

15. H. Luke Shaefer, Kathryn Edin Vince Fusaro, and Pinguie Wu, "The Decline of Cash Assistance and the Well-Being of Poor Households With Children," *Social Forces* 98 (2020): 1000–1025.

16. *Chart Book: Temporary Assistance for Needy Families* (Washington, DC: Center on Budget and Policy Priorities, August 21, 2019).

17. *Chart Book: Temporary Assistance for Needy Families* (Washington, DC: Center on Budget and Policy Priorities, August 21, 2019).

18. Heather Hahn, Laudan Aaron, Cary Lou, Eleanor Pratt, and Adaeze Okoli, *Why Does Cash Welfare Depend on Where You Live? How and Why State TANF Programs Vary* (Washington, DC: Urban Institute, June 2017).

19. Hahn, Aaron, Lou, Pratt, and Okoli 2017.

20. Hahn, Aaron, Lou, Pratt, and Okoli 2017.

21. Danilo Trisi, *Economic Security Programs Cut Poverty Nearly in Half Over Last 50 Years, New Data Show* (Washington, DC: Center on Budget and Policy Priorities, September 18, 2018).

22. Ashley Burnside, *TANF at 23: Over 2.5 Million More Families Could Be Getting Cash Assistance, Work Supports* (Washington, DC: Center for Budget and Policy Priorities, August 20, 2019).

23. Kjetil van der Wel and Knut Halvorsen, "The Bigger the Worse? A Comparative Study of the Welfare State and Employment," *Work, Employment and Society* 29 (2015): 99–118.

24. Abhijit V. Banerjee, Rema Hanna, Gabriel E. Kreindler, and Benjamin A. Olken, "Debunking the Stereotype of the Lazy Welfare Recipient: Evidence From Cash Transfer Programs," *World Bank Observer* 32 (2017): 155–184.

Chapter 14

1. Staff Report, "Woman Charged With Wrongly Receiving More Than $10,000 in Food Stamps," *Village-News.com* (March 25, 2017).

2. "Brothers Sentenced in $1.4 Million Grocery Store Welfare Fraud Scheme," *CBS/AP* (June 20, 2018).

3. Daily Mail Reporter, "I'm Going to Make Millions! Unrepentant Escalade-Driving Surfer Who Lives Like a King on Food Stamps Tells How the Welfare System Has Let Him Strike It Rich With His Band," *Daily Mail.com* (February 26, 2014).

4. Samantha Wyatt, "Fox's Shameless Misrepresentation of SNAP Recipients," *Media Matters for America* (August 9, 2013).

5. *Policy Basics: The Supplemental Nutrition Assistance Program (SNAP)* (Washington, DC: Center on Budget and Policy Priorities, June 25, 2019).

6. *Policy Basics: The Supplemental Nutrition Assistance Program (SNAP)* (Washington, DC: Center on Budget and Policy Priorities, June 25, 2019).

7. Heather E. Bullock and Harmony A. Reppond, "Of 'Takers' and 'Makers': A Social Psychological Analysis of Class and Classism," in P. L. Hammack ed., *The Oxford Handbook of Social Psychology and Social Justice* (New York: Oxford University Press, 2018), pp. 223–244.

8. Donald Trump, "Remarks by President Trump on Tax Reform," St. Charles, Missouri (November 29, 2017). https://www.whitehouse.gov/briefings-statements/remarks-president-trump-tax-reform-2/

9. Linley Sanders, "Americans Believe Benefits Fraud Is Common for SNAP," *Real Time Research* (September 10, 2019).

10. Stacy Dean, *SNAP: Combating Fraud and Improving Program Integrity Without Weakening Success* (Washington, DC: Center on Budget and Policy Priorities, June 9, 2016), https://www.cbpp.org/food-assistance/snap-combating-fraud-and-improving-program-integrity-without-weakening-success; U.S. Government Accountability Office, *Improper Payments: CFO Act Agencies Need to Improve Efforts to Address Compliance Issues* (GAO 16–554) (June 2016), https://www.gao.gov/products/GAO-16-554; U.S. Government Accountability Office, *Food Stamp Trafficking: FNS Could Enhance Program Integrity by Better Targeting Stores Likely to Traffic and Increasing Penalties* (GAO 07-53) (June 2006), https:www.govinfo.gov/content/pkg/GAOREPORTS-GAO-07-53/html/GAOREPORTS-GAO-07-53.html.

11. Josh Levin, *The Queen: The Forgotten Life Behind an American Myth* (New York: Little, Brown and Company, 2019), p. 115.

12. Randy Alison Aussenberg, *Errors and Fraud in the Supplemental Nutrition Assistance Program* (R45147) (Washington, DC: Congressional Research Service, September 28, 2018).

13. Aussenberg 2018.

14. Aussenberg 2018.

15. Aussenberg 2018.

16. Aussenberg 2018.

17. Aussenberg 2018.

18. Aussenberg 2018.

19. Aussenberg 2018.

20. Aussenberg 2018.

21. Aussenberg 2018.

22. Aussenberg 2018.

23. William G. Gale and Aaron Krupkin, "How Big Is the Problem of Tax Evasion?" *Brookings Institution Up Front Report*, April 9, 2019.

24. Stacy Dean, *SNAP: Combating Fraud and Improving Program Integrity Without Weakening Success* (Washington, DC: Center on Budget and Policy Priorities, June 9, 2016), https://www.cbpp.org/food-assistance/snap-combating-fraud-and-improving-program-integrity-without-weakening-success, p. 11.

25. Dean 2016.

26. Aussenberg 2018.

27. Kaaryn Gustafson, "The Criminalization of Poverty," *Journal of Criminal Law & Criminology* 99 (2009): 643–716.

28. Harold Pollack and Sheldon Danziger, "House Republicans Want Drug Tests for Food Stamp Recipients. There's No Good Reason for That," *Washington Post* (August 21, 2013).

29. Pollack and Danziger 2013.

30. Byrce Covert and Josh Israel, *"What 7 States Discovered After Spending More than $1 Million Drug Testing Welfare Recipients,"* *Think Progress* (February 26, 2015).

31. Kaaryn Gustafson, "The Criminalization of Poverty," *Journal of Criminal Law & Criminology* 99 (2009): 643–716.

32. Cindy Rodriguez, "The Clash Over Fingerprinting for Food Stamps," *NPR January 30, 2012.* https://www.npr.org/2012/01/30/145905246/the-clash-over-fingerprinting-for-food-stamps#:~:text=The%20Clash%20Over%20Fingerprinting%20For%20Food%20Stamps%20%3A%20NPR&text=The%20Clash%20Over%20Fingerprinting%20For%20Food%20Stamps%20If%20New%20York,them%20from%20applying%20for%20assistance

33. Harry Murray, "Deniable Degradation: The Finger-Imaging of Welfare Recipients," *Sociological Forum* 15 (2000): 39–63, p. 56.

34. Jennifer Stuber and Karl Kronebusch, "Stigma and Other Determinants of Participation in TANF and Medicaid," *Journal of Analysis and Management* 23 (2004): 509–530.

35. Gideon Yaniv, "Welfare Fraud and Welfare Stigma," *Journal of Economic Psychology* 18 (1997): 435–451.

36. Heather E. Bullock, Gabriel H. J. Twose, and Veronica M. Hamilton, "Mandating Work: A Social Psychological Analysis of Rising Neoliberalism in U.S. Public Assistance," *Analyses of Social Issues and Public Policy* 19 (2019): 282–304.

37. Laura Reiley, "Trump Proposal Would Push 3 Million People Off Food Stamps," *Washington Post* (July 22, 2019).

38. Helaine Olen, "Billionaires and Millionaires against Food Stamps," *Washington Post* (July 24, 2019); Reiley 2019.

39. Mark R. Rank and Thomas A. Hirsch, "The Link Between Population Density and Welfare Participation," *Demography* 30 (1993): 607–622.

Chapter 15

1. See Joe Feagin, "Poverty: We Still Believe That God Helps Those Who Help Themselves," *Psychology Today* 6, no. 6 (1972):101–129. See also Joe Feagin, *Subordinating the Poor: Welfare and American Beliefs* (Englewood Cliffs, NJ: Prentice-Hall, 1975).

2. For more on the LIS, visit their site: https://www.lisdatacenter.org/.

3. A valuable resource for understanding the connection between social policies and poverty in affluent countries is David Brady, *Rich Democracies, Poor People: How Politics Explain Poverty* (New York: Oxford University Press, 2009). See also Lawrence M. Eppard, Noam Chomsky, Mark Robert Rank, and David Brady, "On Culture, Politics, and Poverty," *Contexts* 16 (2017): 8–11.

4. Government is of course heavily involved in determining the *initial* distribution of resources, not just the *redistribution* of resources. The labels "pretax/pretransfer" and "post-tax/post-transfer" are imperfect because they suggest that there is a point at which the government becomes involved in the distribution of resources. Government is involved in the distribution of resources in society in countless ways above and beyond the welfare state.

5. Jared Bernstein, "International Poverty Comparisons: What Do They Tell Us About Causes?" (2012). http://jaredbernsteinblog.com/international-poverty-comparisons-what-do-they-tell-us-about-causes/

6. Jonathan Bradshaw, Yekaterina Chzhen, Gill Main, Bruno Martorano, Leonardo Menchini, and Chris de Neubourg, "Relative Income Poverty Among Children in Rich Countries" (2012). https://www.unicef-irc.org/publications/655-relative-income-poverty-among-children-in-rich-countries.html

7. Max Roser and Esteban Ortiz-Ospina, "Income Inequality" (2013), https://ourworldindata.org/income-inequality. Similar analyses can be found in Orsetta Causa and Mikkel Hermansen, "Income Redistribution Through Taxes and Transfers Across OECD Countries," https://voxeu.org/article/income-redistribution-through-taxes-and-transfers; and Joh Cassidy, "American Inequality in Six Charts," https://www.newyorker.com/news/john-cassidy/american-inequality-in-six-charts.

8. Laurie C. Maldonado and Rense Nieuwenhuis, "Single-Parent Family Poverty in 24 OECD Countries: A Focus on Market and Redistribution Strategies" (2015), p. 10. file:///C:/Users/markr/Downloads/MaldonadoNieuwenhuis-2015-Single-ParentFamily Povertyin24OECDCountriesAFocusonMarketandRedistributionStrategies%20(2).pdf

9. Cheol-Sung Lee and In-Hoe Koo, "The Welfare States and Poverty," in D. Brady and L. M. Burton eds., *The Oxford Handbook of the Social Science of Poverty* (New York: Oxford University Press, 2016), p. 715.

10. Analysis conducted by the authors with the assistance of poverty scholar David Brady utilizing Luxembourg Income Study (LIS) data: http://www.lisdatacenter.org.

11. U.S. Census Bureau, "Historical Poverty Tables: People and Families—1959 to 2019" (2020). https://www.census.gov/data/tables/time-series/demo/income-poverty/historical-poverty-people.html

12. Gary V. Engelhardt and Jonathan Gruber, "Social Security and the Evolution of Elderly Poverty," NBER Working Paper Series, Working Paper 10466 (Cambridge, MA: National Bureau of Economic Research, 2004), p. 24.

13. Kathleen Romig, "Social Security Lifts More Americans Above Poverty Than Any Other Program" (20208). https://www.cbpp.org/research/social-security/social-security-lifts-more-americans-above-poverty-than-any-other-program

14. Romig 2020.

15. David Cooper and Elise Gould, "Financial Security of Elderly Americans at Risk" (2013), p. 3. https://www.epi.org/publication/economic-security-elderly-americans-risk/

16. Joint Economic Committee Democrats, "Medicare: Protecting Seniors and Families" (2018), pp. 2–3. https://www.jec.senate.gov/public/index.cfm/democrats/2018/7/jec-dems-report-on-medicare-protecting-seniors-and-families

17. Zachary Parolin, Megan A. Curran, and Christopher Wimer, "The CARES Act and Poverty in COVID-19 Crisis: Promises and Pitfalls of the Recover Rebates and Expanded Unemployment Benefits," *Poverty and Social Policy Brief* (New York: Columbia Population Research Center, June 21, 2020).

18. Timothy M. Smeeding, "Public Policy, Economic Inequality, and Poverty: The United States in Comparative Perspective" *Social Science Quarterly* 86 (2005): 955–983, p. 980 .

19. Alberto Alesina, Edward Glaeser, and Bruce Sacerdote, "Why Doesn't the U.S. Have a European-Style Welfare State?" Discussion Paper 1933 (Cambridge, MA: Harvard Institute of Economic Research, 2001), p. 39.

20. See Martin Gilens, *Why Americans Hate Welfare: Race, Media, and the Politics of Antipoverty Policy* (Chicago: University of Chicago Press, 1999).

21. See Alberto Alesina and Edward L. Glaeser, *Fighting Poverty in the US and Europe: A World of Difference* (New York: Oxford University Press, 2004). See also Heather E. Bullock, Wendy R. Williams, and Wendy M. Limbert, "Predicting Support for Welfare Policies: The Impact of Attributions and Beliefs About Inequality" *Journal of Poverty* 7, no. 3 (2003): 35–56. See also Matthew O. Hunt and Heather E. Bullock, "Ideologies and Beliefs About Poverty," in D. Brady and L. M. Burton eds., *The Oxford Handbook of the Social Science of Poverty* (New York: Oxford University Press, 2016), pp. 93–116. See also Pew Research Center, "Emerging and Developing Economies Much More Optimistic Than Rich Countries About the Future" (2014) http://www.pewglobal.org/2014/10/09/emerging-and-developing-economies-much-more-optimistic-than-rich-countries-about-the-future/. See also Economic Mobility Project, "Economic Mobility: Is the American Dream Alive and Well?" (2007). https://www.brookings.edu/research/economic-mobility-is-the-american-dream-alive-and-well/

Chapter 16

1. Shai Davidai, "Why Do Americans Believe in Economic Mobility? Economic Inequality, External Attributions of Wealth and Poverty, and the Belief in Economic Mobility," *Journal of Experimental Psychology* 79 (2018): 138–148.

2. CBS News/New York Times (IPOLL Databank, The Roper Center for Public Opinion Research, University of Connecticut, 2012).

3. Pew Charitable Trusts, "Findings From a National Survey and Focus Groups on Economic Mobility" (Washington, DC: Economic Mobility Project, 2009).

4. James R. Kluegal and Eliot R. Smith, *Beliefs About Inequality: Americans' Views of What Is and What Ought to Be* (New York: Aldine De Gruyter, 1986).

5. Liana Fox, Florencia Torche, and Jane Waldfogel, "Intergenerational Mobility," in David Brady and Linda M. Burton eds., *The Oxford Handbook of the Social Sciences of Poverty* (New York: Oxford University Press, 2016), pp. 528–554.

6. Fox, Torche, and Waldfogel 2016.

7. John Ermisch, Markus Jantti, and Timothy Smeeding, *From Parents to Children: The Intergenerational Transmission of Advantage* (New York: Russell Sage Foundation, 2012).

8. Miles Corak, "Chasing the Same Dream, Climbing Different Ladders: Economic Mobility in the United States and Canada" (Economic Mobility Project, the Pew Charitable Trusts, 2010); Miles Corak, "Inequality From Generation to Generation: The United States in Comparison" (Unpublished paper, Graduate School of Public and International Affairs, University of Ottawa, 2011); Marie Connoly, Miles Corak, and Catherine Haeck, "Intergenerational Mobility Between and Within Canada and the United States," NBER Working Paper Series, Working Paper 25735 (Cambridge, MA: National Bureau of Economic Research, 2019).

9. Jonathan David and Bhashkar Mazumber, "The Decline in Intergenerational Economic Mobility After 1980" (Federal Reserve Bank of Chicago Working Paper, Revised WP 2017–5, 2020).

10. Bhaskar Mazumber, "Earnings Mobility in the U.S.: A New Look at Intergenerational Inequality" (Federal Reserve Board of Chicago Working Paper, WP2001-18, 2001); Bhaskar Mazumber, "Intergenerational Mobility in the United States: What We Have Learned from the PSID," *ANAALS* 680 (2018): 213–234.

11. Markus Jantti, "American Exceptionalism in a New Light: A Comparison of Intergenerational Earnings Mobility in the Nordic Countries, the United Kingdom and the United States" Discussion Paper 1938 (Bonn, Germany: Institute for the Study of Labor, 2006).

12. Hilary W. Hoynes, Marianne E. Page, and Ann Huff Stevens, "Poverty in America: Trends and Explanations," *Journal of Economic Perspectives* 20 (2006): 47–68.

13. Raj Chetty, David Grusky, Maximillian Hell, Nathaniel Hendren, Robert Manduca, and Jimmy Narang, "The Fading American Dream: Trends in Absolute Income Mobility Since 1940," *Science* 356 (2017): 398–406.

14. Chetty et al. 2017, p. 400.

15. Chetty et al. 2017, p. 405.

16. Arne L. Kalleberg, *Good Jobs, Bad Jobs: The Rise of Polarized and Precarious Employment Systems in the United States, 1970s to 2000s* (New York: Russell Sage Foundation, 2011).

17. Elise Gould, "The State of Working America Wages 2018" (Washington, DC: Economic Policy Institute, 2018).

18. U.S. Census Bureau, *Income and Poverty in the United States: 2019* (Report Number P60-270) (Washington DC: U.S. Government Printing Office, 2020).

19. Kalleberg 2011.

20. Kathryn J. Edin and H. Luke Shaefer, *$2.00 a Day: Living on Almost Nothing in America* (Boston: Houghton Mifflin Harcourt, 2015).

21. Federal Reserve Bank, "Report on the Economic Well-Being of U.S. Households in 2019, Featuring Supplemental Data from April 2020" (Washington DC: Board of Governors of the Federal Reserve System, 2020).

22. Jacob S. Hacker, *The Great Risk Shift* (2nd ed.) (New York: Oxford University Press, 2020).

23. U.S. Census Bureau 2019.

24. See the OECD data website: https://data.oecd.org/inequality/poverty-gap.htm.

25. Edward N. Wolff, "Household Wealth Trends in the United States, 1962 to 2016: Has Middle Class Wealth Recovered?" NBER Working Paper Series, Working Paper 24085 (Cambridge, MA: (National Bureau of Economic Research, 2017).

26. Joseph E. Stiglitz, *People, Power, and Profits: Progressive Capitalism for an Age of Discontent* (New York: W. W. Norton, 2019); Thomas Piketty and Emmanuel Saez, "Inequality in the Long Run," *Science* 244 (2014): 838–843.

Chapter 17

1. For a good examination of American stratification beliefs, see Matthew O. Hunt and Heather E. Bullock, "Ideologies and Beliefs About Poverty," in D. Brady and L. M. Burton eds., *The Oxford Handbook of the Social Science of Poverty* (New York: Oxford University Press, 2016), pp. 93–116. See also James R. Kluegel and Eliot R. Smith, *Beliefs About Inequality: Americans' Views of What Is and What Ought to Be* (Hawthorne, NY: Aldine de Gruyter, 1986).

2. Clifton Mark, "A Belief in Meritocracy Is Bad for You," *The Week* (April 6, 2019).

3. For an insightful analysis of the problems with meritocratic assumptions, see Stephen J. McNamee, *The Meritocracy Myth* (4th ed.) (Lanham, MD: Rowman & Littlefield, 2018).

4. Jim Cullen, *The American Dream: A Short History of an Idea That Shaped a Nation* (New York: Oxford University Press, 2003), p. 10.

5. We borrow heavily from Pierre Bourdieu and his forms of capital, such as economic capital, cultural capital, social capital, and symbolic capital. For a good explanation of Bourdieu's forms of capital, see Robert Moore, "Capital," in Michael Grenfell ed., *Pierre Bourdieu: Key Concepts* (Stocksfield, UK: Acumen, 2008), pp. 101–117.

6. Raoul Martinez, *Creating Freedom: The Lottery of Birth, the Illusion of Consent, and the Fight for Our Future* (New York: Pantheon Books, 2016), p. 3.

7. See Richard V. Reeves and Kimberly Howard, "The Parenting Gap" (September 9, 2013), https://www.brookings.edu/research/the-parenting-gap/. Studies show that investments in children in early childhood can lead to a 7 to 13 percent societal return per year. These investments therefore "pay off" by the teenage years and lead to societal profit every year after. This is due to the better educational attainment, economic productivity, and health, and less need for welfare or incarceration, for children who are invested in versus those who are not. See James J. Heckman, "There's More to Gain by Taking a Comprehensive Approach to Early Childhood Development." https://heckmanequation.org/assets/2017/01/F_Heckman_CBAOnePager_120516.pdf

8. Reeves and Howard 2013, p. 6.

9. See Jane Waldfogel and Elizabeth Washbrook, "Income-Related Gaps in School Readiness in the United States and United Kingdom," in T. Smeeding, R. Erikson, and M. Jantti eds., *Persistence, Privilege, and Parenting: The Comparative Study of Intergenerational Mobility* (New York: Russell Sage Foundation, 2011), pp. 175–208. Cited in Reeves and Howard 2013, p. 3.

10. Betty Hart and Todd R. Risley, *Meaningful Differences in the Everyday Experience of Young American Children* (Baltimore, MD: Paul H. Brookes, 1995), p. 176).

11. Hart and Risley, 1995, p. 168.

12. Greg J. Duncan, W. Jean Yeung, Jeanne Brooks-Gunn, and Judith R. Smith, "How Much Does Childhood Poverty Affect the Life Chances of Children?" *American Sociological Review* 63 (1998): 406–423, p. 420.

13. Isabel V. Sawhill, Scott Winship, and Kerry Searle Grannis, "Pathways to the Middle Class: Balancing Personal and Public Responsibilities" (September 20, 2012). https://www.brookings.edu/wp-content/uploads/2016/06/0920-pathways-middle-class-sawhill-winship.pdf

14. There is a wealth of online resources that help you examine the inequalities of place. For a few examples, see the Opportunity Atlas (https://www.opportunityatlas.org/), Life Expectancy Map (https://qz.com/1462111/map-what-story-does-your-neighborhoods-life-expectancy-tell/), and EPA's Environmental Justice Screening and Mapping Tool (https://ejscreen.epa.gov/mapper/).

15. Jonathan Rothwell, "The Neighborhood Effect: Localities and Upward Mobility" (November 12, 2014). https://www.brookings.edu/blog/social-mobility-memos/2014/11/12/the-neighborhood-effect-localities-and-upward-mobility/

16. As Robert Putnam notes, "Ultimately, growing class segregation across neighborhoods, schools, marriages (and probably also civic associations, workplaces, and friendship circles) means that rich Americans and poor Americans are living, learning, and raising children in increasingly separate and unequal worlds, removing the stepping-stones to upward mobility." See Robert Putnam, *Our Kids: The American Dream in Crisis* (New York: Simon & Schuster, 2015), p. 41.

17. A correlation of 0.10–0.29 is considered weak, 0.30–0.49 is considered moderate, and 0.50–1 is considered strong. A positive sign indicates that an increase in the independent variable leads to an increase in the dependent variable. A negative sign means the opposite: that the dependent variable decreases when the independent variable increases. For more information, see Barbara G. Tabachnick and Linda S. Fidell, *Using Multivariate Statistics* (6th ed.) (New York: Pearson, 2013).

18. Raj Chetty, "Improving Opportunities for Economic Mobility in the United States," Testimony for the Budget Committee of the United States Senate (April 1, 2014), p. 3. https://books.google.com/books?id=hRvVB2eXf7gC&pg=PA18&lpg=PA18&dq =Raj+Chetty,+%E2%80%9CImproving+Opportunities+for+Economic+Mobility+in+ the+United+States,%E2%80%9D+Testimony+for+the+Budget+Committee+of+the+ United+States+Senate,+(April+1,+2014+),&source=bl&ots=ytepBUyLi2&sig=ACfU3 U3Vl3NT42fxbdwH5ENACtTI9qg0gg&hl=en&sa=X&ved=2ahUKEwisobGD15HsA hVHbs0KHfgUA2UQ6AEwA3oECAcQAQ#v=onepage&q=Raj%20Chetty%2C%20 %E2%80%9CImproving%20Opportunities%20for%20Economic%20Mobility%20in%20 the%20United%20States%2C%E2%80%9D%20Testimony%20for%20the%20Budget%20 Committee%20of%20the%20United%20States%20Senate%2C%20(April%201%2C%20 2014%20)%2C&f=false

19. Gary W. Evans, "The Environment of Childhood Poverty," *American Psychologist* 57 (2004): 423–451.

20. Laura Dwyer-Lindgren, Amelia Bertozzi-Villa, Rebecca W. Stubbs, Chloe Morozoff, Johan P. Mackenbach, Frank J. van Lenthe, Ali H. Mokdad, and Christopher J. L. Murray, "Inequalities in Life Expectancy Among US Counties, 1980 to 2014 Temporal Trends and Key Drivers," *JAMA Internal Medicine* 177 (2017): 1003–1011.

21. U.S. Department of Education, Equity and Excellence Commission, *For Each and Every Child: A Strategy for Educational Equity and Excellence* (Washington, DC: Education Publication Center, 2013), p. 12.

22. Jennifer Hochschild and Nathan Scovronick, *The American Dream and the Public Schools* (New York: Oxford University Press, 2003), pp. 12–13.

23. Erica Frankenberg, Jongyeon Ee, Jennifer B. Ayscue, and Gary Orfiled, "Harming Our Common Future: America's Segregated Schools 65 Years after *Brown*," The Civil Rights Project (May 10, 2019), p. 4. https://civilrightsproject.ucla.edu/research/k-12-education/ integration-and-diversity/harming-our-common-future-americas-segregated-schools-65- years-after-brown/Brown-65-050919v4-final.pdf

24. Frankenberg, Ee, Ayscue, and Orfiled 2019, p. 9.

25. Hochschild and Scovronick 2003, p. 5.

26. Daniel P. McMurrer and Isabel V. Sawhill, *Getting Ahead: Economic and Social Mobility in America* (Washington, DC: Urban Institute Press, 1998), p. 69.

27. Greg J. Duncan and Richard J. Marmane, *Whither Opportunity? Rising Inequality, Schools, and Children's Life Chances* (New York: Russell Sage Foundation, 2011), p. 15.

28. William A. Darity and A. Kirsten Mullen, *From Here to Equality: Reparations for Black Americans in the Twenty-First Century* (Chapel Hill, NC: University of North Carolina Press, 2020); Thomas M. Shapiro, *Toxic Inequality: How America's Wealth Gap Destroys Mobility, Deepens the Racial Divide, and Threatens Our Future* (New York: Basic Books, 2017).

29. See Scott Winship, Richard V. Reeves, and Katherine Guyot, "The Inheritance of Black Poverty: It's All About the Men" (March 22, 2018), https://www.brookings.

edu/research/the-inheritance-of-black-poverty-its-all-about-the-men/. See also Richard
V. Reeves, "The Other American Dream: Social Mobility, Race and Opportunity"
(August 28, 2013). https://www.brookings.edu/blog/social-mobility-memos/2013/08/28/
the-other-american-dream-social-mobility-race-and-opportunity/

30. Ta-Nehisi Coates, "The Case for Reparations," *Atlantic* (June 2014).

31. Patrick Sharkey, "Neighborhoods and the Black-White Mobility Gap." https://www.
pewtrusts.org/~/media/legacy/uploadedfiles/wwwpewtrustsorg/reports/economic_mobility/
pewsharkeyv12pdf.pdf

32. See Edward Rodrigue and Richard V. Reeves, "Five Bleak Facts on Black Opportunity"
(January 15, 2015). https://www.brookings.edu/blog/social-mobility-memos/2015/01/15/five-
bleak-facts-on-black-opportunity/. See also Jonathan Rothwell, "Housing Costs, Zoning,
and Access to High-Scoring Schools" (April 2012). https://www.brookings.edu/research/
housing-costs-zoning-and-access-to-high-scoring-schools/

33. See Ihab Mikati, Adam F. Benson, Thomas J. Luben, Jason D. Sacks, and Jennifer
Richmond-Bryant, "Disparities in Distribution of Particulate Matter Emission Sources by
Race and Poverty Status," *American Journal of Public Health* 108 (April 1, 2018). See also Van
R. Newkirk II, "Trump's EPA Concludes Environmental Racism Is Real," *Atlantic* (February
28 2018).

34. See Michelle Alexander, *The New Jim Crow: Mass Incarceration in the Age of
Colorblindness* (New York: The New Press, 2020). See also Jeffrey Reiman and Paul Leighton,
The Rich Get Richer and the Poor Get Prison: Ideology, Class, and Criminal Justice (10th ed.)
(New York: Routledge, 2016).

35. See Devah Pager, Bruce Western, and Bart Bonikowski, "Discrimination in a
Low Wage Labor Market: A Field Experiment," *American Sociological Review* 74, no. 5
(2009): 786. See also Devah Pager, "The Mark of a Criminal Record," *American Journal of
Sociology* 108 (2003): 937–975.

36. Pager, Western, and Bonikowski 2009. For a related study, see Marianne Bertrand
and Sendhil Mullainathan, "Are Emily and Greg More Employable Than Lakisha and
Jamal? A Field Experiment on Labor Market Discrimination," *American Economic Review*
94 (2004): 991–1013.

37. Gallup, "Race Relations." https://news.gallup.com/poll/1687/race-relations.aspx

38. Today, the top 10 percent of Americans own almost three-fourths of the wealth (73%)
and earn almost half (47%) of the income, up from 61 percent and 34 percent in the 1980s,
respectively. See the World Inequality Database for details: https://wid.world/.

39. Bandy X. Lee, "Causes and Cures VII: Structural Violence," *Aggression and Violent
Behavior* 28 (May–June 2016): 110.

40. Claude S. Fischer, Michael Hout, Martín Sánchez Jankowski, Samuel R. Lucas,
Ann Swidler, and Kim Voss, *Inequality by Design: Cracking the Bell Curve Myth* (Princeton,
NJ: Princeton University Press, 1996), p. 7.

41. "Social capital" refers to the people you know and the resources they can make available to you. The amount of social capital people have and the "value" of that particular social
capital in enabling or constraining upward mobility vary widely by social class. "Cultural
capital" refers to forms of knowledge, expertise, educational credentials, taste, aesthetic and
cultural preferences, and language and verbal skills. The likelihood we will acquire valued cultural capital varies widely by social class. As Leonard Beeghley states, "The class structure is
stable across generations because people in each class pass their resources (wealth, education,

interpersonal contacts) on to their children. . . . The rewards of hard work go mainly to those who start out with some advantages." Quote from Leonard Beeghley, *The Structure of Social Stratification in the United States* (5th ed.) (New York, Routledge, 2008), p. 143.

Chapter 18

1. Joseph Stiglitz, *The Price of Inequality: How Today's Divided Society Endangers Our Future* (New York: W. W. Norton, 2013), p. 2.

2. World Inequality Database, "USA," https://wid.world/country/usa/.

3. Stiglitz 2013, p. 5.

4. World Inequality Lab, "World Inequality Report 2018" (2018). https://wir2018.wid.world/files/download/wir2018-full-report-english.pdf

5. Organisation for Economic Co-operation and Development, "Income Inequality." https://data.oecd.org/inequality/income-inequality.htm

6. Edward N. Wolff, "Household Wealth Trend in the United States, 1962 to 2016: Has Middle Class Wealth Recovered?" NBER Working Paper Series, Working Paper 24085 (Cambridge, MA: National Bureau of Economic Research, November 2017).

7. William J. Chambliss and Daina S. Eglitis, *Discover Sociology* (4th ed.) (Thousand Oaks, CA: SAGE, 2020), p. 175.

8. Jesse Bricker, Sarena Goodman, Kevin B. Moore, and Alice Henriques Volz, "Wealth and Income Concentration in the SCF: 1989-2019." FEDS Notes, https://www.federalreserve.gov/econres/notes/feds-notes/wealth-and-income-concentration-in-the-scf-20200928.htm

9. Wolff 2017.

10. U.S. Census Bureau, "Historical Poverty Tables: People and Families—1959 to 2019." 2020, https://www.census.gov/data/tables/time-series/demo/income-poverty/historical-poverty-people.html

11. Lawrence Mishel, Josh Bivens, Elise Gould, and Heidi Shierholz, *The State of Working America* (12th ed.) (Ithaca, NY: Cornell University Press, 2012).

12. Stanford Center on Poverty and Inequality, "Income Segregation in the United States' Largest Metropolitan Areas." 2020, https://inequality.stanford.edu/income-segregation-maps. See also Sean F. Reardon and Kendra Bischoff, "Growth in the Residential Segregation of Families by Income, 1970–2009," November 2011. https://s4.ad.brown.edu/Projects/Diversity/Data/Report/report111111.pdf

13. Robert D. Putnam, *Our Kids: The American Dream in Crisis* (New York: Simon & Schuster, 2015), p. 187.

14. The National Academies of Sciences, Engineering, and Medicine, *The Growing Gap in Life Expectancy by Income: Implications for Federal Programs and Policy Responses* (Washington, DC: The National Academies Press, 2015), pp. 2–3.

15. Richard V. Reeves, Isabel V. Sawhill, and Eleanor Krause, "The Most Educated Women Are the Most Likely to be Married" (August 19, 2016). https://www.brookings.edu/blog/social-mobility-memos/2016/08/19/the-most-educated-women-are-the-most-likely-to-be-married/

16. Putnam 2015, p. 66.

17. Putnam 2015, p. 65.

18. Joseph E. Stiglitz, *The Great Divide: Unequal Societies and What We Can Do About Them* (New York: W. W. Norton, 2015), p. 159.

19. Economic Mobility Project, "Findings From a National Survey and Focus Groups on Economic Mobility" (March 12, 2009). https://www.pewtrusts.org/-/media/legacy/uploadedfiles/wwwpewtrustsorg/reports/economic_mobility/emp20200920survey20on20economic20mobility20for20print2031209pdf.pdf

20. Richard Wilkinson and Kate Pickett, *The Spirit Level: Why Greater Equality Makes Societies Stronger* (New York: Bloomsbury Press, 2010), p. 157.

21. IGE values range from 0 to 1, with a value of "0" indicating virtually no relationship between parents' income and their children's income in adulthood, and a value of "1" indicating that parental income perfectly predicts children's income. The higher the value, the more significant the impact of one's childhood social class on their adult social class. Values of 0.50 or above indicate a strong relationship.

22. Alan B. Krueger, "The Great Utility of the Great Gatsby Curve," May 19, 2015.

23. Mishel, Bivens, Gould, and Shierholz, 2012), p. 161. See also Miles Corak, "Inequality from Generation to Generation: The United States in Comparison" (May 2016), p. 12. http://ftp.iza.org/dp9929.pdf

24. Raj Chetty, "Improving Opportunities for Economic Mobility in the United States," Testimony for the Budget Committee of the United States Senate (April 1, 2014). https://www.budget.senate.gov/imo/media/doc/Chetty%20mobility%20testimony.pdf

25. Raj Chetty, Nathaniel Hendren, Patrick Kline, and Emmanuel Saez, "Where Is the Land of Opportunity? The Geography of Intergenerational Mobility in the United States," NBER Working Paper Series, Working Paper 19843 (Cambridge, MA; National Bureau of Economic Research, January 2014).

26. See Bhashkar Mazumder, "Estimating the Intergenerational Elasticity and Rank Association in the United States: Overcoming the Current Limitations of Tax Data," in L. Cappellari, S. Polachek, and K Tatsiramos eds., *Inequality: Causes and Consequences* (Bingley, UK: Emerald Group, 2016), pp. 83–129.

27. Bhashkar Mazumder, "The Apple Falls Even Closer to the Tree Than We Thought: New and Revised Estimates of the Intergenerational Inheritance of Earnings," in S. Bowles, H. Gintis, and M. Osborne Groves eds., *Unequal Chances: Family Background and Economic Success* (Princeton, NJ: Princeton University Press, 2005), p. 81.

28. Mishel, Bivens, Gould, and Shierholz 2012.

29. Stiglitz 2015, p. 160.

30. Kerry Trueman, "Looking for the American Dream? Try Denmark," *Huffington Post* (December 7, 2011).

31. Patrick Sharkey, Max Besbris, and Michael Friedson, "Poverty and Crime," in D. Brady and L. Burton eds., *The Oxford Handbook of the Social Science of Poverty* (New York: Oxford University Press, 2016), pp. 626, 631.

32. Lee Ellis and James N. McDonald, "Crime, Delinquency, and Social Status: A Reconsideration," *Journal of Offender Rehabilitation* 32, no. 3 (2001), pp. 23–52.

33. Sharkey, Besbris, and Friedson 2016, pp. 623–627.

34. See Ching-Chi Hsieh and M. D. Pugh, "Poverty, Income Inequality, and Violent Crime: A Meta-Analysis of Recent Aggregate Data Studies," *Criminal Justice Review* 18 (1993): pp. 190–192. See also Steven F. Messner, "Regional and Racial Effects on the Urban Homicide Rate: The Subculture of Violence Revisited" *American Journal of Sociology* 88 (March 1983), pp. 997–1007.

35. Rachel E. Morgan and Jennifer L. Truman, "Criminal Victimization, 2017," U.S. Department of Justice (December 2018). https://www.bjs.gov/content/pub/pdf/cv17.pdf

36. Wilkinson and Pickett 2010, p. 132.

37. Bernadette Rabuy and Daniel Kopf, "Prisons of Poverty: Uncovering the Pre-Incarceration Incomes of the Imprisoned" (July 9, 2015). https://www.prisonpolicy.org/reports/income.html

38. Rabuy and Kopf 2015.

39. See Frank J. Elgar and Nicole Aitken, "Income Inequality, Trust and Homicide in 33 Countries," *European Journal of Public Health* 21 (April 2011): 241–246. See also Hsieh and Pugh 1993.

40. Maia Szalavitz, "The Surprising Factors Driving Murder Rates: Income Inequality and Respect," *Guardian* (December 8, 2017), https://www.theguardian.com/us-news/2017/dec/08/income-inequality-murder-homicide-rates. See also Marin Daly, *Killing the Competition: Economic Inequality and Homicide* (New York: Routledge, 2016).

41. Szalavitz 2017.

42. Martin Daly, Margo Wilson, and Shawn Vasdev, "Income Inequality and Homicide Rates in Canada and the United States," *Canadian Journal of Criminology* 43 (2001): 219–236.

43. "The Stark Relationship Between Income Inequality and Crime," *Economist* (June 7, 2018). https://www.economist.com/graphic-detail/2018/06/07/the-stark-relationship-between-income-inequality-and-crime

44. Elgar and Aitken 2011.

45. U.S. Federal Bureau of Investigation (FBI), "Murder Offenders by Age, Sex, Race, and Ethnicity, 2017." https://ucr.fbi.gov/crime-in-the-u.s/2017/crime-in-the-u.s.-2017/tables/expanded-homicide-data-table-3.xls

46. Szalavitz 2017.

47. Wilkinson and Pickett 2010, p. 133.

48. Szalavitz 2017.

49. Gallup, "Americans' Views on Economic Mobility and Economic Inequality in the U.S. (Trends)" (January 2018). file:///C:/Users/markr/Downloads/180307EconomicOpportunity.pdf

50. Stiglitz 2015, p. xii, 122.

51. Mark Robert Rank, *One Nation, Underprivileged: Why American Poverty Affects Us All* (New York: Oxford University Press, 2004).

Chapter 19

1. Susan T. Fiske and Courtney Bearns Tablante, "Stereotyping: Processes and Content," in M. Mikulincer and P. R. Shaver eds., *APA Handbook of Personality and Social Psychology* (Washington, DC: American Psychological Association, 2015), pp. 457–507.

2. Catherine Cozzarelli, Anna V. Wilkinson, and Michael J. Tagler, "Attitudes Toward the Poor and Attributions for Poverty," *Journal of Social Issues* 57 (2001): 207–227.

3. Andrea Bobbio, Luigina Canova, and Anna Maria Manganelli, "Conservative Ideology, Economic Conservatism, and Causal Attributions for Poverty and Wealth," *Current Psychology* 29 (2010): 222–234; Rosa Rodriguez-Bailon, Boyka Bratnova, Guillermo B. Willis, Lucia Lopez-Rodriguez, Ashley Sturrock, and Steve Loughnan, "Social Class and

Ideologies of Inequality: How They Uphold Unequal Societies," *Journal of Social Issues* 73 (2017): 99–116.

4. Edward J. Rickert, "Authoritarianism and Economic Threat: Implications for Political Behavior," *Political Psychology* 19 (1998): 707–720.

5. Heather E. Bullock and Harmony A. Reppond, "Of 'Takers' and 'Makers:' A Social Psychological Analysis of Class and Classism," in P. L. Hammack ed., *The Oxford Handbook of Social Psychology and Social Justice* (New York: Oxford University Press, 2018), pp. 223–244; Heather E. Bullock, *Women and Poverty: Psychology, Public Policy, and Social Justice* (Chichester, UK: Wiley-Blackwell, 2013).

6. Brett A. Boeh Bergmann and Nathan R. Todd, "Religious and Spiritual Beliefs Predict Poverty Attributions," *Social Justice Research* 32 (2019): 459–485; Catherine Cozzarelli, Anna V. Wilkinson, and Michael J. Tagler, "Attitudes Toward the Poor and Attributions for Poverty," *Journal of Social Issues*, 57 (2001): 207–227; Bullock and Reppond 2018.

7. Shai Davidai and Thomas Gilovich, "Building a More Mobile America: One Income Quintile at a Time," *Perspectives on Psychological Science* 10 (2015): 60–71.

8. Michael W Kraus, and Jacinth J. X. Tan, "Americans Overestimate Social Class Mobility," *Journal of Experimental Social Psychology* 58 (2015): 101–111.

9. John T. Jost, Danielle Gaucher, and Chadly Stern, "'The World Isn't Fair:' A System Justification Perspective on Social Stratification and Inequality," in M. Mikulincer and P. R. Shaver eds., *APA Handbook of Personality and Social Psychology: Volume 2 Group Processes* (Washington, DC: American Psychological Association, 2015), pp. 317–340.

10. Jost, Gaucher, and Stern 2015, p. 321.

11. Cheryl J. Wakslak, John T. Jost, Tom R. Tyler, and Emmeline S. Chen, "Moral Outrage Mediates the Dampening Effect of System Justification on Support for Redistributive Social Policies," *Psychological Science* 18 (2007): 267–274.

12. Wakslak, Jost, Tyler, and Chen 2007.

13. Francesco Duina, *Broke and Patriotic: Why Poor Americans Love Their Country* (Stanford, CA: Stanford University Press, 2018).

14. Kristin D. Mickelson and Emily Hazlett, "'Why Me?': Low-Income Women's Poverty Attributions, Mental Health, and Social Class Perceptions," *Sex Roles* 71 (2014): 319–332.

15. Mickelson and Hazlett 2014.

16. Danny Osborne and Chris G. Sibley, "Through Rose-Colored Glasses: System-Justifying Beliefs Dampen the Effects of Relative Deprivation on Well-Being and Political Mobilization," *Personality and Social Psychology Bulletin* 39 (2013): 991–1004.

17. Susan T. Fiske and Courtney Bearns Tablante, "Stereotyping: Processes and Content," in M. Mikulincer and P. R. Shaver eds., *APA Handbook of Personality and Social Psychology* (Washington, DC: American Psychological Association, 2015), pp. 457–507.

18. Fiske and Tablante 2015.

19. Fiske and Tablante 2015, p. 466.

20. Suzanne R. Horwitz and John F. Dovidio, "The Rich—Love Them or Hate Them? Divergent Implicit and Explicit Attitudes Toward the Wealthy," *Group Processes & Intergroup Relations* 20 (2017): 3–31.

21. Horwitz and Dovidio 2017.

22. Horwitz and Dovidio 2017.

23. Michele Benedetto Nietz, "Socioeconomic Bias in the Judiciary," *Cleveland State Law Review* 61 (2013): 137–165.

24. John M. Darley and Paget H. Gross, "A Hypothesis-Confirming Bias in Labeling Effects," *Journal of Personality and Social Psychology* 44 (1983): 20–33.

25. Darley and Gross 1983.

26. Lee Ross, "The Intuitive Psychologist and His Shortcomings: Distortions in the Attribution Process," In L. Berkowitz ed., *Advances in Experimental Social Psychology*, Vol. 10 (New York: Academic Press, 1977), pp. 174–221, p. 183.

27. Bullock and Reppond 2018; Matthew O. Hunt and Heather E. Bullock, "Ideologies and Beliefs About Poverty," in D. Brady and L. M. Burton eds., *The Oxford Handbook of the Social Science of Poverty* (New York: Oxford University Press, 2016), pp. 93–116.

28. Linda J. Skitka, Elizabeth Mullen, Thomas Griffin, Susan Hutchinson, and Brian Chamberlin, "Dispositions, Scripts, or Motivated Correction? Understanding Ideological Differences in Explanations for Social Problems," *Journal of Personality and Social Psychology* 83 (2002): 470–487.

29. Herbert J. Gans, "The Positive Functions of Poverty," *American Journal of Sociology* 78 (1972): 275–289.

30. Peter Edelman, *So Rich, So Poor: Why It's So Hard to End Poverty in America* (New York: The New Press, 2012).

31. Josh Levin, *The Queen: The Forgotten Life Behind an American Myth* (New York: Little, Brown and Company, 2019).

32. Martin Gilens, *Why Americans Hate Welfare: Race, Media, and the Politics of Antipoverty Policy* (Chicago: University of Chicago Press, 1999).

33. Jake Rosenfeld and Jennifer Laird, "Unions and Poverty," in David Brady and Linda M. Burton eds., *The Oxford Handbook of the Social Sciences of Poverty* (New York: Oxford University Press, 2016), pp. 820–842.

34. Frances Fox Piven and Lorraine C. Minnite, "Poor People's Politics," in David Brady and Linda M. Burton eds., *The Oxford Handbook of the Social Sciences of Poverty* (New York: Oxford University Press, 2016), p. 765.

35. Seymour Martin Lipset, *American Exceptionalism: A Double-Edged Sword* (New York: W. W. Norton, 1996).

36. Mark Robert Rank, Thomas A. Hirschl, and Kirk A. Foster, *Chasing the American Dream: Understanding What Shapes Our Fortunes* (New York: Oxford University Press, 2014).

37. Henrikas Bartusevičius, "The Inequality-Conflict Nexus Re-Examined: Income, Education, and Popular Rebellions," *Journal of Peace Research* 51 (2013): 35–50; Richard Wilkinson and Kate Pickett, *The Spirit Level: Why Greater Equality Makes Societies Stronger* (New York: Bloomsbury Press, 2009); Fiske and Tablante 2015.

Chapter 20

1. Bradley R. Schiller, *The Economics of Poverty and Discrimination* (Upper Saddle River, NJ: Prentice Hall, 2008).

2. Timothy M. Smeeding, Lee Rainwater, and Gary Burtless, "U.S. Poverty in a Cross-National Context," in Sheldon H. Danziger and Robert H. Haveman eds., *Understanding Poverty* (Cambridge, MA: Harvard University Press, 2001), pp. 27–68.

3. Alberto Alesina and Edward L. Glaeser, *Fighting Poverty in the US and Europe: A World of Difference* (Oxford, UK: Oxford University Press, 2004).

4. Hillary W. Hoynes and Ankur J. Patel, "Effective Policy for Reducing Poverty and Inequality? The Earned Income Tax Credit and the Distribution of Income," *Journal of Human Resources* 53 (2018): 859–890.

5. Center on Budget and Policy Priorities, "Child Tax Credit and Earned Income Tax Credit Lift 10.6 Million People Out of Poverty in 2018," *Off the Charts: Policy Insight Beyond the Numbers* (October 31, 2019).

6. Bruce D. Meyer and Douglas Holtz-Eakin, *Making Work Pay: The Earned Income Tax Credit and Is Impact on America's Families* (New York: Russell Sage Foundation, 2002).

7. Schiller 2008.

8. Mark Paul, William Dairty Jr., Darrick Hamilton, and Khaing Zaw, "A Path to Ending Poverty by Way of Ending Unemployment: A Federal Jobs Guarantee," *Russell Sage Foundation Journal of the Social Sciences* 4 (2018): 44–63.

9. David T. Ellwood and Elisabeth D. Welty, "Public Service Employment and Mandatory Work: A Policy Whose Time Has Come and Gone and Come Again?" in David E. Card and Rebecca M. Blank eds., *Finding Jobs: Work and Welfare Reform.* (New York: Russell Sage Foundation, 2000), pp. 299–372.

10. Hyman P. Minsky, *Stabilizing an Unstable Economy* (New Haven, CT: Yale University Press, 1986).

11. David Brady, Agnes Blome, and Hanna Kleider, "How Politics and Institutions Shape Poverty and Inequality," in David Brady and Linda M. Burton eds., *The Oxford Handbook of the Social Science of Poverty* (New York: Oxford University Press, 2016), pp. 117–140; Lane Kenworthy, *Social Democratic Capitalism* (New York: Oxford University Press, 2019).

12. Cheol-Sung Lee and In-Hoe Koo, "The Welfare States and Poverty," in David Brady and Linda M. Burton eds., *The Oxford Handbook of the Social Science of Poverty* (New York: Oxford University Press, 2016), pp. 709–732.

13. Charles Noble, *Welfare as We Knew It: A Political History of the American Welfare State* (New York: Oxford University Press, 1997), p. 3.

14. Rebecca M. Blank, *It Takes a Nation: A New Agenda for Fighting Poverty* (Princeton, NJ: Princeton University Press, 1997), pp. 141–142.

15. Kenworthy 2019, p. 121.

16. Mark Robert Rank, *Confronting Poverty: Economic Hardship in the United States* (Thousand Oaks, CA: Sage Publications, 2021).

17. Jeff Madrick, *Invisible Americans: The Tragic Cost of Child Poverty* (New York: Alfred A. Knopf, 2020), pp. 134–135.

18. H. Luke Shaefer et al., "A Universal Child Allowance: A Plan to Reduce Poverty and Income Instability Among Children in the United States," *Russell Sage Foundation Journal of the Social Sciences* 4 (2018): 22–42.

19. Walter Korpi, "Welfare-State Regress in Western Europe: Politics, Institutions, Globalization, and Europeanization," *Annual Review of Sociology*, 29 (2003): 589–609.

20. Kenworthy 2019.

21. Gosta Esping-Andersen, *Why We Need a New Welfare State* (Oxford, UK: Oxford University Press, 2002), p. 18.

22. Stephen Roll, Michal Grinstein-Weiss, Joseph Steensma, and Anna deRuyter, "Developing Financial Assets for Lower-Income Households," in Mark Robert Rank ed.,

Towards a Livable Life: A 21st Century Agenda for Social Work (New York: Oxford University Press, 2020), pp. 114–151.

23. Elise Gould, "Black-White Wage Gaps Are Worse Today Than in 2000," *Working Economics Blog* (Washington, DC: Economic Policy Institute, February 27, 2020); Kriston McIntosh, Emily Moss, Ryan Nunn, and Jay Shambaugh, "Examining the Black-White Wealth Gap," Brookings Institution, *Up Front* (February 27, 2020).

24. Thomas M. Shapiro, *Toxic Inequality: How America's Wealth Gap Destroys Mobility, Deepens the Racial Divide, and Threatens Our Future* (New York: Basic Books, 2017).

25. Roll, Grinstein-Weiss, Steensma, and deRuyter 2020.

26. Roll, Grinstein-Weiss, Steensma, and deRuyter 2020.

27. William A. Darity and A. Kirsten Mullen, *From Here to Equality: Reparations for Black Americans in the Twenty-First Century* (Chapel Hill, NC: University of North Carolina Press, 2020).

28. Roll, Grinstein-Weiss, Steensma, and deRuyter 2020.

29. Roll, Grinstein-Weiss, Steensma, and deRuyter 2020.

Chapter 21

1. Michael Burawoy, "2004 American Sociological Association Presidential Address: For Public Sociology," *British Journal of Sociology* 56 (2005): 261.

2. Mark R. Rank, "Changing the World, One Website at a Time," *Contexts* 16 (2017): 74–75.

3. Mark Robert Rank, Thomas A. Hirschl, and Kirk A. Foster, *Chasing the American Dream: Understanding What Shapes Our Fortunes* (New York: Oxford University Press, 2014), p. 174.

4. Paul Rogat Loeb, *Soul of a Citizen: Living With Conviction in a Cynical Time* (New York: St. Martin's Griffen, 1999), p. 219.

5. Jacob A. Riis, *How the Other Half Lives: Studies Among the Tenements of New York* (New York: Hill and Wang, 1957), p. 163.

{INDEX}

For the benefit of digital users, indexed terms that span two pages (e.g., 52–53) may, on occasion, appear on only one of those pages.